Rebellion in the Reign of Charles II

To DM

Rebellion in the Reign of Charles II

Julian Whitehead

PEN & SWORD
HISTORY

First published in Great Britain in 2017 by
PEN AND SWORD HISTORY
an imprint of
Pen and Sword Books Ltd
47 Church Street
Barnsley
South Yorkshire S70 2AS

Copyright © Julian Whitehead, 2017

ISBN 978 1 47389 678 9

Printed and bound in Malta by
Gutenberg Press Ltd

Typeset in Times New Roman by Chic Graphics

Pen & Sword Books Ltd incorporates the imprints of Pen & Sword
Archaeology, Atlas, Aviation, Battleground, Discovery,
Family History, History, Maritime, Military, Naval, Politics, Railways,
Select, Social History, Transport, True Crime, Claymore Press,
Frontline Books, Leo Cooper, Praetorian Press, Remember When,
Seaforth Publishing and Wharncliffe.

For a complete list of Pen and Sword titles please contact
Pen and Sword Books Limited
47 Church Street, Barnsley, South Yorkshire, S70 2AS, England
E-mail: enquiries@pen-and-sword.co.uk
Website: www.pen-and-sword.co.uk

Contents

List of Illustrations

Acknowledgements

I am indebted to all the authors of the books listed in the Bibliography, in particular for the various works of Alan Marshall, Richard L. Graves, and John Kenyon. I would also like to thank the National Portrait Gallery and Mary Evans Picture Library for their assistance and agreement to me using their images for illustrations. Finally, I want to thank my wife for her help and support.

Introduction

If the name of Charles II is mentioned to the average person a number of vague thoughts may enter their mind. They probably think of him as the 'merry monarch', a fun loving king with several mistresses including a pretty cockney girl called Nell Gwynn. They might remember that he was the adventurous young man who hid in an oak tree to escape from Cromwell's Roundheads. If asked about the Restoration, most people might think of bawdy comedies with women on the stage for the first time and Samuel Pepys recording the naughty goings-on in his diary. They might also remember the Great Plague that was then wiped out by the Fire of London which in turn allowed Sir Christopher Wren to build a fine stone city. It is just possible that Restoration might also be remembered as the time when the Royal Society was founded with men such as Isaac Newton and Robert Boyle making huge strides in mathematics and science. In general the period would be considered a fun, romantic and positive time. This is a reasonable enough summary as far as it goes but there was a darker side to the period – which is the subject of this book.

The three kingdoms of England, Scotland and Ireland, which Charles II came to rule in 1660, totalled nearly nine million people. These people had been severely traumatised. They had suffered civil wars that had resulted in the loss of 200,000 lives, countless casualties and bitter divisions of communities and families.[1] A Republic had been created, followed by a military coup and Cromwell's Protectorate with what amounted to a police state followed by another Republic that had imploded on itself as generals fought for power. During the turmoil bishops and the whole Anglican Church had been abolished and its property seized. Most Royalist supporters had lost a great deal of their lands and wealth through confiscation or fines and these were now owned by parliamentary supporters or resold to others. Those who felt they had been wronged during the Interregnum now wanted both restoration of their wealth and vengeance against the people responsible for taking it from them. Those who had supported the Republic or Protectorate were in fear that they might be deprived of their gains in that time and retribution would be awaiting them. Above all, this was a deeply religious age and each Protestant sect be it Anglican, Presbyterian, Quaker, Baptist or Congregationalist, had little or no tolerance of each other, and absolutely no tolerance for Roman Catholics. The welcome that was given to the returning king was based upon the hope that the general yearning for peace, stability and prosperity would be miraculously fulfilled. It would be a tall order for any monarch.

The euphoria of the Restoration soon evaporated as the deep problems, divisions and distrust of the past re-emerged. Plots, uprisings and threats to the king's power, throne and even life soon followed. Charles's father had been executed and his successor only managed to keep the throne for four years, yet Charles reigned for a quarter of a century and died in his bed. Charles was an intelligent and energetic man but those qualities were largely devoted to the pursuit of pleasure. Despite indolence and indifference, the Merry Monarch could sometimes show iron determination to retain royal power. In preserving the security of his throne Charles relied upon his secretaries of state with their intelligence, organisation, and means of controlling the press. This book describes the plots, uprisings and subversion that took place, and how they were overcome. The book is written by someone who has spent a working lifetime in government intelligence. It seeks to throw light on the murky world of espionage, covert operations and general dirty tricks that enabled Charles II to overcome opposition and intrigue to be England's last absolute monarch to hold the throne.

Chapter 1

Homecoming
1660

But it was the Lord's doing, for such a restoration was never
mentioned in any history, ancient or modern, since the return
of the Jews from their Babylonish captivity.

John Evelyn

On 29 May in the year of Our Lord one thousand, six hundred and sixty a
minor miracle was taking place. A tall, slim, dark haired man was riding into
London. The last time he had seen his hometown was eighteen years before
when he had left so hurriedly with his parents. He was in the highest spirits.
It was his thirtieth birthday and he was wearing an expensive set of clothes
and mounted on a very fine horse. He had much to think about but little time
for private thoughts as he was not travelling alone. Apart from his escort of
five cavalry regiments, he was accompanied by 300 gentlemen in cloth of
silver, another 300 in velvet coats and hundreds of footmen and servants in
purple or green livery. Then there was the crowd of 120,000 who had come to
welcome him; their loud cheers competing with the sound of every church
bell ringing and the roar of cannon firing salutes. Riding on either side were
his brothers, James, Duke of York, and Henry, Duke of Gloucester, and a little
ahead was the man who had made it all possible, General George Monck.[1]
    Just a couple of months earlier, Charles Stuart had been living in Brussels
unable to afford more than one meal a day and wondering how to get credit
to pay for his meagre board and lodging. Money lenders had known he had
been crowned King of Scotland ten years earlier but they also knew that he
had lost all when he attempted to gain his father's throne in England.
Cromwell had destroyed Charles's army at Worcester and the King of
Scotland had fled to the Continent with a price on his head. Charles then had
to watch from afar as Cromwell, backed by the all-powerful army, was

appointed Lord Protector and king in all but name. When Cromwell died, his son Richard had become Protector but had been ousted by the army's senior generals who dismissed parliament, and government had begun to disintegrate. George Monck, the General commanding Scotland, decided to support the return of parliament and marched down to London unopposed by the other generals. Once there, the reassembled House of Commons made him Commander in Chief and agreed to his proposal to call an election. As Monck had intended, the new parliament had a Royalist majority which, after Monck had won the grudging support of the Army, invited Charles to return as king. Charles was transformed from being a penniless pretender to being King of England, Scotland and Ireland. The climax of this amazing turn of fortune was 29 May, the day he entered his capital to receive the formal acknowledgement of his royal inheritance.

The programme of welcoming events had been exhilarating but also tiring; consisting of a military review, ceremonies by the Lord Mayor and Aldermen, followed by further ceremonies from each of the Houses of Parliament, then a thanksgiving service and finally a banquet. When it was at last time for bed, Charles privately celebrated his birthday with his new lover Barbara Palmer.[2] He did not realise it but this voluptuous, auburn haired, violet eyed beauty would come to dominate his life for many years to come. When Charles woke up the next morning he may finally have had a few moments to reflect upon his situation. Initially, there must have been relief and excitement that he was waking up as king in his palace of Whitehall. Then two principles are likely to have guided his thoughts. Firstly, that now justice had at last been done and he had secured the crowns of his father's three kingdoms, he would never let them go. Secondly, that after enduring so much adversity he would ensure he fully enjoyed all the pleasures that kingship could offer. Charles would always be an amusing and generous person, but the setbacks and humiliations of his years of exile had turned him into a cynic. He knew that the crowds that welcomed him so enthusiastically were made up of the same citizens who had rioted against his father back in 1642 when he had attempted to arrest some members of parliament for treasonous action against him. So strong had been their feeling against the monarchy that his father had been obliged to leave London to ensure the safety of his wife and family. One of the people that Charles I had hoped to arrest was Lord Manchester who had gone on to command the Roundhead Eastern Association against the King. It had been Manchester who, as leader of the House of Lords, had given a grovelling address of welcome when he had entered London the day before. Charles had every reason to be a cynic.[3]

HOMECOMING

As he lay in bed, Charles may have begun idly thinking about the long-term preservation of the throne for the House of Stuart. Now he was king, he would need an heir. He already had children, including a son, James, by a previous mistress Lucy Walter; but obviously they could not be successors. Charles had been transformed into Europe's most eligible bachelor and he needed a suitable royal bride to produce him a successor. However, although the selection of a wife would be a necessary and amusing activity, there was the more immediate matter of consolidating himself upon the throne. He would need a government he could trust, with the ability to guide him in healing the deep divisions in the nation. For this he would naturally turn to his faithful servant Sir Edward Hyde, the Lord Chancellor, who he ennobled to Baron Hyde. Hyde was 51; old for that time and, although his loyalty and acumen were beyond question, he was a fussy workaholic whose diligence and concern for detail was not always appreciated by an innately lazy and easily bored monarch. Nevertheless, Hyde was a safe pair of hands with which to build a government.

Charles had just received a genuinely ecstatic greeting from the London crowds and any amount of sycophantic fawning from the great men of the land who had welcomed him back. For all that, his position was, at best, precarious. Kingship was by its nature precarious. After all, had not Charles's father been executed; his grandfather James I nearly killed by the Gunpowder Plot; his French grandfather King Henry IV, assassinated; his great-grandmother, Mary Queen of Scots, executed; and his great-grandfather, Darnley, murdered. Hardly very promising. There was no doubt about Charles's courage, which he had demonstrated so clearly when leading cavalry charges at Worcester, but he realised he must be on his guard with so many old Republicans and religious extremists who might take it into their head to assassinate him.

Of more immediate concern was retaining the backing of the principal power in the country. It had been the army that had been the basis of Cromwell's power and it had been the removal of the army's support from Richard Cromwell that had forced him to resign as Lord Protector. General Monck had the power to engineer Charles's restoration only because he had the tacit support of the army to do so. But what the army had done, it could also undo. Charles's review of the army at Blackheath on the previous day had been a disciplined affair but there had been no sign of enthusiasm in the ranks. Hardly surprising when virtually all of them had spent their military careers as staunch Republicans, which they called 'The Good Old Cause'. They were mostly drawn from a number of strict Protestant sects with a deep hatred of all things Popish. These grave Republican men found themselves not only welcoming a king, but the man who was known as 'the young Tarquin' for his dissolute ways and was believed to be a Papist or, at the very least, a Roman Catholic sympathiser. They had found themselves going along with the Restoration out of respect for Monck as a leader and in the hope that a new regime might give them the many months of pay they were owed. Although the army was currently loyal to Monck and, by extension, his return of the monarchy, they might soon feel betrayed and rally to one of the other former generals such as Fleetwood. Then there was Monck himself. There was the possibility that he might become disenchanted with Charles as king and lead the army against him. This seemed unlikely, as Charles had already made Monck a Knight of the Garter and in the next two months would make him Earl of Torrington, Duke of Albemarle, Lord Lieutenant of Ireland, Captain General of the army for life, and grant him considerable estates and a substantial pension. With the hindsight of history we know that Monck was to remain totally loyal to his monarch, but in May 1660, Charles might not have had complete confidence in so powerful a man who had already changed sides twice. Among so much uncertainty, there was one thing that Charles knew for sure. If he was to successfully neutralise the actions of those who might attempt to remove him from his newly won throne, he must identify his enemies and uncover their plots against him. For this he would need intelligence.

Under Oliver Cromwell a formidable intelligence apparatus had been built up that helped to make the Protectorate a major power abroad and little short of a police state at home. This intelligence organisation was controlled by the very able secretary of state, John Thurloe. He drew upon military and naval intelligence reported from commanders deployed on operations, correspondence from magistrates and government servants at home, and the dispatches from the colonies of North America and the West Indies and the large number of diplomatic representatives abroad. Beside these relatively overt sources of information, Thurloe had three separate secret means of intelligence collection. There was the intercept of mail, largely carried out through the Post Office, which involved the secret opening of letters, their translation if required, the cryptanalysis of any cipher and finally, transcription. Then there was information provided through examination, or what we would today call interrogation. This could be carried out anywhere but was mainly conducted at the Tower of London. Finally there was agent handling. As well as recruiting and running agents, this included the management of sub-agents and casual informants, some of whom were employed in static or mobile surveillance. The main personalities responsible for this system were Issac Dorislaus at the Post Office, Colonel John Barkstead at the Tower, and Samuel Morland managing agent handling in Whitehall. Thurloe not only carried out the overall direction of the intelligence operation and the assessment of its product, but also took the lead in agent handling.[4] So successful had been this intelligence apparatus that it completely penetrated the Royalist and other resistance groups and it was said that: 'Cromwell carried the secrets of all the princes of Europe in his girdle.'[5]

After Cromwell died in October 1658, Thurloe continued his excellent work in the service of Cromwell's son Richard. When Richard was ousted by General Fleetwood's military junta in May the next year, Thurloe was dismissed. In the same month, Barkstead was removed as Lieutenant Governor of the Tower and fled to Germany. The new Council of State made one of its member's head of a Standing Committee for Intelligence. This was Thomas Scot who was an ardent Republican and had been the previous head of intelligence before Oliver Cromwell became Lord Protector. Scot was only to have five months in post until the military junta dismissed him and the whole Council of State, and replaced it with their own Committee of Safety. Almost immediately, Fleetwood and the other generals were challenged by General Monck. They resigned and Monck recalled the Long Parliament. In January 1660 the restored parliament made Scot secretary of state, but within two months he had fled to Germany realising that the Restoration was imminent. Monck became the de facto ruler of the Commonwealth during the short period of negotiations for the king's return and appointed John Thurloe as a secretary of state. Although Thurloe was a true servant of the house of Cromwell he was also a true government servant and began re-establishing the intelligence apparatus and re-orientating it to the Royalist cause. Monck was a personal friend of Thurloe but he knew that such a formidable opponent of the monarchy could not remain in post for Charles's return. With skilful manoeuvring, Monck had persuaded the Long Parliament to dissolve itself on 16 March and to call a free parliament. A pro-Royalist parliament – known as the Convention Parliament – was elected and assembled on 25 April and within days had invited Charles to return as king. As a demonstration of its new-found loyalty, parliament had ordered Thurloe to be imprisoned in the Tower for high treason. So it was that Charles found himself restored as king, but with an intelligence organisation that was leaderless and had been severely disrupted and staffed by men of questionable loyalty. The resurrection of an effective intelligence organisation was an imperative, but that was detailed work inappropriate for a king and which Charles would make a priority of one of his secretaries.

With the immediate excitement of the welcome over, Charles sat down with his Privy Council to review the situation. The full Privy Council was about forty strong but there were only about ten in the inner council. These consisted of the councillors he had had in exile, that is: his two brothers, James and Henry; his cousin, Prince Rupert, the great Royalist cavalry general and admiral; James Butler, the Marquis of Ormonde, who had been the Royalist leader in Ireland during the Civil War; Sir Edward Nicholas, his secretary of state; and Baron Hyde, his chief minister and Lord Chancellor. To these were added the Royalist grandee, the Earl of Southampton, who became Lord Treasurer. Since returning to England Charles had of course added Monck to the Council, and Charles felt obliged to accept Monck's protégé and relation, the fiercely Presbyterian Sir William Morrice, as his second secretary of state. Other previous commonwealth leaders included Sir Anthony Ashley Cooper, a former member of Cromwell's Council of State who had later supported Monck and had been one of the members of parliament to travel to Holland to invite Charles to return. Despite his Republican background, Ashley Cooper was a rich landowner, married to Southampton's niece, and his considerable political experience led to him being appointed Chancellor of the Exchequer.

By far the most pressing items for discussion in council were the three issues of national reconciliation, re-establishing the Stuart form of government and addressing royal finances. Any consideration of the creation of an intelligence organisation would have to wait its turn in the list of priorities. For national reconciliation it was necessary to draw a line under the past and try to encourage former Cavaliers and Roundheads to put aside their antagonism. Charles had made the Declaration of Breda to parliament before they had formally invited him to return. In this he had proclaimed a general pardon for all offences committed during the interregnum, had urged his subjects to befriend their former enemies and accept the principle of religious toleration. Those fine words were good as far as they went, but now needed to be more specific and turned into legislation. There were many issues closely related to this, including what to do about the Republic's confiscation of Crown and Church lands, and the lands confiscated from Royalist supporters. The second pressing matter was how to arrange a return to the former system of government. This meant ceasing to have the centralised rule of the Commonwealth of Great Britain and Ireland, which had a single House of Commons with MPs from England, Ireland and

Scotland, and returning to a ruler who was separately King of England, Ireland and Scotland, with three separate parliaments. Both these issues needed careful planning and parliamentary legislation to implement.

Finally, and nearest to the king's heart, was the financial situation. Charles had been transformed from being a penniless pretender into a reigning sovereign receiving a grant of £50,000 from parliament and a further £10,000 from the Common Council of London. Unfortunately these large sums were trivial compared with the huge royal debts amassed in exile, which were themselves dwarfed by the £3,000,000 treasury deficit he had inherited. This amounted to three year's revenue. Part of this Treasury debt was money owed in back pay to the army that was still some 40,000 strong. As the army had shown time and again that it could make or break governments, and a massive reduction in the size was essential but there was no chance of it going quietly unless it was paid off. Just like the legislation, Charles would have to rely on parliament to raise the money so vitally required. The return to kingship is called the 'Restoration' though it was clear to Charles that kingship by divine right had not been restored, but rather a situation closer to what we would now term 'constitutional monarchy'. All the acts of parliament forced on his father before January 1642 were still valid. That meant that the power to raise money without parliament's consent had gone. There could be no more royal taxes such as Ship Money. Fortunately for Charles, the Convention Parliament seemed well disposed towards him but even so, the resolution of these three principal issues would take a lot of managing.

As Charles's chief minister, Hyde got busy and immediately took a hand in drafting a Bill of General Pardon Indemnity and Oblivion. To raise the money necessary to replenish the Treasury and reduce the size of the army, Hyde got parliament to pass a Poll Tax in June (an esquire paid £10 1s for each household servant, knights and peers much more) and in August, George Monck, Duke of Albemarle, proposed disbanding the armies of England and Scotland. Albemarle was not only Captain General of the Army but highly respected by officers and rank and file alike. The army was prepared to trust him and his assurances that they would receive what was owing to them on disbandment. To most peoples' amazement, the whole standing army of 42,000 men melted away into civilian life in an orderly fashion without protest. Although the standing army was abolished, Charles got round this by designating Monck's regiment of Coldstreamers and a squadron of horse (the Royal Horse Guards or 'Blues') as his bodyguard. In the fullness of time Charles would use other expedients to expand this group by, for example, establishing the Royal Dragoons supposedly to be a garrison for Tangier and the Royal East Kent Regiment or 'Buffs' supposedly to fight in Holland. In other words he was to create a small army of men totally loyal to the crown that could be used if necessary to crush armed opposition.

During these busy few months constitutional matters were also addressed. George Monck, Duke of Albemarle, had been made Lord Lieutenant of Ireland on top of his many other appointments but, as he remained in England, the country was run by three Lord Justices. This interim and confusing form of government for Ireland did not have the authority to deal with its two related major problems. These were the religious divide between the Catholics and the Protestants and Cromwell's huge confiscation of Catholic land, which had been passed into the Protestant hands of soldiers from the New Model Army. The Catholics who had owned two thirds of Ireland before Cromwell's conquests had been reduced to less than a quarter. This would take some sorting out and in the meantime, deep resentment and distrust continued.

In Scotland, the Committee of Estates was reassembled as an interim government. The king sent the Earl of Middleton to Edinburgh as High Commissioner, where he began the unpopular task of replacing the Presbyterian Kirk with the Episcopal Church. The former Covenanter, John Maitland, was made Earl of Lauderdale and given the vital job of secretary of state for Scotland. As such he became the king's chief Scottish adviser and so directed the policy that Middleton had to implement. A sensitive situation, particularly as both men disliked each other intensely, with Lauderdale continually undermining all Middleton's efforts to restore the bishops. Maitland had been imprisoned after the Battle of Worcester and on being released just before the Restoration, had dashed over to Breda to claim reward for loyalty. This 6ft 5in man with his shock of unkempt red hair was intelligent and could discourse at length in his loud voice in Latin, Greek and Hebrew. He was also a wholly unattractive person who was described by a contemporary (Bishop Burnet) as 'uncouth, boisterous, shaggy, ugly and cunning.'[6] Despite that, he was one of the few Scots that Charles could stand, and so came to direct Scottish affairs to the king's satisfaction and his own considerable profit. With monarchical rule re-established in Ireland and Scotland the final constitutional act was the dissolution of the Convention Parliament on 29 December so that it could be replaced by a free parliament summoned under the king's authority.

Although many of the main destabilising issues facing the monarchy had been addressed by Hyde, there was still the matter of establishing an intelligence system. During the king's exile it had been Sir Edward Nicholas who had directed intelligence, although Hyde had often taken a leading part. Cromwell had Thurloe as a single secretary of state who also was a de facto chief minister and head of intelligence. The king used Hyde, the Lord Chancellor, and his chief minister and adviser. It was the Stuart practice to have two secretaries of state, one for the North who dealt with northern Europe, and one for the South who dealt with the Mediterranean countries and was regarded as the more senior of the two. The post of Secretary had originally been the monarch's private secretary but this had gradually developed to be the head of the government service controlling all correspondence and business for the monarch as head of state. All decisions of government ultimately rested with the monarch but those decisions would be influenced by the king's principal advisers. The Secretaries' role was to implement the king's decisions and coordinate the whole government apparatus from ambassadors, to justices of the peace. As all royal correspondence went through them and they worked so closely with the king, the posts had the potential to be very powerful. The extent of the power depended upon the ambition of the Secretary and the extent to which they won the confidence of the King. Albermarle's nominee, Sir William Morrice had been made secretary of state for the North but, although a reasonably diligent worker, was without ambition and just pleased to be holding an office giving the opportunity for making money. Nicholas, the secretary of state for the South, was now 67 years old, had no personal ambition and was losing what energy he had in the past. For all that, he was a highly experienced Crown servant, totally loyal and incorruptible and a close friend of the powerful Hyde. It was, therefore, natural for him to have sole responsibility for intelligence matters. He began setting up an efficient office for managing his secretariat's share of government business including an intelligence department. Nicholas was well aware of the importance of security especially in covert affairs and swiftly established a full time clerk to carry out enciphering and deciphering correspondence to and from English diplomats abroad.

Both secretaries of state were allocated £700 a year from the Secret Fund, primarily to pay staff and informants. As Morrice was not engaged in espionage it may be assumed that much of the notional intelligence money made its way into his own pocket. In exile, Nicholas had run a few good sources himself but had been severely hindered by lack of funds to pay them. Now he had the money but needed to obtain more sources. He did what he could to resurrect the formally excellent intelligence regime of the Republic. This was a matter of re-establishing the Intelligence apparatus and seeing if he could make use of any of the intelligencers of the Republic. An obvious person to use would have been Samuel Morland, who had been Thurloe's principal secretary for covert activities and agent handling. After Cromwell's death, Morland had begun passing state secrets to the Royalist court in exile in order to ingratiate himself with what he anticipated might be the new regime. His intelligence assessment had proved correct and when Charles returned as king, he was made a baronet in recognition of the valuable intelligence he passed. Morland had hoped that his new-found loyalty to the Crown would be rewarded by him being made a secretary of state but, as we have seen, those posts had gone to Nicholas and Morrice. Morland's new status made him too senior to work in the intelligence department below Nicholas, so he ended up kicking his heels in a minor court appointment.

Had they been trustworthy, it would have been useful to make use of Colonel John Barkstead, who had been Cromwell's governor of the Tower and principal interrogator, and Thomas Scot, the Republic's head of intelligence. Unfortunately there was no question of recruiting them as they had both signed Charles I's death warrant and were exempt from the Restoration pardon. On 17 October, Scot was executed before the king at Charing Cross in the traditional manner for traitors, in which castration was just part of the butchery. Barkstead was to be captured and suffered the same prolonged agonies of a traitor's execution two years later. Then there was the matter of John Thurloe, Cromwell's head of intelligence, who was not a regicide and had tried to make his peace with Charles through Hyde just before the Restoration. He had been released from the Tower in June and according to Thurloe's State Papers, had been given 'free liberty to attend the secretary of state at such times as they shall appoint and for so long a time as they shall own his attendance for the service of the state.'[7] History does not record whether Sir Edward made any use of Thurloe, but it is likely he was not prepared to have dealings with the person who had been Cromwell's right hand man. Although Nicholas found that he could not make use of the wealth of expertise of the Republic's intelligencers, he did obtain a significant legacy from one of them. Before his death, Scot had made a vain attempt to save his life by providing details of all his informants. It was this information, coupled with what Nicholas had obtained in exile, which was to make the basis for the intelligence and security records of the new regime.

Nicholas had to assemble a new team to run his intelligence department. In July 1660, Nicholas had recruited Joseph Williamson as one of his clerks. Williamson was a tall 33-year-old Cumbrian who was the second son of an impoverished vicar. He had been following an academic career as a private tutor and had become an Oxford fellow at the time of the Restoration. Life had been a struggle to make ends meet and being ambitious, he had tried to make connections with those who could further his career. One of these was Gilbert Sheldon, Bishop of London; Sheldon recommended him to Nicholas, who gave him a job in his new intelligence department.[8] The job of a clerk was hardly prestigious but it gave Williamson the foothold he needed to climb to the power and fortune he was determined to grasp. He threw his formidable intelligence and energy into his work with the result that, before very long, he would be dominating the king's intelligence service. This dominance was to last for the next nineteen years.

While Hyde and the two secretaries of state had been managing the pressing problems of government, the king had been otherwise engaged. Naturally he had taken an overall interest in their progress, but had left the day-to-day work to Hyde and had put his energies into enjoying the pleasures of kingship. Charles enjoyed life in many ways but always with considerable energy. A keen sportsman, he would be up at 6 am to play a hard game of tennis or go swimming at Putney. An excellent horseman, he greatly enjoyed hunting deer and stag and as well as being the patron of Newmarket, would take part in races himself. He loved the sea and spent as much time as he could racing his newly commissioned yachts. Many of his afternoons would be spent in the newly opened theatres, which, for the first time, had the added allure of female actresses. He made major improvements to his palaces and their grounds and created an informal but lavish court full of music, dancing, gaming and entertainment, with an inner circle of amusing men and beautiful women. Of the many beautiful women the breathtakingly attractive and enchanting Barbara Palmer was becoming his most regular companion and bed partner. But Charles was an intelligent man who also took pleasures from more intellectual pursuits such as architecture, shipbuilding and the development of science, in fact everything that took the fancy of his enquiring mind. Any Londoner seeing the 6ft tall king striding across St James Park with his spaniels yapping at his heals and courtiers barely keeping up with him, would have had no doubt about his energy for life. To the average person it must have seemed amazing that a year that had begun with General Monck sending his advanced guard from Coldstream into England, had ended with stable governments established in the three kingdoms and headed by a fun loving monarch who was lifting the gloom that had beset the Interregnum. However, before the year was out, there were two events concerning the king's brothers which were to have a major impact on the future.

21

The first event was the sudden death of the king's youngest brother, the Duke of Gloucester, from smallpox in September. On the face of it, this was no more than the sad loss of a promising young man, but it affected the royal succession. As a result of the death, Charles's sister, Princess Mary of Orange, became third in line to the throne and, following her death (also from smallpox) three months later, her 11-year-old son William assumed that position. What might have appeared at the time to be of no more than passing genealogical interest was to have far reaching results for English history. The second event was the news that James, Duke of York, had secretly married Anne Hyde, the daughter of the Lord Chancellor. This was not the doing of Hyde, who was furious about it because of the complete disparity of the match. Hyde was, after all, just the second son of a Wiltshire squire who had achieved a successful career as a Crown servant. The king decided to make him Earl of Clarendon to give him aristocratic status but if anything, this fuelled the jealousy of those who were convinced he had engineered the match for his own aggrandisement. The marriage brought a major backlash against him, not least from Charles's mother Queen Henrietta Maria. She came over from France on hearing the news that her son had not only married the daughter of a commoner, but also a man she hearty disliked. As Henrietta Maria was the daughter, wife, and mother of kings, she found this uneven match just too much to bear. However, she did manage to bring herself to bear it when Hyde arranged for the state to pay off her considerable debts in return for her acceptance of the match.

More interesting than Henrietta Maria's tantrum, was that she was accompanied by her youngest child, who had been born just before she had last left England in 1643. This was Princess Henrietta–Anne, know to her family as Minette. Charles had last seen his sister in December 1659 in Paris and had been completely enchanted by the then 15-year-old blue-eyed brunette with her unstudied charm. From that time he had begun to correspond regularly with her, and the queen's arrival allowed Charles to spend time with his charming, delicate, doll-like younger sister. Charles had a strong brotherly affection for Minette, which was soon to become more intense with the death of the third of his five siblings. For her part, Minette thought the world of her successful and amusing brother who, in some ways, may have taken the role of the father she had never known.

Minette's short visit to England turned her from a being more than just a delightful younger sister, to being a person in whom Charles could trust and confide in above all others. The main purpose of her visit to London with her mother was to complete the marriage settlement for the betrothal to her cousin

Philippe Duke d'Orleans, the younger brother of King Louis XIV. This was a good match and would mean that the following year, she would marry the second most powerful man in France, who would prove to be a brave and successful general in his country's army. The downside was that her fiancé was a flamboyant homosexual with a vicious nature. The difficulties of her future married life would make Charles care for her even more and after she returned to France, she and her brother continued their increasingly close relationship through correspondence. When an English ambassador in Paris was appointed it was the Presbyterian Lord Holles, who hated all things French.[9] It would be through Holles that the king and his sister exchanged letters which developed from friendly banter and family gossip to matters of state. She married the Duke of Orleans early the next year and became a popular, captivating ornament of the royal court of France. King Louis became increasingly fond of his sister-in-law and, by that summer, the two had a brief affair. The French king's ardour was soon directed elsewhere, but Minette remained a close friend and family member with whom he would discuss affairs of state. So it came about that Minette became Charles's secret conduit between him and his cousin Louis.

Although the year had ended in royal mourning for the king's brother and sister, Charles had every reason for optimism. On the personal side, the stunningly beautiful Barbara Villiers was his principal mistress and he was having the time of his life enjoying the recreations and amusements of his ever more extravagant court. After the penury of exile it was a joy to spend as he chose, and thanks to parliament's recent grant of an annual revenue of £1,200,000, it looked as though the lavish life style could go on indefinitely. As for his security of tenure as king, the many threats that could have so easily occurred had not manifested themselves. Scotland and Ireland, with their unresolved religious problems, had remained quiet. The country was not at war, and Spain and France, the two super powers of Europe, both wanted to strengthen relations with him. Most of those who had supported the previous regime were trying to demonstrate that they were now loyal subjects, and diehard Republicans had either gone to ground in England or fled to exile in Holland or Switzerland. There had been no plots or assassination attempts, and the lack of a threat must have been a great relief to Nicholas at a time when his intelligence department was still in the making. To all appearances the Crown was secure but, as the next year would show, appearances can be deceptive.

Chapter 2

Seeds of Dissent
1661

From all sedition, privy conspiracy, and rebellion;
from all false doctrine, heresy and schism;
from hardness of heart, and contempt of thy Word and
     Commandment,
Good Lord, deliver us.

The Litany, 1662 Book of Common Prayer.

It came without warning. No one, including Sir Edward Nicholas's Intelligence Department, had any idea that the first insurrection against the king was about to take place. On the night of 6 January 1661, there was a Fifth Monarchist uprising in London led by Thomas Venner. Now what were the Fifth Monarchists and who on earth was Thomas Venner? The English Revolution had not just removed the monarchy, but brought a fundamental questioning of accepted beliefs in religion and social order. Out of this crucible, radical ideas materialised that gave rise to a variety of fanatical political groups and Nonconformist sects. Some, like the Levellers, would inspire political reform in centuries to come and others, such as the Quakers and Anabaptists, would develop into respected faith movements; but in the 1660s, all were Republican in nature and a potential threat to the king. The Fifth Monarchists were one of these groups. It had begun as a few London tradesmen who interpreted the Book of Daniel as showing that there would be four monarchies (Babylonian, Persian, Greek and Roman) followed by a fifth, the Papacy, which would rule for a thousand years and be replaced by the reign of Christ on earth. It was the obligation of true believers to act as Christ's saints and facilitate His return to earth. There was some disagreement about the precise timing of the Second Coming but it was generally believed it would be in 1666 based on the mystical number '666' recorded in the Book of Revelations.

The most prominent member of the Fifth Monarchists had been one of Cromwell's generals. This was Thomas Harrison, whose decomposed head could to be seen spiked on London Bridge having been hanged, drawn and quartered, along with Scot and other regicides a month or so earlier. Thomas Venner had taken over the leadership from Harrison. Venner was a cooper who had been living in Boston, Massachusetts, but felt obliged to return to England after Cromwell had become Lord Protector. He regarded a Lord Protector as a king by another name and believing as he did that 'There should be no king but Christ', he began organising an uprising against Cromwell. Venner's scheme had quickly come to the attention of Thurloe's intelligence organisation and the Fifth Monarchist's plans were compromised. Early on the day set for their uprising, Venner and about twenty of his supporters were arrested at their assembly point at Mile End Green. Their weapons, banners and pamphlets were seized and Venner was thrown into the Tower. Although not directly involved in the uprising, Thomas Harrison was also arrested and placed in the Tower; it was there that the two remained until released after Cromwell's death.

After his release, Harrison went into retirement in Staffordshire suffering from ill health. Although no longer posing a threat to the crown, he was nevertheless indicted and executed as a regicide. It was partially to avenge the execution that Venner decided to launch his second insurrection. He got his supporters to gather for a sectarian meeting at a tavern in Swan Alley off Coleman Street on the evening of 6 January and bring with them such weapons as they could lay their hands on. Having worked up the fifty or so in the congregation to appropriate zeal, he led them waving a pike towards St Paul's with a view to seizing it, and after that, the Tower. En route, they stopped any citizen they could find and demanded to know who they supported. Anyone who replied 'King Charles' rather than 'King Jesus' was attacked, and a couple of night watchmen were beaten up. The noise and general mayhem brought people out into the streets to protect their property and soon the Trainband militia was summoned. The Fifth Monarchists were thrown back and Venner took his followers off into the night to the safety of Caen Wood between Highgate and Hampstead. Undaunted, the next day Venner led his group to resume their march and went off down Wood Street towards Threadneedle Street. Believing that, as Christ's saints, they were impervious to bullets, they attacked a detachment of the Life Guards of Foot, who tried to block their advance, with fanatical energy. The Life Guards retreated and the Fifth Monarchists then made their way to Compton Prison, intending to release prisoners to swell their numbers, but were beaten back by some troops from General Monck's regiment. The rebels then split into two groups and barricaded themselves in at 'Helmet Tavern' in Threadneedle Street and 'Blue Anchor' in Coleman Street, to prepare for a last stand. Monck's men got onto the roofs of the buildings, broke off the tiles with their musket butts and began firing down on the rebels. It rapidly became clear that Fifth Monarchists were not impervious to bullets and the great majority were killed. Venner suffered nineteen wounds but was captured alive.

Venner neither expected nor received mercy and on 19 January was hanged, drawn and quartered. His head then joined those of other traitors spiked on London Bridge. The Venner uprising had been a surprise but it was no real threat. John Evelyn in his diary for 6 January merely records: 'This night was suppressed a bloody insurrection of some Fifth-Monarchist enthusiasts. Some were examined the next day but could say nothing to extenuate their madness and unwarrantable zeal.' The king was not at all threatened by the uprising as he was in Portsmouth with his mother at the time. Despite disbandment of most of the army, there was no way a poorly armed congregation of fifty had the slightest chance of defeating the remaining Guards regiments and Trainbands. Indeed, the Fifth-Monarchists themselves only thought they could be successful because they believed they would be supported by divine intervention. The incident could have been dismissed as a small demonstration by religious fanatics led by a nonentity, but it was not. The council regarded it as proof that the monarchy might be challenged by dissenters of all types. They convinced themselves that it was not just misguided Fifth Monarchists, but also other Nonconformists such as Quakers and Baptists who might pose a threat to the state. Radical action was taken to counter this supposed challenge to the stability of the kingdom. On 10 January, Charles issued a proclamation banning all meetings of not only Fifth Monarchists, but also Quakers and Anabaptists. Within a few weeks, 4,230 Quakers were thrown into gaol and many Baptists and other dissenters were harassed or imprisoned. [1] They remained without trial in the truly ghastly confines of seventeenth century gaols for five months before being released.

This was to be just the beginning of a period of persecution for Nonconformists of all types. In April the new parliament assembled. It was known as 'the Cavalier Parliament' because it was largely composed of gentry and the sons of aristocrats who were staunchly Anglican and wanted to sweep away all vestiges of the commonwealth years. It might have been supposed that the king would have been delighted to have a parliament so completely loyal to all things associated with the royalist cause. That was not the case because Charles was a pragmatist and was attempting to unite the nation rather than seek vengeance against former opponents. His strong inclination was for religious toleration, but that was the last thing he could expect from this new parliament, which was to last eighteen years and define the religious climate of his reign. These High Anglican gentlemen had no time for Nonconformists and still less for Papists. They immediately showed their robust royalist spirit by ordering that the Presbyterian's Solomon League and Covenant should be burned by the Public Hangman, and that the decomposing corpses of Cromwell and other leading republicans should be dragged from their graves, hacked into quarters and the parts put on public display. They were not to be satisfied by these symbolic expressions of vengeance and began to pass a series of acts ironically known to history as the 'Clarendon Code'. As Clarendon was the king's chief minister, these acts became associated with him, although he in fact disagreed with them as they ran counter to his aims to foster peace and reconciliation.

First came the Corporation Act, which decreed that no one could hold a post in a municipal body unless they received communion in the rites of the Anglican Church. The next year the exact nature of these rites was defined in a new prayer book and an Act of Uniformity was passed making it the only authorised form of worship. This was accompanied by the Quaker's Act, which levied increasingly severe penalties on those attending Quaker services. Soon some 1,300 Quakers found themselves once again in prison.[2] The year after came the Conventicle Act. A 'conventicle' is the name given to any religious gathering which was not following the Anglican Book of Common Prayer. The Act made it illegal for more than five people to attend a conventicle unless they were members of the same family. Again the penalties grew in severity with the number of cases of infringement. This group of Acts had two immediate effects: a major purge of Church of England clergy, and the persecution of anyone following non-Anglican worship, known as 'dissenters' if they were Protestant or 'recusants' if they were Catholic. The purge resulted in about 2,000 parish priests having to give up their livings because they would not accept the Anglican doctrine. They and their families lost the roof over their heads and their income to support themselves. These clergy were also banned from working in schools or universities and so were deprived of the most likely source of alternative employment. Those who managed to seek shelter and support from local friends found that even this was removed when the introduction of the Five Mile Act made it illegal for them to come within five miles of their previous parish.

The persecution of Roman Catholics was nothing new and had been going on since Queen Elizabeth's Penal laws. Under these laws, anyone who did not attend an Anglican service once a week, and take Anglican communion three times a year, was a 'recusant' and subject to severe fines. If they refused to take the Oath of Supremacy acknowledging the monarch as head of the Church in England they were excluded from public office and admission to universities and Inns of Court. It became a felony to attend mass, and the 1585 statute made Catholic priests liable to the death penalty – and the same for any laymen caught giving them shelter. Fortunately, this legislation was not stringently enforced and only about forty Roman Catholics were executed after 1603. By Charles II's reign, recusants were largely members of the gentry who had learned to practice their faith discreetly in their own homes while publicly attending an Anglican Church. At a pinch, some would even take the Oath of Supremacy in order to hold public office. As a result they were largely left alone.

For the Protestant dissenters such as Presbyterians, Baptists, Quakers, Congregationalists, indeed all Nonconformists, the Clarendon Code legislation was a body blow. All these sects had been used to openly practising their own form of religion. Now their services were banned and places of worship closed. If services took place, they would be broken up and fines and other punishments imposed on worshippers. At a time of deep religious conviction, to deprive someone of worshipping in the way they believed God had intended was nothing short of endangering the salvation of their souls. An innocent preacher such as John Bunyon would find himself imprisoned in Reading Gaol for twelve years. He was fortunate compared with the thousands of Quakers who would die in the filthy, overcrowded, disease-ridden gaols about the country.

The implementation of the Code brought considerable human misery, but it also had significant effects on the security of the State. When Charles had reclaimed his crown the previous year, there had been no real opposition. Republicans had either fled abroad or were keeping a very low profile. The whole atmosphere had been one of rejoicing and hope for a stable future. The Clarendon Code resulted in a significant section of the population becoming religious outcasts and second-rate citizens. The great majority of Cromwell's army had been Nonconformists. That army, of some 28,000 men, had just been paid off so there was a pool of former soldiers who now carried the grievance of being religiously persecuted as dissenters. Many of these former soldiers had no jobs to go to and some turned to crimes such as highway robbery. There were also about 2,000 retired Cromwellian officers with the potential to provide leadership for unhappy veterans.[3] Many looked back on the past with nostalgia for what they called the 'Good Old Cause' of Republicanism. Instead of there being no real opposition to Charles, parliament had created the circumstances for part of the population to have deep dissatisfaction with the regime. Worse, it had done so among those who had Republican sympathies and were men of action. It was no surprise there would be sullen mutterings of grievances in the alehouses frequented by such men. These mutterings could lead to seditious talk, which might be the first step to treasonous actions. For the present, they were just small groups of dissatisfied men and any talk of direct action was nothing more than bravado. Nevertheless the potential for resistance and insurrection had been created.

So far from wanting religious persecution, Charles wished to heal the wounds of the past and establish freedom of conscience. He had some empathy with the Roman Catholics. After all, they had supported his father in the Civil War and had been the main group who had arranged his escape after the Battle of Worcester. Also, his mother and beloved sister were Catholics, as were some of his friends in the nobility, so he knew that followers of that faith were not the Papist demons they were made out to be. Charles had little regard for Protestant sects such as Baptists, but he was well aware that it had been a largely Presbyterian parliament that had invited him to return as king. Sensibly, he issued a Declaration of Indulgence to the effect that he had no desire to overturn the Act of Uniformity, but wished to find a way, through parliament, of allowing loyal Protestants and Catholics a measure of freedom of worship. This reasonable proposal was received with horror when parliament reassembled. The Lords immediately began to modify it but before that had got very far, the Commons rejected it outright. Charles was reminded that, although he might be king, he had to rule with parliamentary consent if he wanted them to vote taxes for the royal revenue. So despite his intervention, the Anglican juggernaut of religious persecution rolled on, leaving anguish and the threat of resistance in its path.

As well as this new threat of resistance, the Code resulted in a perceived threat from the dissenters. The fact that dissenters were not allowed to hold public worship meant that they could only worship in secret. It might be in a member's house or in a wood or on a hillside, often under cover of darkness, but wherever a conventicle took place, the location had to be a secret kept among the congregation. Their ministers had to go underground and often resort to disguises to be able to get to and from services. The more secretive these basically loyal and God fearing people became, the more they exhibited the characteristics of conspirators. As suspect persons, it made it even more important for the authorities to clamp down on them and inflict punishments for religious transgression. The greater the repression, the greater the likelihood that even the mildest dissenter might have their loyalty tested beyond breaking point. Soon a few would feel they had no option but to plot armed resistance; such men were to get the common label of 'Phanaticks.'

The result of the Code was that Sir Edward Nicholas's clerks, who were engaged in intelligence, now had a defined group posing a threat to the Crown, even if much of that threat was illusionary. It was against this group that they could now direct their intelligence energies. An indication of how strong was the focus of intelligence action against dissenters is given by reference to Joseph Williamson's personal book of disaffected persons in London. By the following year, the book contained 112 names.[4] The majority were Congregationalists, but there were also some Presbyterians, Baptists and Fifth Monarchists. Ten of them were women, most suspected of providing safe houses for ministers, or helping to organise meetings. Williamson made these 112 the prime targets for his informants and agents. It was notable that there were no Roman Catholics on the list as it was rightly assumed that recusants posed no serious threat. Also, the list contained no Republicans as such, although many of the dissenters may have been nostalgic for the religious freedom of the Commonwealth. Williamson and the others busied themselves recruiting and developing sources to penetrate dissenter activity.

Whereas good agents were always hard to find, and difficult to manoeuvre into penetrating target organisations, general casual contacts and informants were easy to come by. The last twenty years had seen two civil wars and the turbulence of the Commonwealth and Protectorate. Intelligence gathering had become common practice. It had blossomed out of necessity in the Civil War as both Parliamentary and Royalist forces needed to obtain each other's military strengths, intentions and political plans. Then in the Commonwealth and Protectorate, intelligence had been vital for the new Republic to counter Royalist and other threats at home and abroad. Added to that was the need for military and political intelligence against the Dutch and Spanish, with whom England was at war. Cromwell's Secretary, John Thurloe, had run an extensive network of agents and informants for the government, but espionage had also been used by many at a regional level, such as Ormonde during the Civil War in Ireland, and Monck in Scotland during the Protectorate. It is likely that Williamson and his co-intelligencers had little difficulty in finding people willing, and indeed eager, to take the king's money in exchange for information. Some of them may have been working for Thurloe in the past and would have been happy to become a turncoat in order to support themselves.

As well as informants and casual contacts, the period also gave birth to professional spies, or agents as they would be called today. These were usually adventurers, often with a military background, who entered into a semi-formal contract for the provision of clandestine information. A typical person of this type was Colonel Joseph Bampfylde, a professional soldier who had been sent to London by Charles I in 1644 to spy on Parliament. Four years later, when the Duke of York was confined to St James's Palace, it was Bampfylde who organised his escape, disguised the prince in woman's clothes, and got him safely to Holland. He returned to London as a Royalist spy but was captured a year later and thrown into to the Gatehouse prison. He engineered his escape from the Gatehouse and made his way to Charles II's exiled court in The Hague. While on board a ship crossing the Channel, Bampfyled killed Sir Henry Newton in a duel. Newton was the brother-in-law of the lady to whom Bampfylde had offered marriage – while omitting to mention that he already had a wife. Under these circumstances, Bampfylde got a frosty reception at the Stuart Court. Seeing that he had no immediate prospects with the Royalists, he returned to England and offered himself as spy for the Republic.

Bampfylde then returned to the Stuart Court in the pay of John Thurloe, the Republic's spymaster and, in time, managed to get himself accepted by the Royalists to such an extent that he was sent by them on a secret mission to Scotland. On returning, Hyde received an intercepted letter showing that Bampfylde was a spy, but the colonel managed to escape from Cologne and, although no longer a member of the Royalist court, he was able to provide useful information, in particular, of a plot to assassinate Cromwell. He moved about the courts of Europe and, in Paris, managed to intercept correspondence between Charles at his court in Bruges about negotiations with Spain through a sub-source he was running in Madrid. With the fall of the Protectorate and the Restoration of the monarchy, Bampfylde was imprisoned in the Tower for a year and then recruited by Clarendon to spy against Republicans and Nonconformists who had fled to the United Provinces. Bampfylde took service in the Dutch army, as had several other English exiles and, with his spell in the Tower giving him credibility as a Republican, was able to inveigle his way into their confidence.

Clarendon did not normally use agents but felt that, as he was running foreign policy, it would be useful to have his own source on the Continent. Bampfyled had been disloyal, but in Clarendon's own words was 'a man of wit and parts' who could probably be relied upon to use his considerable experience in intelligence tradecraft to the benefit of his paymaster. In this case the immediate paymaster was Sir Alan Apsley, Master of the Hawks, who knew both Clarendon and the colonel, and it was he who had the task of communicating with Bampfylde. Sir Edward Nicholas's staff probably had a few agents with the experience of Bampfylde on their books and were, at this stage, busying themselves in building up a network of informants. As has been mentioned, recruitment was relatively simple, but not so simple was assessing the veracity of the information provided. An informant, or indeed agent, knows that they will only receive money if they provide valuable information. The temptation to invent important intelligence was considerable and could be conveniently combined with making accusations against anyone with whom the informant held a personal grudge. Bearing in mind that in the first year or so after the Restoration the only real opposition to the king had been the trivial affair of the Fifth Monarchist rising, informants would have had little to report on other than the harmless activities of the dissenters. Informant reports based on rumours, or merely concocted for money, would bedevil the work of the intelligence department during the reign. As time passed, Williamson and others would build up their expertise in making accurate evaluations of the veracity of sources and the likelihood of their information being correct.

While Clarendon, Nicholson, and other servants of the crown, were working hard to set up the effective government of the three kingdoms, the king had thrown himself into the pursuit of pleasure. He had his sporting pastimes such as tennis and sailing, intellectual interests such as shipbuilding and chemistry, and amusements such as the theatre and court entertainment. An important element of the amusement department was his mistress Barbara Palmer. Barbara was the daughter of William Villiers, Viscount Grandison, whose father was step-brother to George Villiers, the first Duke of Buckingham. George Villiers had been the most powerful subject in the land under both James I and Charles I until he was assassinated in 1628. George had ensured that some of the massive wealth and royal patronage he enjoyed was spread among his family. His other two brothers were made Viscount Purbeck and Earl of Anglesey, and his sister was married to the Earl of Denbigh. Barbara was therefore a member of one of the richest and most aristocratic families in England, but her high expectations were to be thwarted by the Civil War. Her father had died of his wounds in combat having expended most of his fortune on the king's cause. Although her mother then married her late husband's cousin, the Earl of Anglesey, there was still little money and no chance of aristocrats prospering under the Republic. Barbara found herself living in reduced circumstances, which were not at all to her taste. At the age of 15 she became the mistress of the handsome, fun-loving, Earl of Chesterfield.

Probably in an attempt to take her wayward daughter in hand, her mother had married Barbara off at 18 to a wealthy Buckinghamshire gentleman called Roger Palmer. Barbara was not one to let marriage interfere with her enjoyment and so continued her relations with Chesterfield. In 1659 Chesterfield killed someone in a duel and to avoid the law, fled to The Hague to seek Charles's forgiveness; which he duly received. The Palmers also decided to go to The Hague to pay their respects to the exiled king. When Charles met them he was immediately bowled over by the voluptuous, violet-eyed Barbara. And so it was that Barbara became Charles's mistress while still enjoying relations with Chesterfield – when time permitted. After Charles returned to London as king his infatuation with Barbara continued to grow. She was not only outstandingly beautiful, but also very amusing and great company. At court she was constantly at the king's side, whether it was gaming, dancing, masques or whatever amusing activity was taking place. At night she would dine with the king either alone or with a small group before entertaining him in her bedchamber. It was in the bedchamber that Barbara's highly charged libido and sexual inventiveness totally eclipsed the many other women of the king's experience. She had presented Charles with one child earlier in 1661 and, by the end of that year, was again pregnant. As a result, the unfortunate Roger Palmer was made Earl of Castlemaine so that Barbara could be elevated to a countess. This gave Barbara official recognition as the king's principal mistress and Lady Castlemaine began to assume a position similar to that of a queen consort.

One person who was not impressed by Barbara was Clarendon. He regarded her as a whore and a disgrace to her family, with whom he had been close. Clarendon had been a friend of her father's and a romantic admirer of her aunt, Lady Morton.[4.] There was also the matter of Barbara being showered with gifts by the king that never seemed enough to satisfy her avarice and were becoming a serious drain on the Privy Purse. Finally, and perhaps most importantly, the king was sometimes listening to the advice of his mistress rather than Clarendon, his first minister. For her part, Barbara hated the elderly and rather pompous Clarendon and took every opportunity to ridicule and undermine him.

Barbara was to find a powerful ally in her cousin George Villiers, second Duke of Buckingham. George had been 7 months old when his father was assassinated and was taken from his Catholic mother by Charles I to be raised among the royal children. He was two years older than the future Charles II and in many ways took the role of an elder brother. He fought bravely in the Civil War, had been with Charles at the battle of Worcester and then joined him in exile. George was handsome, intelligent, amusing, good humoured and generous. He was a good horseman, fencer and dancer as well as being a poet, writer and scientist. He was also a libertine and a rake who was self-serving, unprincipled and disloyal. It was these mixtures of talents, virtues and vices that would make Buckingham fall in and out of royal favour.

Buckingham had been at Dover to welcome Charles when he arrived as king, but was received rather coldly – and not without reason. Buckingham had deserted Charles in exile to return to England and marry the daughter of Lord Fairfax to whom parliament had given Buckingham's confiscated estates. There was also the matter of Buckingham having previously made an unseemly attempt to get off with Charles's sister Mary just after her husband's death. However, such were the bonds of shared experience between Charles and Buckingham that his charm and good company soon brought him back into royal favour. He was made a Gentleman of the Bedchamber and carried the orb at the king's coronation. Although Charles could forgive Buckingham, other major figures who shared the king's exile were less generous. Clarendon considered Buckingham a traitor, and a fool for persuading Charles to have his ill-fated alliance with the Presbyterian Scots. James Butler, now Duke of Ormonde, felt likewise. The bad feeling was equally reciprocated by Buckingham – with additional venom for good measure. By the end of the year Ormonde would be out of the way having been made Lord Lieutenant of Ireland but still a member of the Privy Council and retaining the king's favour. As Barbara and Buckingham were both close to Charles in their different ways and shared a dislike of Clarendon, it was natural that these Villiers cousins should become allies in pursuit of their own interests. However, their potentially formidable alliance did little to curb the influence of Clarendon, who largely directed the government of his indolent monarch and was the father-in-law to the Duke of York, who was heir to the throne until such time as Charles produced a legitimate child of his own. Nevertheless, the time would come when both Barbara and Buckingham would have a significant influence on royal policy and an impact on the government intelligence organisation.

Intelligence gathering was just one of the many duties of the two secretaries of state and their staff. Legal matters and the job of principal adviser to the king rested with Clarendon, the Lord Chancellor. Financial matters were the responsibility of the Earl of Southampton, the Lord Treasurer, although much of this was undertaken by Sir Anthony Ashley Cooper, the Chancellor of the Exchequer. As for virtually everything else concerning the running of the country, this lay with the two secretaries and their staff. Of course, Scotland and Ireland affairs were largely the province of Lauderdale and Ormonde. However, as England was the richest and most populous of the three kingdoms as well as the base of the king and his court, the secretaries were often concerned with Scottish and Irish affairs. The first few years after the Restoration were a particularly busy time because on top of routine work, there was the matter of re-establishing a royal administration to replace that of the Protectorate, which had, in any case, become pretty chaotic since the fall of Richard Cromwell. Added to this was the deluge of mail and personal petitions from the vast number of those who had supported Charles and his father and lost their offices and fortunes in that cause. Understandably they expected rewards or, at the very least, recompense for their loyalty. The secretaries had to administer the distribution of titles, offices, sinecures, land and pensions to the Anglican Church and deserving Royalists. There could not possibly be enough largesse to go round the many who considered themselves deserving. The disappointed would continue pressing their cases for years to come.

As secretaries of state were responsible for all royal correspondence it was essential for them that letter communications could be as swift, secure and efficient as possible. Having such an interest in the smooth running of the postal services it was natural that the supervision of these services should be included among their many responsibilities. The English Royal Mail delivery service had been established by Henry VIII. James I had expanded it to cover Scotland and Ireland so that he could better administer his three kingdoms. Charles I had further widened the scope of the Royal Mail from being purely for Crown correspondence to a service open to the general public. It was granted the monopoly for postage with the recipient paying the cost of the transmission. Cromwell's secretary of state, Thurloe, had introduced a number of measures for improvement such as a fixed postage rate and had them enshrined in the General Post Office Act of 1657. At the Restoration, the legislation of the Protectorate was declared null and void and a new General Post Office Act, based on Thurloe's, was passed in 1660. As part of the Act the office of Post Master General was created and the first incumbent was a Colonel Henry Bishop, who had fought for Charles I and had then adapted himself to life under the Commonwealth. It was his financial proposition rather than his loyalty which commended him for the post as he offered to pay the Crown £21,500 to run the organisation for seven years. Under this system of privatisation known as 'farming', the Crown would have a guaranteed revenue without the bother of having to run the service. The farmer would undertake to provide the service but pocket the profit between his costs and the money he could make from postage charges.

Letters consisted of paper folded and sealed with the address written on the exposed fold (envelopes were not used until 1840). The hub of the Post Office delivery network was the General Letter Office at Clock Lane in the City of London (roughly the same site as the present Bank of England). The General Letter Office was staffed by a small management team, three 'window men' to receive the letters and fifty sorters. All domestic mail passed through the General Letter Office and arrived on Mondays, Wednesdays and Fridays and was dispatched on Tuesdays, Thursdays and Saturdays. Overseas mail went through three clerks in the Foreign Office. There were six post routes out of London with mounted postal messengers stationed about every fifteen miles, and then a network of sub-routes to smaller towns or ports. Thurloe had fully exploited the facility of the General Letter Office and its offshoot at the Foreign Office to intercept the correspondence of foreign embassies and of those suspected of plotting against the state. Sir Edward Nicholas was well aware of the potential value of Clock Lane to government intelligence and Joseph Williamson would have been trying to intercept the letters of suspects. Although the General Post Office was nominally under the secretaries of state, they did not, at this stage, have it properly under control and it would take several more years before its potential as a vital intelligence facility would be realised. One of the reasons for this was that the intercept operation was a covert activity. As such it could only be carried out if the relevant General Letter Office staff were both willing to do so, and could be totally relied upon for their loyalty and secrecy.

The majority of the Protectorate General Letter Office staff had continued in their jobs after the Restoration. By carrying out highly secret operations for Thurloe they had displayed their loyalty to the Protectorate; whether that loyalty and discretion could be transferred to the new regime was more doubtful. There was certainly doubt in the mind of parliament when they realised that Post Office employees included such men as the Leveller, Thomas Chapman, the Baptist, Clement Oxbridge and Cornelius Glover, a servant of Hugh Peters, the hated Cromwellian cleric recently executed for treason. That doubt turned to considerable concern when it became known that Colonel Bishop and some of his clerks had been seen on several occasions in a coffee shop called the Nonsuch Club in Bow Street, which had a strong Republican reputation.[6] Worse still, Bishop had been seen at the Nonsuch in the company of John Wildman. To most Royalists, anyone associating with Wildman was suspect because he was a notorious Republican. Wildman was the son of a Norfolk butcher and had obtained an MA at Corpus Christi, Cambridge, having worked for his education as a college servant. After studying law, he was chosen as a principal advisor to the Agitators of the Parliamentary Army. It was he who had urged them to oppose all compromise with the king. He was commissioned as a major in the New Model Army and became a leader of the Leveller movement that believed in the end of inequality and establishing the sovereignty of the people. After a spell in prison for his radical ideas he was elected MP for Scarborough in the First Protectorate Parliament. As a radical Republican he started to plot against Cromwell and was arrested in 1655. At the time of his arrest he was found writing: *A Declaration of the Free and Well-Afflicted People of England now in Arms Against the Tyranny of Oliver Cromwell.* Unsurprisingly, Cromwell had him thrown in the Tower. Following a public petition he was released two years later on the promise of good conduct and remained out of public notice from then to the Restoration. That did not mean he had retired from his clandestine activities.

Wildman was a complex character. Although a leader of the Levellers he had proved a successful businessman and had accumulated a sizable fortune through the purchase of forfeited Royalist lands at knock-down prices. Despite his dislike of the monarchy, he established contact with Charles's exiled court with a view to forming an alliance between the Levellers and Royalists to overthrow Cromwell. Wildman's offer was cautiously accepted and he busied himself in planning an uprising. The plot became more complex when he entered into negotiations with the Spanish in Flanders for their support for a Royalist/Leveller uprising and was party to a series of Leveller attempts on Cromwell's life. As it happened, the assassination attempts all failed and the Leveller uprising never took place. This may be, at least partially explained, because Wildman seems to have become one of Thurloe's sources – his price for being released from the Tower. If Wildman was genuinely working with the Royalists to bring down the common enemy Cromwell, then he was owed Royalist gratitude. If he was genuinely working for Thurloe, he was a traitor. What is most likely is that Wildman was working for himself and trying to further his Leveller aims in whatever way he could. Certainly that was the view Clarendon took of him. Royalists had every reason to be concerned that Wildman was trying to use the Post Office for his own Republican ends and that Bishop could well be an accomplice, especially when it was discovered that Wildman had loaned money to Bishop to help him buy the Post Office monopoly.

Sir Edward Nicholas had been well aware of the Republican reputation of the Nonsuch Club, which had tactfully changed its name from the 'Commonwealth Club' after the Restoration. He decided to put it under surveillance, probably using Peter Crabb and Samuel Wilcox whom he had engaged to build up a list of London suspects. The surveillance confirmed that the Nonsuch was still frequented by well-known radicals such as Praise God Barebone, Samuel Moyer, James Harrington, John Ireton and John Wildman. A separate report came in from the landlady of an alehouse that she had seen two clerks from the General Letter Office secretly opening some mail. It can only be assumed that they were opening letters that they believed might be to (or from) informants, with the intention of identifying those who were in the pay of government intelligence. It also looked as though the clerks were doing this for John Wildman – and with the connivance of Colonel Bishop. However, before this could be investigated further, more pressing intelligence was received about the Nonsuch.

A secret source reported that Wildman, Barebone, Harrington, and other Republicans were engaged in a plot to seize the gates of the City and bring about an insurrection to re-establish the commonwealth under the Long Parliament. Nicholas ordered the arrest of Wildman, Barebone, and the other conspirators, and they were interrogated by members of the Privy Council.[7] As they admitted nothing and the only evidence against them was that of an anonymous informer, there was no way they could be brought to trial without compromising the source. In any case, two witnesses were necessary for a treason conviction so the evidence of a single informer would not have been enough. The problem was that the prisoners were potentially too dangerous to release, but could not be held indefinitely due to habeas corpus. A solution was found by imprisoning them in areas where habeas corpus did not apply and so they were detained in locations such as Guernsey, St Nicholas Island, off Plymouth, and, in the case of Wildman, the Isles of Scilly. It is interesting to note that Barebone was released much earlier than the others in July of the following year after a petition from his wife on grounds of ill health. As it is unlikely that any Royalist would have cared much about Barebone's health, his release may indicate that he was the anonymous informer. Be that as it may, Wildman and the others remained in custody until 1667. Imprisonment was to prevent Wildman from causing too much harm for the next few years. However, intrigue was imbedded in his nature and as we shall see, many future years of conspiracy and sedition lay ahead of him.

Chapter 3

Plots and Risings
1662–3

'The bishops get all, the courtiers spend all,
The king neglects all, and the devils take all.'
London street refrain

The Clarendon Code was not the only legislation that the Cavalier Parliament enacted for the security of the state. Their very first ordinance was a Treasons Act which condemned, among other things: 'All printing, writing, preaching, or malicious and advised speaking calculated to compass or devise the death, destruction, injury or restraint of the sovereign, or deprive him of his style, honour or kingly name.' The Licensing Act then accompanied the Act of Uniformity in May 1662. This Act brought all printed material under state control thus preventing the production of any book that was critical of Anglicanism, the Crown or its government. Printing was only allowed in Oxford, Cambridge and London, and the printers had to be licensed by either the Archbishop of Canterbury or the Bishop of London. The total number of master printers allowed was twenty and they were each restricted to no more than two presses and two apprentices. The presses had to be registered with the Stationers' Company who were responsible for ensuring no press was set up without their approval. The company's charter gave it the monopoly of printing and the right to search for unregistered presses and books and take legal action against offenders. All books had to be licensed and to receive such a licence they had to be approved by an appropriate censor. These censors were the particular authority on the subject matter for publication such as the Lord Chancellor for legal matters, the two secretaries of state for history and affairs of state, and the Archbishop of Canterbury for religious matters. Once a book had been authorised by the correct censor, a warden of the company had to enter the details of the book and printer in the company register.[1]

The overall supervision of the Licensing Act was yet another task given to the secretaries, who were given powers to issue warrants for the search of premises for illegal presses or books. If an illegal press was found, those responsible would be tried for treason and it was for the judge rather than a jury to decide if the material was seditious. In October the next year, a printer had his premises raided at 4 am and was caught printing a seditious book. His punishment was to be hanged, drawn and quartered. This was a fairly strong message to anyone considering publishing an unauthorised book.

The terms of the Licensing Act were comprehensive and you might think that it had tied up censorship pretty effectively. However, more needed to be done because the Act only covered books and did not include other printed material such as pamphlets and newssheets. Fortunately the Common Law could be used to prosecute for the production of material that contained libel, slander, defamation or sedition. An example of this was in 1664, when a stationer called Brewster was indicted for publishing something that was 'a reproach to the king'. The problem was that whereas the Stationers' Company would ensure compliance with the Licensing Act, there was no similar body to police other publications. This was remedied by the issue of a warrant to establish the office of Surveyor of the Press. The person chosen for the post was Roger L'Estrange, the perfect man for the job. He was the youngest son of a Norfolk baronet who had fought for the king in the Civil War and ended up in parliamentary prison. An ardent Royalist, he had produced pamphlets supporting Charles's return and, after the Restoration, became somewhat obsessed with preventing the printing of any material critical of the government, as was made clear in his pamphlet: *Consideration and Proposal in order to Regulate the Press.* Having been given powers to search for illegal press and seditious material of any kind, be they books or pamphlets, he was in his element. He carried out his duties with tireless enthusiasm aided by his rapidly established network of informants. It had been L'Estrange and his agents who had sniffed out John Twyn and conducted the raid that was to lead to his execution. L'Estrange's dedication resulted in him also being given the monopoly to print the news. His newspaper, the only one authorised in the land, was called *The Intelligencer.* The first edition came out in August 1663 and included advertisements, although they were all of a government nature offering, for example, 40s to any informer of a secret press, 10s for unlicensed books and 5s for identifying 'hawkers of seditious publications'. It was not long before L'Estrange had a wide network of informants who brought him details of those who might be involved in the writing, publishing, printing or distribution of seditious material. The normal pattern was for those suspected of minor infringements to be interrogated either by L'Estrange or one of the secretaries of state, placed in gaol, found guilty at trial, then fined and bound over for good behaviour. A flagrant breach of the Act was of course treated as a matter of treason and would result in the death penalty. In time L'Estrange would become a figure of hatred among all those critical of the government; nicknamed 'the Bloodhound of the Press', his effigy received public burnings. He could have hardly wished for greater tributes to his effectiveness as a censor. However, L'Estrange's service to the state went further than stamping out nearly all criticism of the establishment. As his informants were seeking out illegal printing, they naturally concentrated on those who for religious, political, or personal reasons, were dissatisfied or disaffected. The information gathered by L'Estrange's men thus became a useful addition to the secretary of state's sources of intelligence collection.

One of the most important functions of the secretaries of state was to manage the foreign affairs of their respective departments covering northern and southern Europe. As the two great powers of Europe were Spain and France, it was Sir Edward Nicholas's southern department that took the lead. Foreign affairs was a royal prerogative and so alliances were a matter for the king. In this early part of his reign Charles was to some extent guided by his principal minister Clarendon. France and Spain had been at war from 1635–59 and had concluded the Treaty of the Pyrenees just a year before the Restoration. Although the treaty had been sealed with the marriage of the 16-year-old King Louis to Maria Theresa, the daughter of Philip IV of Spain, the rivalry continued by all means – short of open hostilities. Spain was to all appearances the greater power, controlling as it did the Spanish Netherlands, Franche-Comté, Milan, Naples, Sicily and Sardinia as well as its vast colonies in North, Central, and South America and the Caribbean, in fact an empire of 12.2 million square miles. Philip was, of course, closely allied to his Hapsburg cousin Leopold I, Archduke of Austria, King of Croatia, Hungary and Bohemia, Duke of Burgundy and Luxembourg and, as Holy Roman Emperor, titular head of the German states. The 20-year-old Leopold had been raised for the Church and although a natural ally of Spain against France, he had problems of his own. He had the task of trying to pull together the Holy Roman Empire after the devastation of the Thirty Years War, and had the Ottoman Turks threatening him in Transylvania.

Spain was debilitated from endless war, including the continuing war of independence by Portugal. Phillip IV was now a weary man running a country with a stagnant economy, chaotic government finances, and royal authority slipping away in its many provinces. In 1665 he would be dead and succeeded by his son Carlos II, a severely physically and mentally handicapped 3-year-old boy. France too had been weakened by wars, including its own civil war of the Frondes, although Cardinal Mazarin had managed to overcome the rebellions, and strengthen the position of the throne in relation to the nobility in the process. Mazarin died in 1661 and the young Louis decided to rule alone and continue to build royal power at home while taking any opportunity to expand his domains at the expense of the declining Spanish Empire.

Charles wanted peace and friendly international relations while he consolidated his position after the Restoration. This was easier said than done in the case of Spain, which was still technically at war with England and smarting over the English capture of Jamaica and Dunkirk in Cromwell's time. It would take several years before peace could be established and during that time there would be intermittent naval engagements between the two countries, especially in the Caribbean. With his French mother and adored sister living in Paris, Charles was naturally drawn towards favouring France. He also had growing respect and admiration for his young cousin Louis, who could rule as he pleased without the inconvenience of a headstrong House of Commons. It would become one of Charles's aims to establish an alliance with France but it would be almost eight years before this would be achieved.

One of Charles's first foreign affairs decisions was the selection of a wife. There were few suitable European princesses to choose from and the king and Clarendon finally alighted on Catherine of Braganza. Catherine was the daughter of John, Duke of Braganza, who had led the revolt of Portugal against Spain in 1640 and subsequently been elected king. The Portuguese revolt had been supported by France, who was then at war with Spain. When hostilities were ended by the Treaty of the Pyrenees in 1659, France agreed to recognise Philip IV of Spain as King of Portugal. John of Portugal had died four years previously, leaving his severely paralysed and mentally unstable 13-year-old son Alfonso as king, and his widow Luisa as Regent. With Portugal still fighting for independence from Spain and having lost its main ally, Queen Luisa was eager to obtain a marriage alliance with England. It was agreed that England would send Portugal a brigade of 2,000 foot and 500 horse to support the struggle against Spain in return for a mouth-wateringly huge dowry.

Catherine's dowry comprised of two million Portuguese crowns, together with the Seven Islands of Bombay, and the town of Tangier. Bombay, with its large natural harbour, was leased to the East India Company and, surviving some attacks ten years later, would eventually develop into the great commercial city of British India. Tangier was another matter. It had the capability of being the premier trading port for North West Africa and, like Gibraltar, was strategically important as a naval base for controlling the entrance to the Mediterranean. The problem was that it was still claimed by Spain and had been left almost deserted when the Portuguese pulled out. Worse still, it was constantly being harassed by Berber tribesmen and would need a strong garrison to protect it. As we shall see, this wedding gift would become a thorn in England's side. The only positive aspect in the short term was that, like the brigade sent to Portugal, it offered employment for soldiers from Cromwell's disbanded army and took these potential trouble makers far from England.

When the 23-year-old Catherine arrived at Portsmouth, she was met by Charles who was pleasantly surprised to find that 'there was nothing in her face that in a least degree can disgust one.'[2] She was, however, very small with slightly buck teeth and her hair and clothes were in the Portuguese fashion, which looked completely outlandish to English eyes. Although a perfectly presentable and charmingly demure queen, this extremely pious lady had been raised in a convent and could not begin to compare with the Countess of Castlemaine in terms of looks or, indeed, companionship, for neither she nor Charles had any language in common. Charles decided to have his cake and eat it by establishing both his queen and his principal mistress together at court; one for official duties, the other for romance and companionship. After much crying, foot-stamping and anguish by Catherine, Clarendon forced her to accept Barbara Castlemaine as a Lady of the Bedchamber, and the woman with whom Charles openly spent the majority of his time. By the end of the year Catherine had resigned herself to the situation with dignity. Her pragmatism paid off and it won her Charles's respect and affection, if not love. Catherine was not interested in politics and had little or no influence in matters of state. Sadly, she would have three miscarriages and never produce an heir, so was denied the status of the mother of a future monarch. Any feminine influence over Charles was exerted by the manipulative Castlemaine. The whole court knew this and the ambitious and avaricious fell over themselves to seek her favour. As those courtiers who could be considered 'ambitious and avaricious' amounted to virtually the whole court, it was only a very small minority, such as Clarendon, who remained beyond the reach of her charms. It would cost him dear.

While the king and his court occupied themselves with extravagant entertainments, amusing pastimes and open debauchery, secretaries of state were increasingly busy on intelligence matters. St Bartholomew's Day (24 August) was approaching – the date set for the clergy and teachers to accept the rites of the Church of England or be expelled. Rumours of planned resistance in Somerset, Dorset and Bristol had to be investigated, and there was also the need to keep tabs on dissident Nonconformists and Republicans who had fled to the continent. The main way this was achieved was through the ambassadors at Brussels and The Hague. Sir William Temple was ambassador to the Spanish Netherlands in Brussels and he took on the task of recruiting agents to monitor the activities of dissidents in Flanders and the German States.[3] Although he kept track of Richard Cromwell, General Desborough, Cromwell's brother-in-law, and a number of less notable Commonwealth figures, all were more concerned with maintaining their own safety than plotting against the king. Of far greater importance in intelligence-gathering was the ambassador to The Hague, Sir George Downing.

Downing was a very experienced intelligencer and ruthless in the pursuit of his ends. His life had already been highly eventful before he became ambassador in March 1661. Born in Dublin, his parents had immigrated to Massachusetts where he had graduated at Harvard before returning to England at the start of the Civil War. He became a chaplain in a parliamentarian regiment and then moved into military intelligence, rising to be Cromwell's Scoutmaster General in Scotland. He became an MP and, as a trusted ally of Cromwell, was made the Protectorate's resident in The Hague where he was very successful in spying against the Royalist exiles. On the fall of Richard Cromwell, Downing had stayed in post but, assessing that Charles might return as king, began passing Thurloe's secret information to the Royalists. In 1660 he was knighted for his treachery and returned to his former post in The Hague the next year – but this time as the king's ambassador with a fund of £1,000 a year for intelligence gathering.[4]

The largely Calvinist United Provinces were the destination of choice of nearly all Nonconformist dissidents. Their surveillance and the penetration of their meetings was therefore an important task of Downing's agents and informants. Of even higher priority was the surveillance of senior members of the commonwealth who had found sanctuary in Holland, men such as Cornet George Joyce, who had arrested Charles I at Haltom House, and Miles Corbet, a Republican MP who was a regicide – the name given to those who had signed Charles I's death warrant. Two even more prominent regicides, Colonel John Barkstead (who had been Lieutenant Governor of the Tower and Cromwell's chief interrogator) and Colonel John Okey (a staunch Republican who had been colonel of the regiment to which Downing had been a chaplain), were living near Frankfurt, and so were frustratingly beyond Downing's reach. There was an English merchant in Delft called Abraham Kirke who Downing discovered was friends with many of the exiles including Barkstead and Okey. With his usual professionalism, Downing managed to recruit Kirke as an agent and tasked him to report on his Republican friends. Kirke soon proved he was worth his money when he reported to Downing that he was arranging to bring the wives of Barkstead and Okey over from England and had offered his house in Delft as the place where they could be reunited. Okey was aware that Downing, his former regimental chaplain, was ambassador and sent a messenger to him asking if it would be safe for him and Barkstead to go to Delft to meet their wives. Downing sent the contact back with the message that he would take no action against them. Reassured by this, the two regicides travelled to Kirke's house in Delft in March 1661 and stayed without problems awaiting the arrival of their wives. Meanwhile, Downing applied for an extradition order. The application had to be made to Johann De Witt, the Grand-Pensionary of Holland and de facto ruler of the United Provinces. De Witt was a staunch Republican determined to prevent Charles's 12-year-old nephew, William of Orange, inheriting the Stadtholdership when he came of age. Nevertheless, de Witt wanted reasonable relations with England and so reluctantly agreed to the extradition, probably believing that Downing would have insufficient time to put it into effect. So far, so good. Downing then suggested that Kirke invite the third regicide, Miles Corbet, to join them at his house for supper. While the invitation was being sent to Corbet, Downing took a party of English soldiers and some of his embassy staff to Delft. When it was known that Corbet would be arriving, Downing bribed the local magistrate to be prepared to carry out the arrests.

On the evening that Corbet visited for supper, Downing and his party raided Kirke's house. The three men were seized while they were quietly smoking their pipes by the fireside and dragged off to the local gaol before they could put up any resistance. The operation was a success but covert operations on foreign territory seldom run completely smoothly. Dutch municipalities have a tradition of independence and, urged on by the burgers of Amsterdam Delft, the magistrates refused to hand over their captives who they regarded as religious refugees. What was more, many citizens of Delft had sympathy with the three Englishmen and there was talk of them organising a gaol break. Downing obtained the huge sum of £1,200 from

Clarendon and gave such high bribes to the key official that they forgot their scruples. He managed to get Barkstead, Okey and Corbet secretly out of the gaol at night and into a canal boat, which took them to the English ship the *Blackamore* that he had pre-positioned.[5] The three regicides were transported back to England where they endured the horrific executions that the law prescribed for treason.

Downing was not an attractive personality but he must be given credit for successfully conducting a complex and difficult covert operation. He had proved his new-found loyalty to the Stuart regime and in time would receive additional recognition to go with his knighthood. This included the grant of some swampy land in Whitehall on which he built a street of houses that was named after him. The success of the Delft operation demonstrated the long arm of Stuart revenge and served as a warning to other Republican leaders to refrain from plotting for the Good Old Cause. This warning was heeded and republican exiles never posed any real threat to the monarchy for the rest of the reign. As the secretaries of state and the two ambassadors could not be sure that this would be the case, intelligence efforts continued to be directed against these aging and politically spent fugitives. The Republican exile who inspired the greatest fear back in England was Edmund Ludlow. He was a parliamentary general who had been one of the judges at Charles I's trial and signed his death warrant. A staunch Republican, he had opposed Cromwell becoming Lord Protector. On the fall of Richard Cromwell he took command of the troops in Ireland and tried to persuade the army and parliament to re-establish a Republican Commonwealth. He was out manoeuvred by Monck and, being a regicide, fled the country after the Restoration. While all other Republican generals were either safely in prison or had fled to America, Ludlow had been given sanctuary in Vevey in Switzerland and so was the most prominent Republican still at large. Ludlow changed his name to Edmund Phillips and became fully accepted by his neighbours in Vevey. There was no question of obtaining extradition from Switzerland and indeed it would even be impossible to get agreement for extradition again from the United Provinces as was found out when a request was made to extradite Cornet Joyce. Assassination was the obvious way round the problem. However, when Downing had earlier requested permission to assassinate Barkstead, Clarendon had told him that assassination required the king's permission and that Charles was not prepared to countenance it. Downing's hands were therefore tied, but a number of former soldiers turned mercenaries thought they would attempt the assassinations of regicides in the hope of reward. One such was Germaine Riordane, an Irish Catholic who, it is believed, was offered £300 by Charles's sister Minette for the murder of Ludlow.[6] He assembled a gang of seven suitably disreputable Irish accomplices and arrived by boat in Vevey having crossed Lake Geneva from Savoy. Their intention was to shoot Ludlow as he went to Sunday morning church with his small band of fellow exiles. As a first step they decided to sabotage the boats in the Vevey beach to prevent any pursuit. Unfortunately, Riordane and his gang stood out like sore thumbs with their furtive behaviour and long cloaks bulging with concealed carbines. Honest citizens of Vevey warned off Ludlow and then, discovering that their boats had been damaged, went after Riordane and his men who just managed to escape back to Savoy by the skin of their teeth.

There would be no more serious attempts to kill Ludlow but the experience had been an alarming one for Ludlow and his compatriots. One of the exiles with Ludlow in Vevay was John Lisle, who had been another of the judges at Charles I's trial. He decided that it was no longer safe to stay and moved to the town of Lausanne. This turned out to be a bad decision. Riordane heard about his move and sent two of his gang, Thomas MacDonnell and James Cotter, to Lausanne. In what was becoming their modus operandi, the two Irishmen waited for Lisle to walk to church and then shot him in the back. The assassins made their escape on horseback to the Geneva area. When news of Lisle's murder reached England, Riordane and the two assassins were acclaimed as heroes in the government press and received various rewards including commissions in the army. Riordane later returned to being a cut-throat mercenary on the continent then disappears from historical view, and MacDonnell was soon dead with the 'French pox'. Cotter, on the other hand, eventually rose to lieutenant colonel in an Irish regiment, carried out various covert activities abroad for Williamson and for these and other services received a pension of £200 a year and a knighthood. Although it was a perilous path, a discharged army thug could use a career in the seamier side of clandestine operations to rise to the gentry.

Although concerned about republican refugees abroad, the secretaries of state had the immediate problem of the ejection of the clergy and teachers who would not subscribe to the Anglican faith by the 24 August deadline. Security was tightened. In June 1662 Charles ordered the demolition of walls and fortifications of Coventry, Northampton, Gloucester and Taunton to prevent them being held by dissenters, and Lords Lieutenant were directed to check the loyalty of their militia.[6] As it happened St Bartholomew's Day passed quietly. Many Nonconformist ministers decided to take the Vicar of Bray approach and hold on to their livings by accepting the Anglican

Communion. There were, however, 1,760 ministers in England and a further 120 in Wales, together with about 150 university teachers, who would not compromise their beliefs and found themselves with no livelihood.[7] They went quietly and there was little or no violent protest at their going. Most stayed in their local areas and tried to secretly conduct worship for the like-minded of their former congregations. A number moved to the United Provinces, particularly Rotterdam, where their activities fell under the surveillance of Downing's informants. Although several months passed with no indication of either Republican or Nonconformist opposition, subsequent events showed that Sir Edward Nicholas and his intelligence staff were right to have been concerned, but for Sir Edward this was soon to be no longer his problem.

The senior courtiers at Charles's court were invariably richly dressed but one man in particular stood out. He wore expensive clothes but, instead of being in the rich colours of his contemporaries, he tended to be dressed in black. What is more, Sir Henry Bennet had a black plaster covering the bridge of his nose to remind everyone that he had received a sabre wound when fighting for the king in the Civil War. He had joined the Royalist court in exile and being an intelligent and amusing person, won Charles's affection. Indeed, they had much in common and it is said that, like the king, Bennet also had an illegitimate child by Lucy Walter. Charles had knighted him and sent him to be his representative in Spain. He returned to England a year after the Restoration and soon joined the ambitious but pleasure-loving faction of Castlemaine and Buckingham. Charles made him Keeper of the Privy Purse but Castlemaine wanted more for her smooth tongued protégé and encouraged Charles to give him higher office. So it was that, against Clarendon's advice, Bennet was made secretary of state for the South in October 1662 at the age of 44. Bennet's post of Keeper of the Privy Purse was given to Charles Berkeley, a royal favourite and one of Castlemaine's lovers. A man described by Bishop Burnet as 'without any visible merit, unless it was managing the king's amours.'[8] The dependable but aged Nicholas was retired with a pension and the younger man took over. This change further strengthened the Castlemaine/Buckingham power base and undermined that of Clarendon. Charles might well have promoted Bennet without Castlemaine's nagging as he knew him well and could see it was time for a younger man to take the reins. Bennet was a polished and sophisticated courtier who was highly intelligent, fluent in three languages, and someone Charles could trust. Unlike Nicholas, he had strong personal ambition. He could be relied upon to work tirelessly in the king's service in order to hold a position of influence that enabled him to receive the back handers so necessary for funding his wildly extravagant lifestyle.

A measure of Bennet's different approach to the job was that when he took over Nicholas's office and lodgings he had a door made, giving direct access to the king's apartments.[9] He decided to set his own stamp on the Secretaryship and dismissed some of Nicholas's staff to be replaced by his own men. One person dismissed was Joseph Williamson who was known to be Nicholas's protégé. It would seem that Bennet soon realised his mistake when it became clear that Williamson alone knew where many documents were filed, and also held much vital information in his head that had not been committed to paper. Williamson had proved indispensable and was very soon back at his desk. So began what was to be an incredibly fruitful intelligence partnership. Bennet, the ruthless and astute politician with the king's ear, and Williamson, the hard working bureaucrat who would use any means to ensure the security of the state. There was no particular friendship in this team, the relationship was one of master and servant, but it was to be so successful because both men were natural intelligencers who worked hard in the king's (and their own) interests and neither were burdened by moral scruples.

About the time of Bennet's appointment, two informers separately reported to the recently retired Lord Mayor of London, Major General Sir Richard Browne, what was to be known as the 'Tonge Plot.' Sir William Morrice, the secretary of state for the North, afterwards described the plot as 'an inconsiderable design, not formed nor any determinate way agreed on the execution.'[10] It is true that there were no people of importance involved in the plot but it was nevertheless an attempted insurrection and was a matter of concern at the time. The informants were William Hill, an ejected minister who was the son of a Cromwell supporter, and John Bradley, a former messenger for Cromwell's Council of State. With this background they were able to become privy to some of the seditious discussions of adherents to the Good Old Cause. Hill and Bradley, like nearly all walk-in informants, wanted some reward and the more dramatic their information, the more likely the reward was to be sizeable. They appeared to have discovered that Captain John Baker and Edward Riggs were planning an uprising of dissenters and Republicans. Both men were down on their luck. Baker had been a member of Cromwell's Life Guard and was now reduced to being a knife grinder, and Riggs had been a Nonconformist minister, ejected from his parish and was now a brewer's clerk.

Having reported the plot to Browne, Hill and Bradley were of course told to get as close as possible to the conspirators and report back. There is every likelihood that in their enthusiasm for the task, the informants became *agent provocateurs* who actively participated in developing the plot. Whether or not this was the case, they were eventually able to give Brown the details of the intended uprising. The plan was to seize Windsor Castle with 500 supporters and then capture the Tower of London. After this they would capture the king and General Monck in Whitehall, recall the Long Parliament, and arrange for General Lambert to escape from his Guernsey prison to become their leader. Thomas Tonge, a retired soldier, now a distiller, who lived at Tower Ditch became central to the success of the plot. He was in touch with some of the Windsor guard who had agreed to assist in giving entry to the Castle. Tonge also knew some of the yeoman warders at the Tower, whom he was confident he could bribe to facilitate entry. The date set for the attack was All Hallow's Eve, but it never got off the ground.

On 28 October, Browne ordered Hill to take a party of soldiers to where Tonge and some of his follow conspirators were meeting so they could be arrested. Tonge and others were duly captured and further arrests followed. It was then time for the conspirators to be interrogated or 'examined' as it was termed in those days. Bennet led the examinations along with members of the council and the king himself took part in the questioning. Examinations in England did not include torture and were formal legal affairs to produce written statements. This did not stop the practice of showing subjects the rack which could result in them confessing there and then. Also, anyone interrogated under suspicion of treason knew that their life hung in the balance and that many a man had gone to a horrific death on fairly flimsy evidence. It was, therefore, sensible to provide incriminating evidence against others in the hope of a reciprocal pardon or lenient sentence. The examination process also offered the intelligencer the opportunity to do a deal with the suspect and turn them into an agent for the State. Such a suspect would then be released after a decent interval to return to their seditious friends and report back on them. This was the case for Edward Riggs who, when interrogated by the king and Duke of York, was given the option of being hanged, leaving his wife and children destitute, or of becoming a government agent. He chose the latter and was returned to the Tower where he remained until April the next year when he was released on security of £500. Four months later he was settled in Rotterdam working as a physician and getting himself accepted into the ex-patriot radical community. Fairly rapidly he became privy to the scheming of the dissidents, which he reported direct to Williamson for an annual payment of £35.

From the examinations, others who had been loosely associated with the plot were named and arrested. The prisoners provided more and more information, some real and some made up, anything to save their lives. It was said that there was going to be a rising of ex-soldiers in Dorset, and one in Kent led by a Colonel William Kenrick. There were many reports of General Ludlow being seen in England although he had remained in Switzerland completely unaware of the plot. On 11 December, Tonge and several others went on trial and were hanged at Tyburn eleven days later. The examination of more suspects continued, the most fruitful of which was of a man called Baker who implicated Captain Robert Johnson, a former member of Cromwell's Life Guards. Johnson had had little to do with this plot but was in close touch with a number of radicals. Realising his life was in danger he gave valuable details of a network of radicals in Scotland, France and the United Provinces. There were further arrests and executions. The death or imprisonment of all those even loosely associated with Tonge had completely crushed that particular plot. However, those convicted were people of little account and the most valuable gain for the government was a much better understanding of the wider activities of Republicans, dissenters and others who might take up arms against the king. Among those whose names came to intelligence attention were former Cromwellian officers: Colonel Gilby Carr a strong Presbyterian, Colonel Henry Danvers who was also a Nonconformist minister, Captain Nathaniel Strange, a Fifth Monarchist, and Captain John Lockyer, all of whom were to take part in other plots. As for the two informants, they both received rewards. John Bradbury was made a king's messenger; William Hill was rather surprisingly made a naval chaplain.[11] As both had openly testified in court, their public appointments served as an encouragement to others to consider the advantages of taking up the informant's trade. In the years to come the government would need all the reliable informants it could recruit.

Chapter 4

Plots Spread
1664

'Plots true or false are necessary things
To raise up commonwealths and ruin kings'
John Dryden *Absalom and Achitophel*

As far as Charles was concerned, the uncovering of the Tonge Plot had been a success and, by extension, showed that his new secretary of state was on top of his intelligence duties. On 4 November 1663 he wrote to Minette:

You will have heard by now of the Alarm we have had of the risings of the Anabaptists. But our spies have played their parts so well amongst them, as we have taken many of them, who will be hanged very speedily, so as I believe for this time, their designs are broke.[1]

Williamson and others of Bennet's staff were occupied with collating and exploiting the information from the Tonge Plot when their attention was suddenly directed to Ireland. Ormonde had been sent to Ireland as Lord Lieutenant, that is the king's ruler of a population of 1.7 million, bitterly divided by family and religious loyalties. He was very experienced at running the complex affairs of Ireland, which was just as well as he was to be confronted with two significant problems. The first was that Ireland was a predominantly Catholic country, although there was a sizable Protestant population of Scots and English settlers who were mainly Nonconformist. The implementation of the Clarendon Code had meant that dissenting clergy had been driven from the churches and that Catholics and Nonconformists alike were second-class citizens to Church of Ireland Anglicans. The second problem was the matter of settling the redistribution of land. Some land had been granted by Charles I for loyal service; this and other land had been confiscated from both Royalists and the Church and large amounts of land had been taken from their Catholic owners, who were then resettled in the less fertile area of Shannon. The lands confiscated by Cromwell had been given to supporters of the Protectorship, mainly soldiers of the New Model Army. At the Restoration of Charles it was decided that those granted land under Cromwell would keep it, but that formerly confiscated land should be returned to the Church, Royalist supporters and Catholics who had played no part in the rebellion. This was all very fair but had the disadvantage that there would be nothing like the amount of land necessary for its implementation. A Court of Claims was established to adjudicate on the many conflicting land claims in an attempt to resolve the problem. Unfortunately, when over 500 Irish Catholics had their land restored, the court was seen to be favouring them at the expense of English Protestants. By 1663, many English Nonconformists were so aggrieved by the attacks on their religion and their property that they were considering rebellion.

In spring 1663, a plot was formulated to carry out a rebellion beginning with the seizure of Dublin Castle and the arrest of Ormonde. The principal leader was Colonel Alexander Jephson, MP for Trim in County Meath, and he was joined by a number of former soldiers and Nonconformist ministers. However, the man who was most remembered for the plot was Thomas Blood; he would soon become infamous as the most wanted man in England. Blood was a tall, pockmarked, roughhewn man who owned some land near Dublin in County Meath. He was a committed Presbyterian and had originally supported the king in the Civil War but then changed sides and went to England to join the Parliamentary Army when the Irish Royalists allied with the Catholics. He had returned to Ireland in 1649 with Cromwell as a Lieutenant and was granted some confiscated land for his service. When Cromwell died and Richard Cromwell fell, Blood had joined other officers in supporting General Lambert. They took over Dublin Castle and arrested the commander Colonel Jones. Then Monck defeated Lambert and ordered Jones to be released. Blood was discharged and returned to civilian life. He might have settled down to managing his small estate in Meath and lived happily ever after with his wife Mary but for the fact that both his estate and his religion were now under threat.[2]

Blood and a relation who was a Presbyterian clergyman called William Lecky went to Ulster to see what support there might be for an uprising. They established a small group of supporters and another Presbyterian minister, Andrew McCormack, arranged for communications to be set up between the plotters in Dublin and their sympathisers in Ulster. A manifesto was produced demanding that all the English and Scottish landowners should be restored to the estates they had possessed as of 7 May 1659, and that Religion should be settled according to the Solemn League of the Covenant. Other Presbyterian and Congregationalist minsters including John Crookshanks and Michael Bruce joined the plot, as well as some former soldiers, most notably Colonel Gilby Carr who had been involved in the Tonge Plot. These were not mere protesters, but men who meant business in trying to overthrow the government. Crookshanks, for example, had translated the sixteenth-century defence of tyranniside: *De juri regni apud Scotus*. Given a chance, they would like to put it in to practice, starting with a full uprising in Ireland. Their plan developed into an expectation that once Dublin had been taken, the strongholds of Cork, Limerick, Waterford, and Clonmel would follow suit. After Ireland had risen, so might Scotland and England.

The final plan was to launch the uprising at about 6 am on a suitable day in May 1663 when a group of six men would enter Dublin Castle by the Great Gate and walk to Ship Street near the rear gates to join petitioners queuing to see the Lord Lieutenant. Once Ormonde had arrived, a man disguised as a baker would drop a basket of loaves at the back gate to cause a diversion. While the guards came to help the baker, the six men would attack and overpower them. They would then open the gates and let in about eighty accomplices who had been hiding outside. This larger force would then take over the castle and arrest Ormonde. Although this plan does not appear very promising, it was a bold one that might just have been enough to spark the highly combustible Protestant resentment and lead to a general rising. As it was, one of the conspirators, Philip Alden, had been passing detailed reports about the plot to Ormonde virtually from the beginning. If that was not enough, Colonel Jephson had tried to enlist Sir Theophilus Jones into the plot, but Jones had gone straight to Ormonde to tell him about it. Ormonde had been letting the plot progress in order to reveal the full extent of those involved. Ormonde knew the date for the operation, but when that was postponed because the conspirators found it difficult to get all their supporters mobilised in time, Ormonde decided to wait no longer. On 21 May he sent out the order for the arrest of 'certain wicked persons of Phanatick and disloyal principles'. Colonel Jephson, and twenty-three other conspirators were immediately arrested. Philip Alden, the main informant, was included in those arrested to preserve his cover and so that he could be used as a stool pigeon. A few months later, arrangements were made for him to escape and he went to England where he became one of Williamson's agents and eventually retired on a secret service pension of £100 a year. More arrests were carried out and by June, the number of accused had risen to seventy. A pretty effective clean up – although a few conspirators did manage to evade arrest. Most notable of these were three dissenting clergy: John Crookshanks, Andrew McCormack, and Michael Bruce, as well as two former soldiers: Gilby Carr and Thomas Blood. The ministers escaped to Scotland where they were to become prominent among the Phanaticks in the South West. Colonel Gilby Carr managed to reach the safety of Holland. Blood had a £100 bounty on his head and went to ground first in Antrim and then England, where he lived under various false names and disguises.

When those arrested were brought to trial, Jephson and two others were sentenced to hang while the rest received imprisonment. In his scaffold speech, one of the condemned men accused Blood of being the main person responsible for the plot and so brought Blood to public attention and began what was to become almost legendary notoriety. The investigations into the plot by Ormonde's council revealed that as well as Jephson, a number of other MPs had been implicated. There was not enough evidence to charge them, but seven were deemed sufficiently suspect that the House of Commons of Ireland not only deprived them of their seats but 'made them incapable of exercising employment civil, military or ecclesiastical, with in this Kingdom.'[3] It is now thought that up to ten MPs had been aware of the plot. If so, it shows that, unlike the Tonge Plot, it had the backing of a number of prominent people and just might have sparked the desired widespread rebellion.

Blood's relation, Reverand William Lecky, would have received the death sentence but managed to convince the court that he was insane by insisting that he was Jesus Christ. Lecky was sent to Newgate prison where, about six months later, he received two lady visitors. The 'ladies' were Phanaticks in disguise and filed through his chains and managed to get Lecky out of the gaol – also disguised as a woman. No one knows for sure, but it was thought by many that one of the 'ladies' was Thomas Blood. As it happened, there was confusion amongst the 'ladies' fleeing from the prison during which Lecky became separated from the others and was later recaptured. This time he received the death penalty. A very large crowd of over a thousand came to watch his hanging, but then a rumour went round that Lecky was going to be rescued by Blood and his gang. There was panic in the crowd and many ran away – including the hangman, leaving Lecky on the scaffold with the rope round his neck. After some time it became clear that Blood was not going to carry out a rescue so the crowd and hangman returned and the sentence was carried out.[4]

Despite the failure of the Dublin Plot and the punishment of those implicated, there still remained considerable resentment in the Protestant community of Ireland on both property rights and religious intolerance. The problem of religious intolerance was not to go away but was to some extent alleviated by Ormonde's reasonably tolerant implementation of the Clarendon Code. Two years after the Dublin Plot, the Act of Explanation was passed which favoured Protestants in resolving land ownership and so very much reduced cause for unrest. Ormonde's role in the Civil War had given him considerable experience in running informants and he made good use of them to identify Phanaticks, Republicans and other potential troublemakers. He also increased the size of the militia and purged the army and public service of any whose loyalty he held doubts. There would be further plots, not least by Thomas Blood, but these security measures help to explain why there were no insurrections in Ireland for the rest of the reign. That was not to be the case in Charles's other two kingdoms.

With the Dublin Plot coming on top of the Tonge Plot, rumours of uprisings were rife throughout the three kingdoms. A large amount of information on conspiracies was coming in to the authorities, most of it completely spurious. There was no doubt that there was widespread dissatisfaction from persecuted Nonconformists, Commonwealth men hankering after the 'Good Old Cause', and hostility to the new 'hearth tax' imposed at a time of great extravagance in the royal court. These grounds for discontent resulted in people voicing resistance to the government but, despite the many house searches and arrests that took place, nothing substantive came to light. Clarendon wrote: 'The continual discourse of plots and insurrections had so wearied the king, that he even resolved to give no more countenance to any such information to trouble himself with inquiry into them.'[5] It was not just Bennet, Williamson, and his clerks who were receiving these reports, but magistrates and deputy lieutenants from all corners of the realm. Among these numerous reports was one by John Cosin, Bishop of Durham, received at about the same time as the Dublin Plot. As Cosin was a Prince Bishop he was also Lord Lieutenant and had made it his business to rigorously monitor the activity of radicals. A Baptist from Northumberland called John Ellerington had been referred to the bishop as he had alleged that his conscience was bothering him about his involvement in a plot. Conscience or not, he was still eager to exchange his information for payment and could have been just another of the volunteer informants hoping for some money. With the advantage of hindsight we now know that this was the first indication to the authorities of what was later to become the Northern Plot.

Ellerington told the bishop that Phanatick conspirators were meeting at

Derwentdale and Muggleswick Park, Durham, to plan an uprising. They were mainly Baptists and Congregationalists rather that Presbyterians as had been the case in Dublin, but they had connections with other dissenter groups. Ellerington gave the names of the leaders as John Ward, John Joplin, Captains Gower and Doffen, and a few members of the gentry such as Sir Henry Witherington, and explained that his role was to act as courier taking letters between groups.[6] As there was nothing definite for the bishop to act on he told Ellerington to continue his activities with the conspirators and regularly report back. Ellerington was later able to report that the uprising had been postponed because the group were hoping that parliament would issue a dispensation for 'tender consciences' that would meet their main objectives. When it was clear that parliament was in no mood to modify the Clarendon Code, the uprising was again postponed to await the return of Dr Edward Richardson from the United Provinces. Richardson was a clergyman who had been ejected from his church in Ripon and had then joined other Phanaticks in Holland. In spring, Richardson did return to England and settled in Harrogate practising as a physician and assuming the role of leading figure in the Northern Plot. Unfortunately, as time passed, the dissidents began to become suspicious of Ellerington and stopped using him as a courier so his value as a source was greatly reduced just at a time when Richardson was providing the leadership for the conspiracy and greatly widening its support.

Sir Thomas Gower was the Sheriff of Yorkshire and Deputy Lieutenant of the North Riding. Gower was even more ardent in his pursuit of radicals and Phanaticks than the Bishop of Durham. He had a small army of agents and informants and these were able to provide him and the authorities in London with a reasonable outline of the progress of the plot. It was learnt that Richardson had set up a council, which included Captain John Lockyer, who had returned from Holland after the Dublin Plot, Captain Roger Jones, who had been involved in the Tonge Plot, Captain Robert Atkinson, a Presbyterian, and a London representative called Timothy Butler who was holding a cache of 2,000 weapons in Thames Street. Also on the council was Lockyer's friend Thomas Blood, never one to miss an opportunity for intrigue. As it happened, Blood disengaged from the conspiracy after a short time. He may have removed himself because, as a wanted man, he was worried the authorities were about to catch up with him. Alternatively, he may have just become disenchanted with all the wrangling in the council to try to reconcile the differing objectives of Congregationalist, Presbyterians, Quakers and Fifth Monarchists. Whatever the reason, after much heated council debate, an uprising declaration was eventually produced with the engaging title 'A door of hope in the Valley of

Achor for the Mourners in Sion out of the North.' The plan at this stage was to attack York and have an uprising in London to seize the king and have other uprisings elsewhere in the country. Captain John Mason, who had joined Richardson's council, had dissident contacts in the West of England and South Wales who he expected would join a rising. Richardson believed that 20,000 horse and 30,000 foot could be counted on to take part and ammunition from the United Provinces would arrive via Bridlington. After further acrimonious debate a new date for the uprising was set for 6 August, the day of the opening of the York Assizes when most of the Royalist gentry would be present and could therefore be captured. Major Joshua Greathead, who had served under General Lambert, was going to command the West Riding contingent, however, he had been so annoyed with the selection of the date for the uprising that he decided to change sides and reported the plot to Sir Thomas Gower. Understandably, Gower told Greathead 'to dissemble till they had drawn in all the friends they could to join with them, and then give evidence against them.'[7] Gower now had an agent in the very heart of the plot's decision making.

Gower informed Monck, the Commander of the Army, that, disregarding the optimistic figures of the plotters, he estimated about 1,500 men were on the verge of rebellion. As a result, a Colonel Freschville was ordered to secure York, and the Duke of Buckingham, who held the position of Lord Lieutenant of the West Riding, was sent from London with reinforcements. When Richardson heard that government reinforcements were on their way, he asked Greathead to take a force to ambush Buckingham en route. Greathead made various excuses and refused. Gower decided to carry out some disruptive arrests. Richardson was a prime target for arrest but somehow gave Gower's men the slip and managed to escape back to the Unitied Provinces. About 100 other suspects were arrested, but charged with frequenting conventicles rather than treason so they would not realise that their plot was compromised. After providing security they were then freed, but Gower's men were now familiar with most of the conspirators and where they lived. Following this disruption the conspirators' council met again with John and Robert Atkinson as the main leaders. Refusal to ambush Buckingham had made Greathead suspect, but he was still able to report that the rising was now set for 12 October. By 28 September, Gower was in the envious position of having two other well-positioned sources to confirm Greathead's reports: Colonel Smithson and Joseph Strangeways; with Ellerington still providing what information he could. In addition, Bennet was receiving information about Richardson and other supporters of the rising in Holland, including that two former Tonge plotters, Tyler and Cole, had sent 1,000 carbines and a consignment of pistols from Amsterdam. These reports came from Edward Riggs, the man who had been turned after the Tonge Plot and showed he was worth his £35 a year agent's pay.

The plan was still to capture York, but also to secure the Severn and Trent by capturing Gloucester and Nottingham. Hull and Tynemouth would be taken in order to have communication with the Scots, and Boston to enable the receipt of supplies from the United Provinces. There was also hope of risings in Dorset, Somerset and Wiltshire. Once troops had left London to deal with the rebellions, a Colonel John Pearson would capture the king and other dignitaries, then seize Whitehall, at which time there would be an uprising in London. The rebels also hoped that when the uprising had started, General Ludlow would return to England and become their leader. Having been informed of the extent of the plot, the king directed the Deputy Lord Lieutenants to call out the militia in the West Riding, Cheshire and Lancashire, and for key garrisons to be reinforced. On 10 October most of the ringleaders were arrested, including Greathead, and a total of about 100 were put in custody. Undeterred, some of the remaining rebels under Lieutenant Colonel Walters went ahead and gathered at the planned rendezvous at Topcliffe Bridge in readiness to seize weapons from Northallerton prior to attacking York. The weather was appalling and there was such a poor turnout that they decided to disband and go home. On the same day the same situation repeated itself when Robert Atkinson found that only fifty-nine men had turned up for the rendezvous at Appleby in Westmoreland, Captain Thomas Oats only got a turnout of about fifty at Farnley Wood near Leeds, and even less gathered under Captain Roger Jones in Durham.

The Northern Plot, which might have been a serious threat to the state, came to nothing because of inept leadership and planning by the conspirators and an effective government intelligence system. As Buckingham had assembled at least 1,000 men including the militia, it would have been hard for the rebels to defeat such a force. That said, without the intelligence, Buckingham's force would not have been raised, the government would have been caught by surprise and the rebels would not have suffered the massive disruption of the 100 arrests on the eve of the uprising. The failed rising was followed by many more arrests and investigations into suspects continued for several years. Despite the efforts of the authorities, relatively few people were tried for treason because of the old problem of needing two witnesses for a conviction. Also many of the conspirators, such as Mason, managed to evade capture and escape to Holland. In January 1664, twenty-six of the leaders were sentenced to be hanged, drawn and quartered, and these included

Thomas Oates and Robert Atkinson. Atkinson had originally escaped from custody, but decided to give himself up in the hope of making a deal for his life. He had been taken to London and interrogated by the king to whom he gave a full account of the plot and offered to become a government informant. As Atkinson was considered completely untrustworthy, his offer was rejected.

Most of the heads of the twenty-six were displayed on spikes at York but some were sent to areas of rebel support such as Doncaster and Northallerton. The problem of severed heads losing their impact by becoming unrecognisable was overcome by the normal practice of the executioner parboiling them in a mixture of salt and cumin, which delayed putrefaction and kept the birds away. Dr Richardson, the main organiser of the plot, remained safely in Rotterdam. George Downing tried to obtain extradition but was refused by De Witt. In typical Downing fashion, he considered kidnapping Richardson but gave this up as politically too difficult when Richardson moved to Haarlem, purchased Dutch citizenship and became a respected preacher in Haarlem's English church. As might be expected, some of those captured decided to save their lives by becoming informers. An escape was arranged for William Leving, a Durham radical, after he had agreed to inform on his fellow Phanaticks.

The following extract from the king's speech to parliament acknowledges the importance of intelligence in foiling the plot:

> *You may judge by the late treason in the North, for which so many men have been executed, how active the spirits of many of our old enemies are withstanding all our mercy. I do assure you that we are not at the bottom of that business. This much appears manifestly, that this conspiracy was but a branch of that which I discovered as well as I could to you about two years since and had been then executed nearer-hand if I had not, by God's goodness, come to the knowledge of some of the principal contrivers so secured them from doing the mischief they intended. And if I had not, by the like providence, had timely notice of the very hour and several places of their rendezvous in the North, and provided for them accordingly by sending some of my own troops, as well as drawing the trainbands together, their conjunction would have been in greater numbers than would have been convenient.[8]*

So far Charles had had plots in two of his kingdoms, but a graver plot was brewing in his third kingdom – one that had the potential to be very inconvenient.

Chapter 5

The Apocalypse Years Begin
1665

From lightning and tempest; from plague pestilence and famine;
from battle and murder, and from sudden death
Good Lord Deliver us.
The Litany, 1662 Book of Common Prayer.

The king was a man of considerable energy, usually starting his day at five or six in the morning. This energy was largely devoted to the pursuit of pleasure, at which he excelled.

For Charles, there were three broad areas of pleasure. There was sport. He was an outstanding horseman who loved hunting and racing and was also a keen swimmer and tennis player. Then there were his intellectual interests. These were very wide ranging and included anything that took his fancy at the time – from a new scientific experiment to garden design. Although very much a dilettante, he did have a strong interest in chemistry, town planning, and all things to do with the sea, from shore defences to ship building, and was never happier than when sailing one of his yachts. Lastly, but probably his highest priority, were activities for his amusement. These again were wide ranging from entertainments such as the theatre, spectacular balls or firework displays, to the collection of beautiful things – whether they be works of art or attractive women. Charles was scrupulously polite, never drunk or given to gambling for high stakes. Nevertheless, it amused him to encourage outrageous behaviour in his court, whether it was the loss of fortunes at the gambling table or the appallingly loutish conduct of the young reprobates he kept about him. Absurd extravagance, vulgar talk and insulting remarks could all be forgiven if they emanated from a beautiful woman, or a witty man – such as the brilliant but totally debauched John Willmott, Earl of Rochester.

To the continual exasperation of Clarendon, Charles's pursuit of pleasure left him little time for affairs of state. He hated paper work, found council meetings tedious and was easily distracted from his role in routine government administration. Under these circumstances Clarendon, the secretaries of state, Ormonde and Lauderdale, were largely left to get on with the running of the three kingdoms with Charles becoming involved when he found the subject of interest, such as interrogating a prisoner or formulating foreign policy. While his ministers had been busy countering plots, Charles had been preoccupied with two personal matters, his son and a new love in his life.

1663 brought the 14-year-old James Crofts to court. He was the king's illegitimate son by Lucy Walter when she had been his mistress in Holland. The attractive but unstable Lucy was a strumpet who died two years before the Restoration 'of a disease incident to her profession.' Prior to that, her son had been removed from her to be brought up by a William Crofts. Charles had felt it was time to be reunited with his son and recognise him as a royal bastard. James was a very good-looking boy and Charles developed a deep fatherly love for him. James became the darling of the court and Barbara, Lady Castlereagh, took him under her wing. Barely a year after his arrival in England the king made James Duke of Monmouth and Knight of the Garter, and provided for him financially by marrying him to the 12-year-old heiress, Anne Scott, Countess of Buccleuch. This thoroughly spoilt boy would turn into a thoroughly spoilt young man whose headstrong actions would pose a serious threat to the monarchy.

The year 1663 had been difficult for Castlemaine. She had converted to Roman Catholicism, probably to ingratiate herself with Queen Henrietta Maria who had set up residence at Somerset House and had a strong influence over Charles. Few took Castlemaine's conversion seriously and Charles remarked that he was more interested in a lady's body than her soul. Buckingham was one of the few who did take the conversion seriously. He did not approve of Catholics and so a rift developed between the cousins. Of more concern to Castlemaine was that Charles's sister Minette had sent Frances Stewart, one of her Maids of Honour, over to London. In Minette's words 'She is the prettiest girl in the world and one of the best fitted of any I know to adorn a Court.'[1] The 15-year-old Frances was indeed pretty and courtiers soon gave her the name 'la belle Stuart'. Perhaps unsurprisingly given her age and sheltered background, she was immature to the point of being childlike. Frances was a simple, virtuous and artless soul who enjoyed party games. In short, she was very different from the voluptuous, sophisticated and witty Castlemaine; and Charles fell madly in love with her.

Castlemaine was pregnant at the time with her second son, probably fathered by Charles Berkley, and found herself side-lined.[2] In typical Castlemaine fashion she attempted to retrieve the situation by befriending Frances so that she could arrange to be in her company whenever the king was present.

Charles had hoped to make a swift conquest of Frances but it was not to be, despite his best efforts in professions of love and expensive presents. In order to fully regain the king's favour Castlemaine tried to encourage Frances to become Charles's lover. On one occasion as a court amusement, Castlemaine arranged a mock wedding between her and Frances. This included being put to bed together in front of the assembled throng and Castlemaine then slipping out of bed to make way for the king. Unfortunately for Charles, Frances would not let matters go beyond a game. Although Charles was still bedding Castlemaine as well as a number of passing females, he grew increasingly frustrated at not being able to have his way with Frances. This situation was to continue for four years and, just as Anne Boleyn had steadily increased Henry VIII's passion for her by resisting his advances, so it was with Frances.

To further complicate matters for Castlemaine, Queen Catherine had been seriously ill after a miscarriage at the end of the year and Charles had rallied round her as an affectionate husband. Castlemaine was in danger of either being usurped by Frances, or having a recovered queen taking up her rightful place at the centre of court. However, Castlemaine although no longer able to dominate the king as she had in the past, still managed to hold her position and receive royal funding to cover her sumptuous lifestyle and astronomic gambling debts. Having fallen out with Castlemaine, Buckingham was putting his full support behind Frances in the hope that she might become queen if Catherine died, and give Charles the chance of producing an heir. As always, Bennet was taking a full part in court life and intrigue and, while remaining friends with Castlemaine, was ensuring he had good relations with Frances. Despite being able to keep up with the late nights and exhausting social round of court, Bennet was consolidating his position as secretary of state, particularly in respect of intelligence matters.

There was the unfinished business of ensuring the loyalty of the Post Office staff.

Bennet introduced a government ordinance that all postal workers had to produce a certificate of conformity to the Anglican Church within six months or face dismissal. He followed this up by reinforcing the government monopoly of the postal service. Private postal services had sprung up such as that of Zachary Standard in Bear Lane, who had been running his own postal service with a network of thirty messengers. Bennet moved against Zachary and his like by directing all mayors and magistrates to arrest anyone carrying letters without a licence from the Post Master General. The politically suspect Henry Bishop was encouraged to hand over his post of Post Master General to Charles's faithful Groom of the Stool, Daniel O'Neale, on payment of £8,000.[3] Unfortunately, O'Neal was only to hold the position for a year-and-a-half before dying of a stomach ulcer, but an indication of his loyalty is given in a letter from Charles to Minette: 'He is as honest a man as ever lived. I am sure I have lost a very good servant by it.'[4] During his fairly short time as Post Master General, O'Neal carried out a major purge of postal service staff who could not produce a certificate of conformity. The sort of people who were removed were Cornelious Glover, a servant of Hugh Peter, who had been Cromwell's leading preacher, the Leveller Thomas Chapman, and Clement Oxbridge, who was not prepared to renounce being a Baptist. The purge was not limited to London, for example William Brown, the Post Master of Wakefield, was removed as he was thought to be distributing the mail of Phanaticks. In total some fifty postal staff were removed.[5] The Royal Mail was getting itself into the position of being able to fully exploit its intercept potential.

With conspiracies and uprisings still occurring, the control of the press remained increasingly important. L'Estrange, the Surveyor of the Press, continued in his zeal to supress all unlicensed printing matter. He was aided in this by his official staff, named 'agents for discovery and intelligence', as well as his small army of informants. The control of the press was no easy task because of the use of small mobile printing presses and the publication of seditious material in Holland, which was then secretly shipped to England, Scotland or Ireland. The underground press was helping to spread radical ideas and inspire the disaffected to rebellion. Captain Roger Jones, who was part of the Northern Rising, had written the highly influential pamphlet *Mene Tekel: 'A Treatise of the Execution of Justice or the Down Fall of Tyranny.'* This stated that it was the people's right to resist tyranny and they should rise up to depose and execute the king. L'Estrange's men arrested a printer called John Twyn for producing copies of the pamphlet, he was subsequently hanged, drawn and quartered. Although that was a good result for the government, it proved hard to prevent copies of *Mene Tekel* being secretly distributed among radicals and Phanaticks. It is known that 1,000 copies printed in Holland were destined for Scotland and Ireland, but it is not clear how many actually got through, or how many other such shipments were made.[6]

THE APOCALYPSE YEARS BEGIN

There were, of course, two aspects of controlling the media: the suppression of seditious material and the production of government propaganda. L'Estrange had taken over the only two legally authorised newspapers but he did not have the same flair for editorship as he did for censorship. Bennet decided to take direct control and have only one official newspaper, *The London Gazette*, and give Williamson the task of running it. This meant that Williamson could ensure that the information released to the public was strictly in accordance with government policy. It has to be said that *The London Gazette* was not a page-turner and did not enjoy wide circulation among the general public.

The government had been successful in countering the plots in London, Dublin and the North of England, but many of the leading conspirators had managed to escape so Williamson and Bennet remained on the alert for further signs of sedition. This was just as well because another plot was brewing in London among some of those former conspirators who had managed to avoid capture and were now living secretly in the city. Those who had been involved in the Northern Plot were: William Leving, Timothy Butler and Captains John Mason, John Lockyer, Thomas Gower and Roger Jones. Also, of course, there was the inveterate plotter Thomas Blood, who had recently started calling himself 'Captain'. Butler had been at the London end of the Northern Plot, responsible for the arms cache; Mason had recently escaped from prison in the North, and Jones was the author of the notorious *Mene Tekel*. These mainly Presbyterian men had joined the leaders of what was left of the Fifth Monarchists, Nathaniel Strange and Jeramiah Marsden, in a united front against the government. They met together in London's Petty France and began making a plan to capture the Tower and then attack Whitehall. Their basic plan was for a small group armed with pistols to take the Tower, gaining entry on the pretext of visiting the Armoury. They were in contact with Scottish Phanaticks who they hoped would carry out an insurrection at the same time, and busied themselves in raising money and finding ways of procuring sufficient weapons for an uprising in London.

What Blood and his fellow plotters did not realise was that their group had been infiltrated by two government agents. A Leonard Williams, who was an informant reporting direct to Henry Bennet, the secretary of state, and John Atkinson, who had turned informant in exchange for immunity after the Northern Rising was being handled by Joseph Williamson. Bennet decided that a raid would be carried out on the conspirators' meeting place in Petty France on 21 September 1664, but the operation was a failure. Not only did the conspirators fail to meet, but had fled and dispersed back into anonymity.

The probable reason was that Atkinson might have tipped them off because, while he was happy enough to receive payment for being a government source, he did not want his former colleagues arrested. Be that as it may, it was a setback not to have been able to arrest the majority of the leading Phanaticks, but at least another plot had been disrupted. The Phanaticks and radicals had, by now, been involved in a number of failed uprisings and on each occasion they had been thwarted by government action. They realised that this was probably because of informants and had become very security-aware, holding courts to try those of their number whom they believed to be government agents, with Thomas Blood often taking a lead on this, even among the Fifth Monarchists. Their problem was that, in order to organise a widespread uprising, quite a large number of potential supporters needed to be given at least some knowledge of the conspiracy. Given the fact that there were so many people prepared to make money out of being government informers it was very difficult to keep a conspiracy secret. However, new opportunities were presenting themselves as there was now growing talk of war with the United Provinces. If England went to war with the United Provinces, then the radicals and Phanaticks might obtain active support from Holland – including a possible invasion. As an added bonus, the government intelligence operation might be distracted from their surveillance, leaving Phanaticks and radicals free to plan an uprising in greater secrecy.

Despite having provided him with a haven during his exile, Charles disliked the Dutch. He disliked their Calvinist religion and puritan ways, he disliked the fact that they were a Republic and were giving shelter to English rebels, and disliked the Grand Pensionary, Johann De Whitt, who was doing all he could to prevent Charles's nephew William from taking his rightful place as Stadtholder. For all that, Charles had no wish for war even though he was well aware that the United Provinces were his kingdoms' main rival in trade and fishing. In the City of London and other financial centres such as Bristol, there was growing appetite for a war to destroy an increasingly successful commercial rival who practised free trade and therefore undercut the tariff-paying English merchants. Many looked back to the naval victories in Cromwell's war against the Dutch and assumed that the Hollanders could soon be put in their place. None of this might have mattered if James, Duke of York, and Prince Rupert, had not been founders and major shareholders in the Royal African Company, as was Secretary of State Bennet. Unfortunately it was found that the company was unlikely to prosper, as the Dutch would not allow English ships to trade in Africa. Charles's brother was Lord High Admiral and an unfulfilled general and, in the autumn of 1663, he directed Admiral Robert Holmes to take a fleet to Africa, where he seized most of the Dutch trading stations and shipping along the Gold Coast.

James also set up the Royal Fishery in the North Sea to prevent Dutch fishing and then, disliking the Dutch presence in New Amsterdam, had it captured and later renamed New York. Parliament was completely behind these actions and followed them up by sending De Whitt a long list of trading demands and calling for reparations for disadvantaging English trade! At this stage Charles still thought that de Whitt would back down and Downing, the ambassador in The Hague, was reporting that the Dutch had no stomach for a fight. They were both wrong; De Witt's response was to send their Mediterranean fleet, under Admiral de Ruyter, to Africa to restore the situation. Egged-on by his brother and mistress, Castlemaine, Charles decided that the deployment of de Ruyter was a declaration of war. Louis, who had an alliance with the United Provinces, tried to persuade Charles against war, as did Charles's principal minister Clarendon, both without success. After parliament had voted the enormous sum of £2,500,000 to pay for what became known as the Second Dutch War, war was proclaimed by two heralds in London on 4 March 1665. The king's decision to declare war was a setback for Clarendon, who had strongly opposed it, and a boost to Bennet, who had advocated it and was now given the title Baron Arlington.

The war began well for England with a great victory at the battle of Lowestoft in June, where twenty-six Dutch ships were sunk or captured to the loss of only one English ship. Although a victory, the vulnerability of the Stuart dynasty became clear when a Dutch cannon ball took Charles Berkley's head off while he has standing next to the Duke of York – splattering his brains over the latter's coat. The poet Andrew Marvel quipped that it was the first proof that Berkley had shown of brains. But the more important point was that, as the king was childless, his brother was heir to the throne and should not be placed in such potential danger. As a result, Charles decided that the Cromwellian-turned-Royalist admiral, the Earl of Sandwich, should be put in charge of the fleet. Unfortunately, the country was facing more pressing matters than the naval command structure. Plague had hit London. In July, Charles moved the court first to Salisbury and then to Oxford, leaving George Monck, Duke of Albemarle and Captain General, responsible for the safety of London and ensuring there would be no Phanatick or radical uprisings. With his usual ruthless efficiency, Monck soon uncovered a plot by former Republican officers to seize the city and the eight ringleaders were captured and hanged; there were no further attempts after this. Some Phanaticks and radicals, such as Thomas Blood, remained in

London but were less concerned with plotting an uprising than surviving the greatest epidemiological catastrophe since the Black Death. However, the plague did not reduce Monck's zeal in his search for seditious activity. Arrests continued. The most notable was that of the former Cromwellian officer, Colonel John Rathbone. He and several other former officers were executed for plotting to capture the Tower of London and kill the king. As those who provided evidence against Rathbone and his associates were highly suspect, it is more than likely that, although Rathbone may have uttered disloyal views, no actual plot existed. A few innocent men may have died but it reinforced Monck's message that, plague or not, there would be no toleration of seditious behaviour.

While the plague raged, 70,000 of London's 400,000 strong population were to die, and all aspects of business and everyday life were turned upside down.[7] Several thousand citizens fled to the countryside, and so spread contagion and alarm to the villages they stayed in. Among those who had fled were, of course, the courtiers who, despite the plague, were making the most of life in Oxford. The university was appalled at the behaviour of the courtiers, many of whom defecated in fireplaces or anywhere they found handy, were rowdy and drunken, and spread the pox among the Oxford maidens. They were scandalised that many of the ladies took to wearing men's clothing as an amusing diversion and by the high stakes won and lost in gaming. Barbara Castlemaine alone lost £4,580 at the gambling tables at one sitting. This was at a time when a parson might hope to earn £50 a year and the average country gentleman, to receive an annual income of £240 from their estate. Barbara's antics in particular outraged the academics of Oxford and someone pinned a note on her bedchamber door at Merton College: *'Hanc Caesare pressam a fluctu defendit onus'* [The reason she is not ducked? Because by Caesar she is fucked].[8] Henry Bennet, now Lord Arlington, was, as usual, taking a full part in the court's social life as well as fulfilling his many duties as senior secretary of state. He and Joseph Williamson had the new task of obtaining intelligence to support the war effort.

Williamson already had quite good coverage of the activities of his rebellious countrymen in the United Provinces from using agents such as Edward Riggs, who was practising as a doctor in Rotterdam. This was, of course, important because the English, Scottish and Irish radicals could well assist the Dutch by helping to support an uprising back at home. However, it was even more important to obtain political intelligence on Dutch intentions, and military naval intelligence on the strength and deployment of their fleet.

Amazingly, the English ambassador George Downing managed to remain in station for the first couple of months of the war and provided both political and military reports. There was some political intelligence collection already in place using agents such as Colonel Joseph Bampfylde, but there was no coverage of naval intelligence, other than that provided by Downing and that was soon to cease. Williamson and his staff therefore busied themselves in recruiting new informers and re-tasking existing agents to cover matters relevant to the war.

As well as using the normal intelligence collection methods of espionage and intercept, Williamson came up with a new approach, he engaged the services of Henry Oldenburg, the Secretary of the Royal Society. Oldenburg was a scholar; born in Bremen, he became the London envoy for that city during Cromwell's Protectorate. He spent some time as the tutor of a family in England, but continued to travel to different European countries making contact with other scholars. When the Royal Society was established in 1662 he was appointed Secretary and in that role forged strong links with members of the scientific and academic communities on the continent. He was, therefore, in an ideal position to maintain those links during the war and obtain the views of those with whom he had established friendships. Williamson arranged for Oldenburg to be given the anagram cover name 'Monsr Grubendol' for correspondence and all letters received by the General Post Office in that name were sent unopened to Oldenburg. He would then translate them, if necessary, extract any information of intelligence interest and forward it to Williamson. Williamson also used Oldenburg for the translation of other intercepted correspondence that was written in German.[9] Unlike many of Williamson's agents and informants on the ground whose reliability required constant assessment, Oldenburg's reports provided honest extracts from the letters of his correspondents.

It might have been assumed that there was no longer much need of intelligence because of the reduced threat from the United Provinces after the major defeat of their fleet off Lowestoft. Indeed, the Dutch had sent a delegation to Charles to sue for peace but it was firmly rejected, not least because Castlemaine could not accept peace with the nation that had blown off the head of her lover. De Witt responded by embarking on a major ship-building project that was not only to restore, but greatly strengthen, his battered fleet. He also replaced a number of incompetent naval officers and made Admiral de Ruyter supreme commander. However, these actions would only bear fruit in the future, and De Witt now faced a threat on land. The belligerent Bishop of Munster, encouraged by the promise of an English subsidy, now attacked the United Provinces. Despite this apparently happy turn of events, England was rapidly becoming weaker. The plague and the war had completely disrupted commerce resulting in a major reduction in trade and therefore a major reduction in the royal excise takings. The king and his government were out of money and were beginning to have to pay sailors in credit notes rather than cash. Equally difficult was the attitude of Louis XIV who had designs on the Spanish Netherlands. King Philip IV of Spain had died in September leaving the Crown to his 3-year-old mentally retarded son Carlos. Louis decided to claim the Spanish Netherlands on behalf of his wife on the pretext that her dowry had not been paid – and even the Crown of Spain if Carlos died without an heir. If the United Provinces was successfully invaded by Munster it could be brought under Austrian Hapsburg domination, thus making it far harder for Louis to take the Hapsburg Spanish Netherlands. In January 1666, Louis decided to rescue the United Provinces by declaring war on England and persuading Denmark to do the same. The Elector of Brandenburg was bought off by De Witt and began to threaten Munster, leading to the Bishop making a hasty peace in April. It need hardly be said that he had never received England's promised financial subsidy.

The plague had begun to subside in London so Charles decided to return the month after Louis's declaration of war. Charles was accompanied by both the queen and Castlemaine, with Frances Stewart in tow. The former had just had another miscarriage and, to make matters worse for her, in the same month Castlemaine had given birth to a healthy boy. This child, the future Duke of Northumberland, was the fifth of Castlemaine's children to be acknowledged by Charles as his own, although he understandably had serious doubts about the paternity. Court life resumed in Whitehall but hundreds continued to die from the plague until it gradually faded away over the next six months. Charles was without money and at war without any allies against a strong coalition which included France, the very country he had always hoped to win as his own ally. Things had gone badly wrong and there was now a real chance that England might be invaded. The outcome of the war now rested on the success of the seriously underfunded English navy.

By spring, the newly built Dutch navy was ready under its seasoned commander de Ruyter. Lord Sandwich had been removed from command of the English fleet and, having been accused of misappropriating bounty from a captured Dutch merchantman, had been sent off to be ambassador in Spain. With his brother the Duke of York confined to shore, Charles needed someone to command the fleet. He decided to split the responsibility between George

Monck, who had been a successful General at Sea in Cromwell's Dutch War, and his cousin Prince Rupert, who had commanded the small Royalist navy during the Commonwealth. In May the English fleet of eighty ships set sail under Monck and Rupert to locate the Dutch. They had barely left when Arlington received intelligence that the French fleet in the Mediterranean was on its way to join de Ruyter. To prevent the risk of an engagement with the combined Dutch/French fleet, Charles sent orders for Rupert to take twenty ships to intercept and defeat the French before they could join forces. This all made lots of sense, the only problem was that the intelligence was incorrect and the French fleet was still in the Mediterranean. Rupert had gone off on a wild goose chase leaving Monck with only sixty ships when he encountered de Ruyter's fleet of eighty-five ships and battle commenced. This division of the English fleet had been caused by a major intelligence failure that may have been brought about by disinformation being fed to English spies by the French. Had it not been for this faulty intelligence there is a good chance that England would have won the battle and achieved the knockout blow to win the war.

Monck and de Ruyter's forces were to slug it out from 1–4 June in the longest naval engagement in British history. By 2 June, Monck only had forty-four operational ships but fortunately, Rupert's squadron returned to the fleet the next day and prevented complete disaster. On 4 June there was a fog and the two fleets, both short of powder, eventually disengaged, with both sides claiming a victory. On the king's orders celebratory bonfires were lit and bells rung in London. But as the English fleet had lost ten ships, with 5,000 sailors dead or wounded, and the Dutch only four ships and 2,000 men, there is little doubt where the advantage actually lay. With neither side having achieved the necessary superiority, the war dragged on. England even had a minor victory two months later in the St James Day battle where the English lost one ship but destroyed two of the Dutch. However, London was about to be concerned with something far more important than the progress of the war at sea.

Chapter 6

Fire and Sword
1666

'The noise and crackling and thunder of the impetuous flames,
the shrieking of women and children, the hurry of people, the
fall of towers, houses and churches, was like a hideous storm...
a resemblance of Sodom or the last day.'

John Evelyn *Diary*

London began to return to normality and there was heartening news in August
when reports arrived of 'Holmes's bonfire'. Admiral Holmes had received
intelligence from a Dutch deserter that the United Provinces' merchant fleet
was lying behind the Frisian Islands in the Vlie Estuary. He immediately
sailed to the estuary, sacked the Dutch town of Terschelling and set fire to
130 of their anchored merchant vessels. A few days later, on Sunday 2
September, London was to share the experience of a conflagration when a
fire broke out at a bakery in Pudding Lane. Fanned by the wind it swiftly got
out of control and was to last for three more days destroying 436 acres, that
was eighty-five per cent of the area within the city walls. The crisis
transformed Charles from an amiable libertine to a man of action. With
considerable energy and courage he and his brother, the Duke of York, threw
themselves into stopping the fire. Both worked by hand trying to extinguish
the flames and, more usefully, ordered buildings to be blown up in the path
of the fire to stop it spreading. The devastation from the fire was enormous
but would have been much greater without Charles's leadership and sound
judgement. In total, 13,200 houses were destroyed and eighty-seven
churches, including St Paul's Cathedral. Warehouses were lost, places of
business such as the Exchange and all fifty-two guild buildings were
destroyed and England's financial and commercial centre was brought to a
standstill. Hundreds of thousands of homeless Londoners camped out in the

woods and hills to the north, as far as Islington and Highgate. There was now a danger of rioting and insurrection.

It was not known how the fire had started, so rumours were rife – as were the cries for revenge. Could it have been the Dutch to repay the 'Holmes's bonfire'? Or possibly more likely, it might have been English Phanaticks working as agents of their Dutch allies. Then the obvious answer occurred to most people that it must have been the papists. Since the Gunpowder Plot, it had been the default position of many Protestants to blame Catholics of any supposed treason. This conclusion was given greater credence when a mentally unstable young Frenchman called Robert Hubert, who was visiting from Rouen, publicly confessed to starting the fire. Although evidence at his trial showed that he had not even landed in England until two days after the fire began, Hubert was hanged. Charles realised the danger that Hubert's conviction would be regarded as proof that a Catholic was responsible. He therefore went to some effort, visiting the camps of the homeless to distribute food and explain that the council's investigation had concluded that fire had been caused by the hand of God, a great wind, and a very dry season. Above all, there was no evidence of Catholic involvement. Charles popularity had been greatly improved by his conduct during the fire and many were prepared to accept his explanation that it was caused by accident. As a result, revenge attacks on Catholics were avoided. Unfortunately, a large number of people retained a lingering suspicion that the fire was caused by papists and those suspicions would be exploited in years to come.

Charles was later to take a considerable interest in the rebuilding of the city, but soon after the fire he left for Newmarket and busied himself in devising the rules for an annual autumn race meeting. Perhaps it was his way of dealing with the stresses of kingship, but the fact remains that he returned to his life of pursuing pleasure and his own interests. On one thing he was clear: the need for peace, and he instructed Clarendon accordingly. The catastrophes of the plague and the fire had brought the country to its knees. A formidable military coalition was now opposing England. Although the Royal Navy had just about held its own off England's shore, French and Dutch privateers were severely harassing trade and overseas, the English territories of St Kitts, Antigua, Monserrat and Surinam had been taken by either the French or the Dutch. Peace was needed urgently, but bringing about a peace was easier said than done. There had been an attempt to gain Spanish support through a number of nefarious meetings that had failed. The king's relationship with Louis was at a low point and the war had prevented correspondence between Charles and Minette, which might have provided a conduit to smooth relations. As it was it would probably have made no difference because Minette was out of favour with Louis for taking his queen's side in the dismissal from court of Louis's pregnant mistress, Louise de La Valliere. Louis was in a dominant position at home and abroad and not minded to offer any olive branch to his English cousin.

An attempt had been made to come to terms with the Dutch but that had gone spectacularly wrong. Henry Bennet, now Lord Arlington, was carrying out informal soundings about a peace with De Witt. The channel for these secret communications was an officer in the Dutch army called Henri Buat. Buat's father was a Huguenot who had been colonel of a French regiment in the service of the Dutch Republic; Buat had followed his father into the army and become Captain of the Stadtholder's Life Guard. As such he was a strong Orangist and remained loyal to William of Orange after the Stadtholdership had been abolished and De Witt became Grand Pensionary. Arlington thought it would be prudent to have a fall-back position if no progress could be made in these informal peace negotiations. This plan was to encourage an Orangist coup against De Witt which, if successful, would establish the young William of Orange as Stadtholder and so facilitate a peace agreement between him and his uncle King Charles. The man Arlington was using to help plan the coup was Sir Gabriel Sylvias who had moved to the court at Whitehall having been previously in the service of Charles's sister, Mary Princess of Orange. Buat had agreed to help organise the proposed coup and was able to approach other trusted Orangists about it. His position as a messenger between Arlington and De Witt provided the cover for him to be able to travel freely between the two countries. In September, Sir Gabriel provided Buat with written details of the plot and he took these documents with him to the United Provinces, along with Arlington's latest draft negotiations. Buat had his audience with De Witt and duly handed over Arlington's documents exploring the possibilities for peace. After the meeting however, Buat must have had a horrible sinking feeling when he realised that he had mistakenly given De Witt the documents from Sir Gabriel about the coup. He rushed back to De Witt to try to retrieve the incriminating documents – but by then they had been read. Buat was arrested and subsequently beheaded. Warrants were issued for the arrest of the Orangists named in the plot documents and although two Rotterdam Regents managed to escape to England, a number of potential supporters were imprisoned. De Witt took full propaganda advantage of the plot and the Orangist cause received a major setback. Needless to say, De Witt lost any trust he might have had in Arlington as a negotiation partner and the peace process came to a halt.

FIRE AND SWORD

As well as exploring covert diplomatic initiatives to end the war, Arlington had been busy with Williamson in directing clandestine operations against the enemy through agents and informants. Coverage was needed of the United Provinces, but also of France because Lord Holles, the ambassador, had left Paris in the spring following the French declaration of war. There followed a major recruitment drive for agents and a flow of additional information but as it happened none was of real value to the war effort as it did not provide intelligence about either the country's military or strategic intentions. Williamson also needed to continue obtaining intelligence on Phanaticks and radicals both at home and overseas. In this he had more success. The war gave the radicals a major opportunity to stab the government in the back while it was distracted by the war. To many Nonconformists, the bloodshed of war, together with the disasters of the plague and fire, were a clear indication of God's judgement on a debauched monarch and his corrupt court. As these disasters occurred in the year 1666, there could be little doubt that they had been foretold in Chapter 13, Verse 18 of the Book of Revelations which refers to the 'Beast', whose number is 'six hundred, three score and six.' Beliefs of this sort could only encourage Phanaticks in seeking to overthrow the government.

The outbreak of the Dutch War in 1665 had offered the opportunity of obtaining sufficient aid from the United Provinces and France to ensure a successful uprising. Having survived the plague, the likes of Thomas Blood returned to their conspiratorial meetings. Blood had gone to Liverpool to meet English radicals such as William More to discuss coordinating a rising in the three kingdoms. The purpose of the rising would be to overthrow the monarchy and the House of Lords, recall the Long Parliament and establish General Ludlow as leader. Blood then travelled to Ireland with George Ayres to enlist support for a rising there but, finding little enthusiasm for his plan, the operation was postponed. In February 1666, Ormonde had been tipped off about Blood's activities by a Captain Robert Oliver, whose wife had been approached about the plot by Robert Taylor, a former Cromwellian officer. Taylor was given a pardon in exchange for a full confession and warrants were again issued for Blood's arrest. Ormonde then informed Arlington that he had received information that Blood had gone to London to continue plotting with Roger Jones and a Ralph Alexander. Although this information was correct and searches were carried out in London, once again Blood had managed to avoid capture. Blood seems to have made an impact on his visit to Liverpool because, in September, a Captain Brown was in Liverpool and formulating yet another plan to take Dublin castle – but this time was trying to get financial backing from the Dutch. One of his associates, a Captain Robert Oliver, decided to betray him to Ormonde and the plan came to nothing.

Despite the favourable situation of the war, the Radicals and Phanaticks seemed to be getting nowhere in launching an uprising. What they really needed was an effective leader of standing rather than former junior officers. Blood had understood this and had travelled with John Lockyer to Lausanne to meet Ludlow and encourage him to lead an uprising. Blood came away from the meeting singularly unimpressed by Ludlow as a man, and angered by his refusal to commit himself. In Blood's word he was 'very unable for such an employment.'[1] Although Blood thought little of Ludlow, he was one of the three Republicans not held in gaol who was sufficiently well known to be a suitable leader of an uprising. The other two were General John Desborough and Colonel Algernon Sidney. Desborough was Cromwell's brother-in-law and a successful general in the Civil War but had been out of London at the time of King Charles's trial so was not a Regicide. On Cromwell's death he had opposed his nephew, Richard, as Lord Protector and sought to restore a republic but lost support, with his soldiers mutinying against him. At the Restoration he had been arrested for suspected sedition, but was later released and had fled to the United Provinces where he took some part in the schemings of the expatriate radical community. After the Dutch War began Clarendon issued an order naming prominent Republicans to return to England or be indicted for High Treason. Desborough decided he had enough of exile and the threat of assassination so, in April 1666, had returned to England and given himself up. He was sent to the Tower but released a year later and lived out the remainder of his life in obscurity.

The third major figure was Algernon Sidney. He was the rather unusual combination of being an aristocrat and a radical political theorist. Sidney's father was Earl of Leicester and his mother was the daughter of the Earl of Northumberland, so he was related to some of the foremost families in the country. In the Civil War he supported parliament and rose to Colonel in the New Model Army before retiring through ill health. He became a prominent member of the Long Parliament and was one of the Commissioners at the trial of Charles I. As political theorist and writer, he supported a Republic and strongly opposed Cromwell becoming Lord Protector. That does not mean he was a boring puritan – indeed he was a lover of Lucy Walter before she became Charles's mistress. It was a small world for the aristocracy. After the death of Cromwell and the fall of his son, Sidney was sent on a diplomatic mission to Sweden and so was abroad at the time of the Restoration. Realising it might be dangerous for him to return to England he remained on the continent and twice escaped assassination from Royalist bounty hunters. At the start of the Dutch War he went to The Hague and had several meetings with De Witt. Sidney tried to persuade De Witt to sign a treaty with the exiles and invade England to coincide with an uprising that Sidney would coordinate, hopefully with Ludlow. De Witt was happy to encourage a Republican/Phanatick uprising in England, but had no stomach for an invasion so was very noncommittal about the project. Privately he felt that if somehow a republic was re-established in England it would be even more anti-Dutch than a Stuart monarchy. After expending a fair amount of effort trying to win over De Witt without success, Sidney decided to try his luck with King Louis after France had entered the war.

Sidney's aristocratic background and prominence in diplomatic circles enabled him to gain access to Louis. Sidney's proposal to Louis was that he should be loaned 100,000 écus to finance an uprising in the three kingdoms Although Louis saw an uprising as a useful distraction from England's war effort, he had no wish to see a republic established and his cousin removed from the throne. Louis was only prepared to offer Sidney 20,000 écus, which Sidney declined, realising it was insufficient to make the scheme viable. All the time Sidney had been negotiating, first with De Witt and then Louis, he had been trying desperately hard to encourage Ludlow to put himself forward as the leader of either an invasion force or an uprising. Ludlow refused to commit himself. He did not trust De Witt after the Dutch had cooperated with the extradition of the Regicides. He also distrusted Louis who, as an absolute monarch, would be unlikely to fully support Republicans such as himself and Sidney. Ludlow was also mindful of his own safety following the attempts on his life and was therefore unprepared to put himself at risk in a partnership with those in whom he had no confidence. So it was that the Phanaticks and radicals in the three kingdoms were unable to obtain the leadership and foreign backing necessary to give an uprising a reasonable chance of success.

Any hope that English Phanaticks and radicals might have obtained from the expatriates in the United Provinces during the war was also hampered by the penetration of government agents and informants. Established agents such as William Leving (using the name Leonard Williams) were regularly reporting to Williamson (cover name 'Mr Lee') about ex-patriots. Also, new agents had been established, including William Scot, a person of impeccable republican credentials as the son of the Regicide Thomas Scot. He was recruited by Aphra Behn who may have previously known him in Surinam when they were both there in 1663. There are few hard facts about Aphra's early life other than she was the daughter of a Canterbury butcher named Johnson, whose wife was nurse to the Culpepper family. She spent some time in the English sugar plantation in Surinam and in 1662, married a Dutch merchant called Johann Behn who died soon after. She then returned to England and somehow got herself attached to the court, possibly through the Culpeppers, or because of her good looks. After the outbreak of war her need for money and a Dutch connection made her a suitable person to be engaged as an agent. She was taken on, offered payment of £50 a year, and given the code name 'Astraea'. If she had known Scot previously, it is likely that she was specifically tasked with his recruitment as she was sent to Antwerp where Scot was believed to be staying.[2] As an agent Behn had some success, not only reporting on radicals, but also about a Dutch agent in England who was spying on the movement of English merchant vessels – information that would enable them to be seized by the Dutch. Although she appeared to have turned Scot, it is not clear whether he merely became a double agent and fed her such information as would help the Republican cause. If this was the case she was in a dangerous position and it is credit to her ingenuity that she survived at all in the murky world of espionage. However, an agent's life is not an easy one especially when, instead of finding it remunerative as she had been led to believe, royal finances were such that Behn was seldom paid and was obliged to pawn her rings to survive. Even when she returned to England at the end of the war, she still received no payment and spent a bit of time in a debtor's prison. She then managed to get a clerk's job with the King's Company, which eventually led her to become one of the most celebrated writers of her time and an inspiration to feminists today. Although she chose the pen name 'Astraea', it is doubtful that she missed espionage and had any regrets as a result of her career change. She is the only former agent to be buried in Westminster Abbey.

Agents and informants were to prove the undoing of most of the plots during the reign, but not of the most serious rising. Scotland had so far been the only one of the three kingdoms not to attempt a rebellion. That was to change. Like other parts of Charles's realm, Scotland had also suffered during the war having lost trade with its main commercial partner, the Dutch, which also resulted in the loss of excise revenue for the government, resulting in the imposition of high taxation for defence. Although Lauderdale was the secretary of state for Scotland, the man on the spot running the country was Lord Rothes, whose appointment Lauderdale had arranged to replace his enemy Lord Middleton as the King's Commissioner. Rothes fully supported James Sharp, Archbishop of St Andrews, who was using his recently created church courts to enforce Anglicanism. Sharp had been a leading Presbyterian minister who had felt it prudent to back Monck in his plot to bring about the Restoration. He had done his best to persuade his fellow Covenanters that the kirk and Presbyterianism would be safe if the king was restored, although he knew full well that Anglicanism and the episcopacy would follow. The Primacy of Scotland was the reward for his treachery. Bishops were restored and Presbyterian clergy removed. A total of 262 of the 952 Scottish clergy lost their livelihood for refusing to take the oaths of allegiance. The South West of Scotland had seen the greatest number of Presbyterian clergy expelled but also the greatest number of illegal conventicles held secretly in woods and fields.[3] Landlords were made responsible for ensuring that their tenants and servants attended Anglican services and were fined if they failed to do so. To bring Nonconformists to heel, it was decided that troops should be quartered on those who had not paid indemnity fines. Thomas Dalziel, the Lieutenant General of Scotland, was not known for his compassion, he had experienced the horrors of the Thirty Years war and served as a mercenary for the Tsar. It was not by chance that he was called 'the Beast of Muscovy'. Dalziel chose Sir James Turner, a likeminded Thirty Years War veteran with his regiment of Scottish Foot Guards, for the task. Turner and his men carried out their orders with the utmost severity, forcefully extracting fines from dissenters and behaving like a conquering army over a defeated nation. Violence was used in the collection of fines and they made free with the goods, chattels and livestock belonging to the houses where they were quartered, eating the owners out of house and home.

On 13 November a small incident sparked off a reaction to the religious persecution and military lawlessness. At Daly in Kirkcudbrightshire a party of Turner's soldiers apprehended an old peasant who was unable to pay his fine for not attending church. They beat him up and threatened to roast him on his own gridiron. Four Covenanters saw this happening and came to the old man's rescue, shooting one soldier and disarming the rest. One of the rescuers was MacLellan of Barscombe and he and another laird, John Nelson of Corsock, were so incensed that that they gathered some of their tenants and overran the sixteen-man garrison at Balmaclellan. They were then joined by 150 armed men including fifty on horseback and, in the early hours of the fifteenth, went to Turner's lodgings in Dumfries and took him prisoner in his nightshirt. The next day the rebel numbers had swelled to 250 and they reached Dalry where they renewed their oath to the Solemn League and Covenant, declared loyalty to the king and begged him to stop the persecution. Phanaticks joined the rebels including Colonel Gilby Carr, who had been on the run after the failure of the Dublin Plot. The government then issued a proclamation ordering the Covenanters to surrender within twenty-four hours or face charges of high treason. The proclamation had no effect. The rebels decided to march on Edinburgh and it seemed there was no stopping their momentum.

Leading dissidents flocked to join the rebels, including Andrew McCormack and John Crookshanks who, like Gilby Carr, had been part of the Dublin plot. Not one to miss the opportunity of an uprising, Thomas Blood went to offer his services. With additional recruits the rebels now numbered 3,000. Although only armed with whatever weapons they could lay their hands on, their numbers made them a significant force – especially as their command had been taken over by Colonel James Wallace of Auchen, an experienced soldier. Lord Rothes was away visiting in London while the rising was taking place, having left Archbishop Sharp as his deputy and president of the council. Sharp ordered General Dalziel to take his men to pursue the Covenanters and called out the militia to join him. The Scottish weather now played its part, with bitter cold and torrential rain for the Covenanters' advance on appalling roads towards Edinburgh. Morale was hit and the rebel numbers began to drift away as men returned to the warmth of their own homes. Nevertheless, the rebels arrived just five miles from Edinburgh. It then all went completely wrong; the city refused to join the uprising and shut the gates against them. The Covenanters had no option but to retreat through snow to the Pentland Hills with Dalziel's force now just eight miles behind them.

On 28 November Dalziel's force of 3,000 soldiers caught up with the rebels at Rullion Green and a battle took place. The rebel numbers had now dwindled to 900 but Wallace had deployed them in a commanding position on the upper slope of the hills. The government forces made several charges against the wings of the Covenanter force but were beaten back each time. Then, with the light failing, Dalziel ordered his whole force to charge against the rebels' centre, which disintegrated. The Covenanters were put to flight, trying desperately to save themselves in the darkness. Fifty of the rebels were killed in the battle including the two clerics Andrew McCormack and John Crookshanks; 120 rebels were captured, thirteen had surrendered on promise of mercy. When the thirteen appeared before Archbishop Sharp he gave his judgement: 'You are pardoned as soldiers but you are not acquitted as subjects.' They were hanged along with another twenty-six prisoners. The heads and limbs of those executed were distributed for display at various towns from Edinburgh to Kilmarnock to help teach obedience to the Anglican faith. Despite the rout, most of the main leaders escaped including John Maclellan and Colonel Wallace, who made his way to the safety of Rotterdam. Thomas Blood was wounded in the battle but also escaped and got to Ireland, although he was soon recognised and so had to escape yet again, this time to link up with Phanaticks in Lancashire and then Westmoreland.

Those who were suspected of supporting the rising but not fortunate enough to escape were to be tracked down over the next few years. Both Lord Rothes and Bishop Sharp were in no mood to show mercy and executions continued to such an extent that there was public disgust – even among staunch royalists. In Ayr, for example, the local hangman refused to execute twelve condemned men. This difficulty was overcome by granting one of the condemned his life if he carried out the job, which he duly did. The repression went on unabated with even larger fines, further billeting and all prisoners who refused to take the oath of allegiance sent as slaves to Barbados or Virginia. Torture was legal in Scotland and 'the boot' was used to encourage suspects to give evidence. An iron boot was fitted to a prisoner's legs and then wooden wedges were hammered in. This sounds pretty painful, but was in fact considerably more painful than it sounds. The next year, fifty-six of the rebels who had not been caught were indicted for high treason in absentia and so were to be executed if they were captured.[4] Severe repression by the authorities ensured that there were no more uprisings for the next few years, but that did not mean that the Covenanters were broken.

Despite the dangers, Covenanter conventicles continued to be held in secret locations and these could be attended by as many as 1,500 faithful; rather more than might be expected at an average Anglican Sunday congregation. The Presbyterian population was ground into apparent submission but their resentment was little diminished. James Mitchell was one of the rebels who escaped capture after Rullion Green and two years later tried to assassinate Archbishop Sharp as he entered his coach in Edinburgh. Mitchell fired his pistol but the bullet missed Sharp and hit his unfortunate travelling companion, the Bishop of Orkney. Mitchell got away and was on the run for a year or so before being captured. There had been no witnesses to Michell's attack on Sharp so it took some time for justice to take its course. As Mitchell refused to confess even after torture with the boot, he was imprisoned on the desolate Bass Rock. There he remained until 'witnesses' could be arranged to commit perjury and provide the evidence required for a guilty verdict and his execution. For Archbishop Sharp it was all most satisfactory, he had been lucky to have survived an assassination attempt and got revenge on his assailant. Sharp would not be so lucky the next time there was an attempt on his life.

The king had not been much concerned about the Scottish uprising or the repression that had been its cause. Scotland was a poor, far away country with a population of just one and a quarter million compared with almost seven million in England and Wales. Charles also had a strong dislike of Scotland in general and Covenanters in particular. This stemmed from his time there in the 1650s when he had been obliged to subordinate himself to the dictates of the Elders of the Kirk. He was therefore more than happy to see the Covenanters brought to heel, however harshly. The dire state of the Privy Purse was probably far more on his mind than events in the windswept glens of Scotland. No peace was in sight and the finances of the king and the country were going from bad to worse. As well as the huge disruption to trade and industry caused by the war, plague and fire, there was a recession in agriculture. The winter of 1666 saw riots in many parts of the country caused by unemployment and high taxation. Dissatisfaction was widespread and much of the blame was laid at the door of the king and his court.

For all that, life at court continued as normal. The Duke of Buckingham had been very put out about not being given a command during the war – after all, his father had been Lord High Admiral. He correctly blamed both Clarendon and the Duke of York for this, and so the existing bad feeling between them increased further. Buckingham decided to use the Lords to oppose Clarendon for the handling of the war and also to attack Ormonde, another old foe, over the importation of Irish cattle to England. His comments about Ormonde were so cutting that they provoked Ormonde's son, Lord Ossory, to challenge him to a duel. Buckingham reported the challenge to the Lords with the result that Ossory was sent briefly to the Tower. As Arlington was Ossory's brother-in-law, the incident further embittered the relationship between him and Buckingham. Before the year was out, Buckingham got himself into another scrape when he had an argument with the Marquis of Dorchester in the Lords, which resulted in him pulling off the marquis's wig, and hair pulling commenced. As a result, both peers were sent to the Tower for a short period. Charles was finding Buckingham's opposition and antics tedious and banned him from court for a month. For his part, the king was reasonably content with his private life and happy to have his son Monmouth around; while still enjoying his relationship with Castlemaine, he was also preoccupied with the major challenge of wooing Frances Stewart.

Chapter 7

Toppling the Chancellor
1667–8

His sceptre and his prick are of a length,
But she who plays with one may sway the other
John Wilmot, Earl of Rochester.

A personal tragedy enabled the beginning of the difficult journey towards Charles's sought-after alliance with France and the end of the costly war. Minette's 2-year-old son, the Duke of Valois, suddenly died. She was devastated. It was a double blow because not only had Minette doted on the little boy, but he was her husband's only son and heir. Louis forgot his squabble with Minette over Louise de La Valliere and returned his normal close affection for his grieving sister-in-law. Louis had lost a nephew but so had Charles and both were united in grief for the loss and concern for Minette.

Although Louis and Charles were now closer, there was still some way to go to resolve the longstanding differences between them. Charles, relaxed and informal in most things, would not countenance an erosion of his status as sovereign – even in ceremonial matters. Such matters included the insistence that the English ambassador to France had precedence over French Princes of the Blood on state occasions, and that French ships saluted English ships in the English Channel. No one could accuse Louis of being without pride and he found Charles's demands irritating to say the least, regarding it as outrageous that Charles still styled himself 'King of France' and displayed the fleur-de-lis on the royal coat of arms.[1] Despite these long standing problems it was in the interest of both cousins to cooperate and covert negotiations began. Queen Henrietta Maria had returned to France after the outbreak of plague in London and she and Minette were the conduit for the negotiations. As a gesture of goodwill, Charles agreed that French ships sailing south of Brittany were no longer required to salute English ships. An imperfect but temporary agreement was reached and a secret treaty signed in February 1667. In the treaty, Louis undertook to return some captured English islands in the Caribbean and cease to actively support the Dutch in the war with England. Charles agreed not to ally with Spain for a year, thus assisting Louis to attack the Spanish Netherlands. The ink was hardly dry on the treaty before Turenne took an army of 50,000 to the Flemish frontier. The next month, England began peace negotiations with the Dutch in Breda. De Witt was not aware that he had been betrayed by his ally Louis and so had no indentation of making peace until he obtained revenge for Holmes' Bonfire. The war continued.

With government finances in crisis there was no money to continue funding the English fleet. Sailors returning to port were unpaid and riots broke out that had to be put down by soldiers who themselves were in arrears of pay. Things came to a head in February when the Navy Board reported that £500,000 was required to pay and fit out the fleet. Something had to be done. The decision was made to layup the major warships at Chatham and just keep some smaller vessels in service to patrol the coast and ward off privateers. Charles and Clarendon banked on peace being agreed with the Dutch but De Witt had other ideas and the war went on.

At court, Buckingham was trying to get back into Charles's favour, taking the curious route of posing as a popular hero against those who held power: Clarendon, Ormonde and Arlington. Knowing that virtually all ministers received bribes, he called for a bill making embezzlement of public money a capital offence. This got nowhere but enabled him to be seen as an advocate of honest government. This, and his known dislike of popery, began to make him a rallying point for many against an unpopular government. Unpaid seamen in particular regarded Buckingham as their advocate. Arlington was concerned about Buckingham's bid for power and decided to take action. He used some of his informants to gather information about Buckingham and discovered that he had been in contact with an astrologer called Dr John Heydon who may have been a radical sympathiser. Heydon was arrested and his house searched; during the search a document was found which seemed to suggest that Buckingham was asking Heydon to cast the king's horoscope. Buckingham, like Charles, was interested in science – particularly the chemistry experiments to turn base metal into gold. Astrology, like alchemy, was regarded as a science and so it is plausible that Buckingham could have asked Heydon to cast the horoscope of Charles. The only problem was that a horoscope might include foreseeing the king's death and 'to compass or imagine the king's death' was technically treason. What was more, William Leving, who had become one of Arlington's agents after the Northern Rising, was able to report that Buckingham had been in league with radicals. A triumphant Arlington was able to draw all this to Charles' attention. The king ordered Buckingham's arrest and the duke went into hiding. Although Buckingham was temporarily out of action as a potential leader of opposition he was not inactive. It is no coincidence that two of the witnesses against him were found poisoned in mysterious circumstances. One of them was George Middleton who was believed to have received £100 from Arlington for saying that he had heard Buckingham speak treason against the king.[2] Court rivalries did not bring out the best in people.

To Barbara Castlemaine's continued annoyance, Charles was still wildly infatuated with Frances Stewart. Barbara's own relationship with Charles had been going through a difficult patch, not least because she was having an affair with Harry Jermyn and was pregnant with her sixth child. Charles had offered to make Frances a duchess and even replace Barbara as his principal mistress but with no result. Frances had no wish to be a mistress and began thinking of getting married to put an end to Charles's advances. She settled on the Duke of Richmond and Lennox. The 27-year-old duke's second wife had died a few months earlier and he had lost no time in secretly wooing the beautiful Frances. Barbara discovered about the secret liaison and paid the Keeper of the Privy Stairs, William Chaffinch, to tip her off when Richmond next visited Frances. As soon as she heard that Richmond was to visit she rushed to tell Charles, who went to the bedchamber and found Frances lying in bed with Richmond seated in a chair next to her. Worse still, Frances announced that the two of them wanted to get married. Charles was devastated, but he still held a trump card. As Richmond was a relation of the king he could only marry with Charles's consent – and that was not forthcoming. Charles then got Clarendon on the case to find suitable reasons why Richmond was an unsuitable husband. After some enquiries, Clarendon came back and reported that he could find no impediment to the match. This was completely the wrong answer. Charles was furious and believed that Clarendon had betrayed him. He thought Clarendon wanted Frances married off so she would not be available for Charles to marry if the queen should die, and therefore, not able to produce an heir who would displace Clarendon's own grandchildren from succession. By this time, Richmond and Frances had tired of waiting for Charles's approval, so they eloped and got married at the duke's estate in Kent. Charles was at once both devastated and furious. Barbara, on the other hand, was over the moon that her scheme

85

had worked so effectively and there was now no challenger to her position as the king's principal mistress.

While these affairs of the heart were occupying the king and his court, De Witt was planning his revenge. He ordered his fleet to sea under de Ruyter to undertake a bold and complex operation against the Thames Estuary. This operation had been a long time in the planning and had begun two years earlier when a Dutch spy had been sent to Chatham to report back to De Witt on the dockyard defences. De Witt had also prepared for amphibious operations by establishing the United Provinces' first marine unit, and ensuring that his fleet included officers who had good knowledge of the Thames Estuary through their previous peacetime trade with London. Many English dissidents in the United Provinces volunteered to join the expedition as either sailors or marines. For good measure, two English sailors and prisoners of war were persuaded to act as pilots to help navigate the Medway.

Clarendon and Arlington were aware that the Dutch fleet had gone to sea but did not believe that they would attack. Louis had been informed of De Witt's major offensive but did not tip off Charles. So much for family ties and the new secret treaty of friendship. It came as a very unwelcome surprise, therefore, to discover their fleet in the Thames Estuary with what appeared to be an invasion force. As in any crisis, Charles transformed himself into a man of action. He borrowed money from the City and supervised the strengthening of the country's defences, including sinking ships to block the Thames. Troops were rushed into position but it was all too late. De Ruyter's first objective was the fortress of Sheerness. The fortress was in a bad state of repair and quickly fell to an attack by 800 Dutch marines before any English troops had time to arrive. The next obstacle to the Dutch attack was the chain barrier across the entrance to the Medway. This had not been left tight enough and was cut through, enabling De Ruyter's fleet to reach Chatham and the laid up English fleet on 13 June. Three great ships, the *Royal Oak*, the *Loyal London* and the *Royal James* were destroyed by Dutch fire-ships, others were seriously damaged and the English flagship the *Royal Charles* was captured to be sailed back as a prize to the United Provinces. The English could only watch aghast from the shore as these humiliations took place. The only consolation was that the actions of Monck and Rupert prevented even greater catastrophe. Monck sank some ships to block the Thames, and Rupert set up a battery of artillery at Woolwich. London was saved and so was the Chatham dockyard, but De Ruyter had succeeded in delivering the greatest naval defeat in British history.[4]

With the great ships of the English fleet lost and the Dutch navy sailing at will along the English coast, peace was now absolutely essential. A peace treaty was therefore signed at Breda the very next month. As it happened the treaty was not as bad as it might have been because the Dutch and the English both kept their conquests, except England had to hand back most of the forts it had taken in West Africa. Although the terms could have been a lot worse, and there was a great relief that the debilitating war was at last over, there was no getting away from the fact that England had been humiliated. Coming after the disasters of the plague and fire, this staggering naval defeat was deeply felt. Parliament and the country wanted someone to blame. Arlington, probably fearing he might be blamed for the failure of intelligence, ordered the arrest of the German, Henry Oldenberg, for 'dangerous desseins [sic] and practices'. In other words, for communicating with foreigners overseas. The fact that Williamson, and very probably Arlington, knew that Oldenberg was corresponding with academics overseas in order to support English intelligence-gathering does not seem to have bothered them. Oldenberg ended up in prison for two and a half years.[5] Not very fair, but he was the best scapegoat that Arlington could come up with at the time.

Parliament hardly noticed the arrest of Oldenberg because for them, the obvious person to be blamed for the naval disaster was the king's principal minister, Clarendon. No matter that Clarendon had been against the war from the outset, envy of his position and pompous manner had made him many enemies. Both Lords and Commons seized on him as a scapegoat, as did the general public. Demonstrators cut down the trees in front of his mansion in Piccadilly and then proceeded to smash all the windows. Despite the storm that was breaking over him, Clarendon could draw strength from knowledge that he would be supported by the king, who owed him so much.

In June 1667 Buckingham came out of hiding and gave himself up, having previously sent Charles a grovelling letter of apology. He had also mended his fences with Castlemaine, who had regained her power once more. This would not be the last time that the relationship between these strong willed and self-centred cousins would change from hot to cold and back again. In typical Buckingham fashion he gave himself up in style. Having officially surrendered himself to Secretary Williamson, he set off for the Tower accompanied by a throng of supporters from watermen to several nobles, including the Duke of Monmouth. He stopped at the Sun Inn at Bishopsgate and sent word to the Lieutenant of the Tower that he would be along once he had enjoyed lunch. During his leisurely lunch he took time to appear on the inn's balcony and receive the acclamation of the crowd before making a triumphal progress to the Tower. The next month he appeared before the council and, through lack of proof, the charges were dropped against him; hardly a surprise considering the witnesses were now dead or missing.

Charles had been irritated by Buckingham's popularity; indeed the council had accused Buckingham of trying to foster his popularity when he appeared before them. His answer was: 'Whoever was committed to prison by my Lord Chancellor or my Lord Arlington could not want to be popular.'[6] There could be no doubt that Buckingham would be seeking revenge but first he needed to return to the king's favour. Barbara Castlemaine arranged a meeting in her rooms between Charles and Buckingham and, as so often in the past, the king was reconciled with his amusing old companion. The king's forgiveness resulted in Buckingham being restored to the Privy Council. The way was now open for him to attack Clarendon and he patched up his differences with Arlington to carry out a joint assault on the man who stood in the way of both their ambitions. Although parliament was not sitting, a number of MPs began planning to impeach Clarendon, with the wholehearted support of Buckingham.

Charles had grown tired of Clarendon and his annoying habit of lecturing him on spending too much time in the pursuit of pleasure rather than the running of the country. Buckingham and Arlington were, of course, against Clarendon, and Barbara Castlemaine had long been nagging for his removal. Charles decided that Clarendon must be dismissed as Lord Chancellor, as much for his failure to prevent Frances Stewart's marriage as being a useful scapegoat for the Dutch War. Considering Clarendon's beloved wife had only died the month before and the Chancellor was suffering from a bad attack of gout, the dismissal was carried out without compassion. Clarendon, having been told that Charles had decided to dismiss him, obtained a two-hour audience with the king during which he reminded Charles of his long service and devotion. The crux came when Clarendon was foolish enough to criticise Castlemaine, at which point Charles got up and left the room without a word. Four days later someone was sent to collect the Great Seal from Clarendon. This was not the end of the matter as, although the Commons wanted impeachment, it would be hard for a charge of treason to stick. Clarendon knew this and prepared to defend himself rather than accepting Charles's dismissal. In his anger, Charles looked into setting up a special court of twenty-seven selected peers in the Lords, with Buckingham as president. Clarendon knew that his life was now in serious danger and so fled to France on 30 November. The next month parliament passed a bill of perpetual banishment against him. The old era of the Restoration was over and the future now lay with younger men who would surpass Clarendon in personal ambition if not in loyalty.

With Clarendon gone, Buckingham became the most prominent person on the Privy Council. Although Buckingham's larger-than-life character meant that he appeared to dominate the king's government, just as his cousin Barbara dominated court life, this was largely illusionary. He was the most important subject in England with a personal income of £25,000 a year, but the only office Buckingham held was Master of Horse, whereas his rival Arlington was the senior secretary of state. Charles was fond of both men but, whereas Buckingham was amusing and a splendid companion to take him off for a night of debauchery, he was also undependable and untrustworthy. Arlington was also amusing, but knew just how to handle Charles. In the words of Bishop Burnet: 'He had the art of observing the king's temper and managing it beyond all men of that time.'[7] Although that was true, having at last got rid of his mentor, Charles was in a mood for making his own decisions while leaving the tedium of administration to others. To ensure no minister became over-mighty, Charles decided to play Buckingham and Arlington off against each other. Charles still wanted to have a solid alliance with France against Spain and the Dutch, and this was supported by Buckingham who, despite being anti-Catholic, wanted revenge for the Medway. Arlington had been pro-Spanish since his time in Madrid and was wary of Louis' continued conquest of the Spanish Netherlands, so favoured an alliance with the United Provinces. His pro-Dutch stance had been strengthened by his recent marriage to Isabella van Beverweed, whose father was the illegitimate son of Prince Maurice of Orange, making Isabella the cousin of William of Orange. Not only was this a social step-up in the world for Arlington, but his bride brought a dowry of 100,000 guilders.[8] Both were most welcome to a man of outstanding ambition and extravagant tastes.

In accordance to the king's wishes, negotiations were begun with France but Louis rejected Charles's demands for an alliance against the Dutch in exchange for recognising the French conquests in the Spanish Netherlands. In order to try to make Louis see the value of an alliance with England, Charles decided to make an alliance with the United Provinces. Using Sir William Temple, the English ambassador, as the negotiator, a treaty was signed with De Witt on 13 January and by the end of the month a further treaty was signed with Sweden. There was now a triple alliance, whose aim was to stop further French expansion by bringing about peace. With the help of Lord Sandwich, the English ambassador in Madrid, peace was agreed between Spain and Portugal, thus robbing France of its Portuguese ally in the war against Spain. In preparation for a general peace, Louis decided to swiftly conquer Franche-Comté and offered to give that up in return for keeping the Spanish land he had conquered in Flanders. This was agreed, a treaty signed, and the European powers could give a collective sigh of relief and return to peace. Just how long this peace would last would depend on whether or not Louis's ambition would be satisfied with the area he had carved out of Flanders.

Buckingham had been busy taking a full part in diplomacy and government affairs, but not too busy to neglect building up a personal power base. For some time he had nurtured a number of political allies, such as the Chancellor of the Exchequer Sir Anthony Ashley Cooper, who had been made Lord Ashley and so a member of the Lords. Ashley, like Buckingham, supported toleration for Nonconformists and shared his hatred of Clarendon and Ormonde. At Court, as well as Barbara, Buckingham had an equally important ally in Monmouth. Charles doted on his 18-year-old son who was being given ever-greater responsibility, having just been made Commander of the Life Guards. Outside parliament and the Court, Buckingham's power base was Yorkshire. A number of able Yorkshiremen became his protégés and were given offices to widen his influence. Most notable of these was Sir Thomas Osborne who, with Buckingham's patronage, became in quick succession: High Sheriff of Yorkshire, then an MP and Treasurer of the Navy. Buckingham's sympathy for the Nonconformist was the one matter he could agree on with Arlington. This resulted in some of the restrictions on dissenters being lifted and many of the imprisoned released. The implementation of this leniency was a patchy affair. The inoffensive John Bunyon who had been arrested for preaching without a licence in 1660 remained stuck in Bedford jail for several more years whereas the inveterate conspirator John Wildman was released from Pendennis Castle on condition that he kept the peace. 'Keeping the peace' was not one of Wildman's strong points. As a man closely connected to radicals and Phanaticks, he was just the sort of person that Buckingham began gathering about him; in fact Wildman was taken on as the duke's lawyer and financial adviser. Wildman was a man of substance and despite his past, at least had an air of respectability now; indeed two months after his release, Buckingham had him appointed as one of the commissioners for the Audit of Public Accounts. However, Buckingham also began dealing with what might be termed the opposition underworld. In this he tended to use his Steward, Henry North, as a go-between. The people Buckingham sought were of Phanatick, radical or just criminal persuasion who could carry out his murkier tasks, such as removing those who might bear witness against him. They were also people with a little financial backing who could organise a London rabble on the streets to support him if required.

90

Watermen, and those who had cheered him on his way to the Tower, had looked on him as something of a hero who had taken up their cause against what they regarded as the corrupt government of Clarendon. He was seen by many as champion of Protestantism against Popery and it might now prove useful to be able to get supporters on the streets as a champion against any unpopular measures that could be blamed on Arlington.

It was about this time that Buckingham is believed to have struck up at least indirect contact with Thomas Blood. As we have seen during the Dutch War, Blood had been secretly trying to organise an uprising, preferably under Ludlow, but all this had come to nothing. His activities had all been in secret, but he was to suddenly return to public attention. It had been decided that Captain John Mason, one of the captured leaders of the Northern Rising, should be transferred from the Tower of London to stand trial in York. He would be escorted by a party of six troopers under a Corporal Darcy and the group would include another prisoner, William Leving, who was a Crown witness. Blood heard that this journey was taking place, possibly through Buckingham who had been in previous contact with Mason using his Steward, Henry North. Blood knew Mason from their time with the Northern Rising and decided to rescue him. For the operation, Blood took with him two seasoned Phenaticks: Captain John Lockyer, who had been part of the Northern Rising, and Timothy Butler, who had been the custodian of Phanaticks' arms cash in London. Blood and his gang eventually located and ambushed Darcy and his group in the Doncaster area, resulting in several casualties. Blood fell off his horse in the skirmish and, fighting on foot, was shot in the arm and wounded by a pistol blow to his face. Nevertheless, Blood and his gang managed to grab Mason and make their getaway. Riding through the night they eventually reached the house of a friend in Yorkshire were Blood had his wounds dressed. Once again a proclamation was issued, offering a reward of £100 for Blood's capture. Leving had hidden during the attack, fearing that Blood and the gang would kill him for being an informer, but gave himself up to Darcy when it was safe to do so. After Leving had informed a local magistrate that he had recognised Blood and his two accomplices, Darcy continued the journey to York with Leving and delivered him to prison in York Castle.[9] Leving, although under arrest for highway robbery, was going to be a star witness against a number of people including Buckingham. Just at the time Buckingham was about to appear before the council for the Heydon affair, Leving was found dead in his cell; he had been poisoned. There is no proof that Buckingham arranged the murder, but the duke had a lot of influence in York and the timing was certainly very convenient.

The murder of Leving had deprived Arlington of a useful source. It was true that Leving had become rather out of control and taken to highway robbery, but that was probably because the £20 a year he had been promised as an agent was not coming through. In this he was no different from most government employees. When Leving was caught and arrested as a highwayman, he sent a letter for help to Joseph Williamson. Although still a prisoner, he came under Williamson's protection as a valuable source who could testify against other rebels currently in custody such as John Atkinson, Roger Jones and Robert Joplin presumably in exchange for a pardon. Leving's death had put paid to that plan. The extraordinary situation now existed that the king had two principal advisers who disliked each other intensely. Although both men were equally self-serving, they both genuinely wanted to serve the king in his best interest. However one, a secretary of state, was responsible for intelligence and combating sedition, whereas the other was secretly working with some of the very people who were scheming rebellion.

Since becoming the senior secretary of state, Arlington had been active in intelligence. He was astute enough to realise that good information brought power, whether it be to protect the state, or his own interests. There were three branches of intelligence collection at his disposal: spies, interrogation, and communication intercept. As we have seen, the primary branch was spies, that is the use of casual informants and salaried agents. Those who become agents or informants normally do so for money, but they may also do so for ideological reasons or because of some form of duress such as blackmail. Charles II's reign saw no shortage of volunteers for this employment, but the motivation for the great majority was money. In order to receive payment, informants and agents had to have information that was worth the money. There was, therefore, a huge temptation to invent dramatic information. There was also the temptation to repay an enemy by naming them as someone engaged in illegal activity – whether it was attendance at a conventicle or plotting sedition. The information of ideologically motivated agents and informants is generally more trustworthy than those motivated purely by financial gain. However, there were few if any ideologically motivated government spies. Staunch Royalists would no doubt inform the authorities of someone suspected of Republican activity. Strong Anglicans might report Nonconformist conventicles or Catholic recusants, but this was more a matter of straightforward reporting rather than secret intelligence collection. On the other hand, duress was made considerable use of to motivate spies and here, there was a cross-over to interrogation.

Interrogation of prisoners and suspects was a judicial procedure and was referred to as 'examination'. In England, the use of torture was only allowed with the king's express permission and it was never authorised by Charles. Indeed, the English had a strong aversion to the use of torture and one of their many grievances against the Dutch was that they were believed to have water-boarded captured English seamen. In Scotland there were no such qualms, and physical incentives such as the boot were used to encourage a prisoner to talk. While these painful techniques often resulted in confessions, these may or may not have been true and rarely provided valuable intelligence. The examination of prisoners in England was simply one of asking questions and recording the statements made. Where a suspect was captured while taking part in a rebellion or otherwise red-handed, it was clear to all concerned that the evidence was so strong against them that the outcome would be a conviction. Even if there were not the requisite two witnesses necessary for a conviction of treason, ways could be found to hold a suspect indefinitely either through transportation or incarceration on an island. The examination process was also used as a means of turning suitable rebels into government agents. By men such as Edward Riggs and William Leving, government employment, admittedly of a rather risky nature, was seen as greatly preferable to lengthy imprisonment or capital punishment.

Williamson and his intelligence staff not only had the task of recruiting suitable agents and informants, handling them (including arranging covert communications and payment), but most importantly of evaluating their product. This was difficult enough with purely government-sponsored spies, but was even more difficult for the evaluation of information received second-hand from Crown officials whether they were magistrates, sheriffs, bishops, generals or governors of overseas colonies, many of whom ran their own spies. Although Williamson became an expert in assessing the reliability of agents and the degree of accuracy of their information, this was not an exact science and there could be no complete certainty about such information. The area of intelligence collection where there was often greater certainty was communications intercept. From the time he had been first appointed by Sir Edward Nicholas, Williamson had been making use of the Post Office to intercept the mail of suspects, but that had been difficult while it was under the influence of Wildman. Things improved following the purge of Republican staff, but the Post Office had still not come under full government control. Arlington had wanted to be Postmaster-General, but that had been blocked by Clarendon and had been one of his many causes of resentment against the Lord Chancellor. With Clarendon gone, Arlington at last became Postmaster-General, which not only became an additional source of income – very necessary to help pay for his extravagant lifestyle at his Euston Hall estate in Suffolk and Goring House (future Buckingham Palace), but gave him complete control over the Post Office.

The hub of the postal system was the General Letter Office in Clock Lane, Dowgate, with its fifty or so clerks.[11] The General Letter Office had been burnt down during the Great Fire but the same process continued in new premises. That is domestic mail, including that from Scotland and Ireland, arrived on Mondays, Wednesdays and Fridays, and was dispatched to its addressees on Tuesdays, Thursdays and Saturdays. Overseas mail was handled by Post Office staff in the Foreign Office. This mail could arrive any time depending on shipping and weather, but was dispatched to France and southern European countries on Mondays and Thursdays, and for the Netherlands and Northern Europe, on Mondays and Fridays. Some of the Republican Post Office staff had survived the purge, most notably Isaac Dorislaus. He had been put in charge of opening and exploiting overseas mail by Cromwell's secretary of state, John Thurloe, and was so good at his job that he was retained and continued his good work in a special room next to the Foreign Office. Dorislaus's method of covertly opening letters was rather basic as he just used a hot knife to raise the wax seal and then a drop of new wax to reseal it. Arlington had been approached by Sir Samuel Morland, who offered an improved method of covertly exploiting correspondence. Morland had also worked for Thurloe but then changed sides just before the Restoration. He was an amateur scientist and invented a method of opening letters without leaving a trace and producing several exact copies. Quite what this process entailed is still not known, but he demonstrated it one night to Arlington and the king, who were so impressed that the method was brought into general use and two rooms allocated for the equipment in the General Letter Office. Unfortunately the equipment was all destroyed in the Great Fire and for some reason was never replaced. Government covert intercept returned to using the hot knife.

It was one thing to be able to open correspondence and copy it, but another thing to be able to read it. It was well known that mail stood a good chance of being opened and so those with something to hide took countermeasures. A surprising number of correspondents had a touchingly naïve confidence in secret ink. This was usually based on either urine or lemon juice and the writing would become visible if the paper was heated. It need hardly be said that Dorislaus and his assistants would routinely check suspect correspondence against a lighted candle for any invisible ink. The more sophisticated method of trying to ensure the confidentiality of letters was the use of cryptography, which is the use of codes and ciphers. Codes replace a word or phrases by another word or symbol. For example 'Mr Phoenix' might mean the 'King of France'. Ciphers conceal the meaning of a message by replacing each letter in the original wording with another letter or symbol. When a document is enciphered, the original wording is replaced by a scrambled version that is unintelligible to the reader. A key is necessary for the particular encryption algorithm to enable the sender to encipher and the recipient to decipher. The two basic methods of encryption were transportation and substitution. For the former, the letters of words are rearranged thus 'king' might become 'gnik'. In substitution, each letter changes its identity but retains its position, for example, the letter 'a' could be changed to 'c' and 'b' to 'd' etc, so king would become 'mkpi'. (*a more detailed explanation of cryptography is at Appendix 1*). As the encryption algorithms could be complex and might be a combination of both transportation and substitution, understanding the content of enciphered correspondence was quite beyond the scope of Dorislaus or other Post Office clerks.

Fortunately, Williamson was able to use the services of the eminent mathematician Dr John Wallis, who was Salvian Professor of Geometry at Oxford. When Wallis had been chaplain to a leading Puritan lady at the start of the Civil War, he had demonstrated that he could decipher some captured Royalist correspondence.[10] From that time onwards he had been employed by parliament and then Cromwell to decipher any encrypted material. In 1649 he had been given the Oxford professorship in recognition of his services and continued working in support of the government until the Restoration. Although a Puritan who had worked for Cromwell, he had signed a document opposing the execution of Charles I. This signature served him well at the Restoration as he was made a royal chaplain, confirmed in his professorship, and eventually brought back into deciphering encrypted correspondence. Wallis contributed to the origins of calculus and is regarded as the greatest English mathematician before Newton but, like many geniuses, was not the easiest person to get on with. He was a grumpy member of the Royal Society and managed to have bitter quarrels with most of the leading thinkers of his day including Hobbes, Descartes and Boyle. However, he seems to have had no difficulties in working with Williamson and the Post Office because he enjoyed the challenge of breaking ciphers. That it was vital work in helping to secure the throne of an Anglican monarch of questionable morals was of secondary importance to the dour Puritan. The fifty guineas a quarter he received as a retainer from Arlington may have contributed to his willingness to work for the Crown.

By about 1668 the king had a most effective intercept service supported by John Wallis who was very probably the greatest cryptanalyst of his age. As well as intercept, the Post Office also provided a valuable service in agent handling. Agents needed to report information to their handler, normally Williamson, and to receive tasking and payment from them. Obviously this communication had to be carried out in secret. Sometimes it was possible to have personal contact. This could be at the secretary's offices at night, or more securely by meeting at a safe house. It was far more secure to have no personal contact after recruitment and indeed this was essential for communications with agents overseas or outside London. The procedure was for agents to be given cover names or 'borrowed names' as Williamson called them. The agent would be given one or more fictitious names and addresses in London to send their reports. Dorislaus was entrusted with Williamson's list of these addressees and would ensure that any letter with such an address would be extracted from the General Letter Office and passed unopened to Williamson for him to evaluate and action as necessary. In some cases the letters would be passed on to Arlington who liked to handle high value agents personally, particularly if he had been involved in their recruitment. However, this was the exception rather than the rule and Arlington left the running of the government's intelligence department to Williamson. Arlington's contribution was to make sure that intelligence was recognised as an essential part of the king's apparatus of government and give it the support and resources that it required. It was in 1668 that, despite the dire state of Royal finances, Arlington managed to get the Secret Intelligence Fund to be increased to £400,000 a year. It has to be said that one of the reasons Charles agreed to the increase was so that some of the money could be covertly used to help finance his mistresses. Even so, it was a considerable help to cover the Intelligence Department's cost for bribes and the payment of agents and informants.

As senior secretary of state, Arlington was, in reality, Charles's principal minister, but the even more flamboyant Buckingham, the king's greatest subject and close friend from his childhood, appeared the most powerful. Charles was well aware that Buckingham, for all his wit and good company, could be relied upon to be unreliable. In January, Buckingham had got into another of his scrapes. He was having an affair with the Countess of Shrewsbury, which resulted in him having a duel with the Countess's husband. Each of the principals in the duel had two seconds and the result was that of six men, one was killed and two were seriously wounded. One of the wounded was the Earl of Shrewsbury who died some time later. The king was strongly opposed to duelling but Buckingham and the others were pardoned, probably on the insistence of Barbara Castlemaine. Buckingham then set up the Countess of Shrewsbury in his own house. Understandably Buckingham's wife Mary voiced objections to this arrangement but was told that if she did not accept it, he would be only too pleased to order a carriage to return her to her parents. This raised eyebrows even in the relaxed moral atmosphere of the Restoration court. Although back in favour, Buckingham was using up his credit with the king, and Arlington became the beneficiary when he was given the chairmanship of the powerful Committee of Foreign Affairs with Joseph Williamson as the secretary.

The king's love life was not going smoothly. He had still not got over Frances Stewart and the rows with Barbara were getting greater as she became ever more demanding. She had an affair with the handsome rake Henry Jermyn who then went off with Lady Falmouth, but had left Barbara pregnant. The king knew the child was not his but Barbara insisted that he recognise it as his own. A huge row ensued, ending with Barbara making Charles get on his knees before her and promise not to offend her again in the future. In the words of Pepys, she had become 'a tyrant to command him'. Even Barbara realised she might have gone too far and nothing was heard of the baby again. Although Barbara remained principal mistress, Charles began a series of affairs; the first important one was with the actress Moll Davies, described by Pepys as an excellent dancer but 'the most impudent slut in the world'.[12] This former milkmaid was set up in a fine house in Suffolk Street and produced Charles a daughter called Mary. Buckingham had once again fallen out with Barbara and decided that the king should have a Protestant mistress to replace his Catholic cousin. It had been he who had introduced Moll to the king, but she was by no means the only lady to journey up the back stairs to the king's bedchamber. The roll-call included aristocrats such as the Countess of Kildare and the Countess of Falmouth, as well as ladies about the court such as Winifred Well and Jane Roberts, ladies of the stage such as the singer Maria Knight, and numerous, nameless common prostitutes.[13] Among this group was an actress called Nell Gwynn, who Buckingham had also introduced to the king.

Nell had not had a good start in life. Her drunken mother worked as a servant in a brothel and her sister Rose was married to a highwayman. Nell had been working as an orange girl when her chestnut hair, sparkling hazel eyes and small but shapely figure had caught the attention of Drury Lane's leading actor Charles Hart. She had become his mistress and he went to some lengths to teach her to act. Her natural talent meant that she had become a leading lady by the time Charles was introduced to her and invited her to join him for supper. Nell had demanded £500 a year for joining the ranks of royal mistresses, but this had been turned down so she remained a full-time actress, merely sharing the king's bed when required. Over time she was to become more than just another good-looking actress as her impudent honesty and sense of humour made her a woman with whom Charles could really relax. Barbara could only watch with mounting anger at her potential rival for the king's affections. She decided to get her own back by having other affairs of her own, in particular with Charles Hart. The relationship between Charles and Barbara become complex, with a constant round of rows, recriminations, and reconciliations. Barbara's hold over the king would manage to last another two years, but it was all very exhausting.

The public too were becoming exhausted with the king's amours and scandals at court. On Easter Monday 1668 riots broke out in Poplar as crowds of apprentices began smashing up the brothels. The reason for what became known as the 'Bawdy House Riots' was because there had been a recent crackdown on conventicles and Nonconformist Londoners were demonstrating against the government, which was turning a blind eye to illegal brothels, but using the full weight of the law against those who wanted freedom of worship. The next day the rioters had swelled to 500, armed with staves, axes and iron bars, and began dismantling the brothels in Moorfield, East Smithfield, Shoreditch, and Holborn. The Guards and militia were called out and arrests were made, with the ringleaders being taken off to the new prison in Clerkenwell. The rioters' blood was up and they broke into the prison and released their comrades. By Wednesday, the rioters had grown to several thousand (some say as many as 40,000) and were destroying brothels and other property in Moorfield. Eventually the Life Guards and militia under Lord Craven used maximum force to restore order.

Although fifteen of the main rioters were tried for treason and four were hanged, drawn, and quartered at Tyburn, this had been a spontaneous uprising with no real leaders. For example, there is no record that Thomas Blood and other Phanaticks and radicals in London at the time took part. Although the cause of the riots had been frustration over religious intolerance and a certain puritan spirit among Nonconformists, in some ways the attack on the bawdy houses represented an attack on the court – the greatest bawdy house of all. Barbara Castlemaine was particularly unpopular because of her mind-boggling extravagance. About this time, Pepys records in his diary that Barbara had won £15,000 in one night of gaming, but lost £25,000 a few days later. This was gossip and may or may not have been true, but it would hardly endear her to poor apprentices who could hope to earn a mere £20 a year once they were established as craftsmen. A very popular satire was published called *The Poor Whore's Petition,* which was addressed to the Countess of Castlemaine and asking her to support the plight of her 'sisters'. Sequels were also published, one called *The Gracious Answer,* in which Barbara was portrayed as a vain Papist whore, gloating over her jewels and saying that 'venereal pleasure, accompanied by looseness, debauchery and profaneness are not such heinous crimes'. She did not enjoy the joke.

Charles realised that he had lost the popularity he had gained for his action during the Fire of London and there was mounting resentment against high taxation, the humiliation of the Medway attack, and a decadent court. Then there were the continued grievances of the Nonconformists. In February, Buckingham, with Charles's support, had tried to end the persecution of Nonconformists by proposing a Toleration Act in the House of Lords. This had been thrown out, so the running sore remained. Although the attempt at toleration had failed, there was a growing public mood that it was necessary and, related to this, was an increasing concern about Roman Catholics. It appeared that Catholics were gaining influence at court with the king's principal mistress being a professed Papist. On top of Charles's wearing and difficult relationship with Barbara, he had the constant worry of debt. The annual royal customs receipts were down to £700,000 a year and there were debts from the war of £1.5 million. Charles's reluctance to provide ever more money to fund the extravagances of Barbara and her offspring was a continuing cause of arguments between them. Of greater concern was that there was little enough money to run the government and definitely not enough to rebuild Charles's pride and joy, the royal fleet. Parliament, although not hostile to the king, was showing little interest in voting adequate sums for revenue. What was more, an informal opposition called the 'Country Party' had developed. This was by no means a political party, but rather a group of MPs who were united in attacking the king's ministers and continuing to find scapegoats for the failure of the Dutch War. There also remained the fundamental worry that the queen had not produced an heir and her recent miscarriage was making it less and less likely. All together, this was not a happy period in Charles's life and he seemed to be as far away as ever from creating his long sought-after alliance with France and avenging the Dutch destruction of the fleet. At least in respect of a French alliance there was about to be a change for the better, but that was to bring even greater problems for the future.

Chapter 8

The Secret Treaty
1669–70

Restless he rolls from whore to whore
A merry monarch, scandalous and poor.
John Wilmot, Earl of Rochester

Charles had gone along with Arlington's Triple Alliance with Sweden and the United Provinces to prove to Louis that he needed him as a friend. This plan seems to have worked because in August 1668, Louis sent Colbert de Croissy as his new ambassador to London with express instructions to get Charles to break with the Triple Alliance. De Croissy was also told to bribe Arlington if required in order to achieve this aim. With Arlington not only the senior secretary of state, but chairman of the Foreign Affairs Committee, there is no doubt that he could be a major impediment to improving Anglo–French relations. Indeed, it might be as well if any such negotiations were carried out without drawing them to Arlington's attention. Of course Minette had been advocating secret negotiations for some time. In her letter to Charles as long ago as April 1664 she had written:

> *I beg you to consider if some secret treaty could not be arranged which you could make sure of this, by giving a pledge on your part that you will help in the business he* [Louis] *will soon have in Flanders, now the king of Spain is ill, and which will certainly be opposed by the Dutch, but will not be contrary to your interests.*[1]

Now that Louis wanted Charles as an ally, it seemed as though secret negotiations might begin between the two kings using Minette as an intermediary, and an alliance might be quickly achieved.

To Charles's disappointment, the alliance with France remained elusive.

100

THE SECRET TREATY

Although Louis wanted to break up the Triple Alliance, it did not necessarily mean that he wanted a treaty with England. There were many old problems to be resolved, such as ambassador precedence, and Charles including 'King of France' among his titles. Louis would welcome an alliance with England against the United Provinces but it would have to be on his terms. Time dragged on and Charles tried to force the pace in a letter to Minette of 20 January 1669, when he said he wanted a special relationship with Louis with her as the go-between. Charles added: 'I send you here a cipher, which is very easy and secure. The first side is the single cipher and with such names I could think of necessary to our purpose.'[2] What he termed a cipher was in fact a code with, for example: 363 = Duke of York, 271= France, 341= Buckingham, 360, 334 or 386 = Charles II, 100 or 152 = Louis XIV, 129 or 103 = Minette, 290 = Catholic, 315 = religion. An extract from a letter from Charles on 27 March shows how this code is difficult to understand to the uninitiated reader: '363 is come into the business and for that reason I desired you not to write anything to anybody upon the business of 271. 341 knowns nothing of 360 intentions towards 290. 315 nor the person 334 sends to 100.'[3]

Bearing in mind that Buckingham was a keen advocate of a French alliance, the question arose whether he should be brought into the secret negotiations. The decision was to keep him out of it because of his notorious unreliability. In any case, Buckingham was currently distracted from foreign affairs by pursuing his long-standing vendetta against Ormonde. Although Ormonde had made some mistakes as Lord Lieutenant of Ireland, particularly over financial management for which he had little aptitude, he had stamped out rebellion and was providing a reasonably benign and honest government for the country. For all that, he was far from Whitehall and the corridors of power and many looked on his post with envy – none more so than his enemy Buckingham. Ormonde despised Buckingham but had done little or no harm to him; Buckingham however, was someone who, once he felt slighted, would never rest until he had exacted revenge. Impeachment proceedings against Ormonde were started by Buckingham and, to Buckingham's delight, the king dismissed Ormonde from his post. Buckingham had been hoping to be made Lord Lieutenant himself so was disappointed when Charles gave that to the ineffectual Lord Roberts, but at least he had achieved his revenge. For his part, Ormonde accepted his removal from office with dignity and remained totally loyal to his ungrateful monarch.

The idea of secret negotiations through Minette did not go smoothly. Minette was indisposed, being pregnant for most of the year and, having had one still birth child and lost her only son, was concentrating on a successful birth. At the same time she was suffering from pains in her side and indigestive problems, which had begun the previous year and were getting steadily worse. On top of that, relations with her husband, the Duke of Orleans, were fraught, not helped by his longstanding infatuation with the grasping, unscrupulous Chevalier de Lorraine, who used all his influence to make life difficult for Minette. Minette suffered a further blow in September when her mother Henrietta Maria, to whom she was devoted, suddenly died. To make matters worse still, even before the funeral had taken place, Orleans was taking action to grab all the former queen's property in France. Minette appealed to Louis and managed to have her mother's property handed over to Charles. Marital relations deteriorated still further.

With negotiations faltering through Minette, other means of negotiation had to be found. Arlington's friend Ralph Montagu had been sent as ambassador to France in April 1669 with instructions to improve relations but, as had happened in the past, he soon got bogged down over the fraught questions of precedence. De Croissy, the French ambassador in London, was in talks with Buckingham, but as the duke was not in Charles's confidence, little came of them. Louis had sent over the Abbe Pregnani as a possible go between but that had not gone well. The Abbe was a well-known astrologer and was invited to Newmarket Races to provide sound tips for the royal party. Unfortunately the stars were not behaving as hoped and all his predictions for winners were incorrect. Both Buckingham and Monmouth lost considerable sums on what they had counted on being a scientific betting system. The Abbe lost credibility and returned to France leaving Anglo–French relations slightly worse than before his visit.

There is some evidence that Charles had taken it into his head to convert to Catholicism in January 1669 and had confided this to his brother the Duke of York, who had also become a closet Catholic at that time.[4] Be that as it may, the king decided that he would pass a message to Louis that he intended to convert. Charles was by no means a devout Christian but he seems to have privately leant toward Catholicism. He was to convert to Catholicism on his deathbed in 1685, but whether he had genuinely decided to become a Catholic in 1669 it is hard to tell. Also, it would be one thing to become a secret Catholic and quite another as Supreme Head of the Church of England to publicly announce his conversion. It is possible that he might have thought that to inform Louis of his conversion would be enough to induce Louis to commit to an alliance. Whatever the case, in March 1669 Charles sent a Catholic, Lord Arundel of Wardour, to Louis to say he had decided to convert. Arundel was chosen for this secret mission because he was a Catholic, and as Master of Horse for Henrietta Maria, he could easily explain his reasons for travelling between Charles and Louis. The next month Arundel reported back saying that Louis would abandon his 1662 treaty with the Dutch if Charles would abandon his 1668 treaty. Louis also suggested that Charles put off announcing his conversion for the time being while he raised an army for war with the Dutch after receiving funding from Louis. With an army in place Charles could announce his conversion and at that time, Louis would give him an additional sum of money. Negotiations continued over the months as the details of the draft treaty were hammered out. By October the main points had been agreed and Louis asked Charles to inform Ambassador De Croissy of his conversion. Such was the need for secrecy that it was decided that Ralph Montagu, the English ambassador in Paris, should remain in the dark. By this time Arlington had been brought into the king's plans and like the ambitious courtier he was, immediately cast aside his personal convictions and threw himself into pursuing the French alliance. It was, however, Sir Thomas Clifford, the Catholic Controller of the Household, who became Charles's right-hand-man in organising the treaty and by December, he and De Croissy had produced a final draft.

The provisions for the treaty were that Charles and Louis would go to war against the United Provinces with France attacking on land supported by a 600-strong English contingent, and England would attack by sea providing fifty men-of-war supported by thirty French men-of-war, all under the command of the Duke of York. What Louis would get out of this would be the conquest of the Spanish Netherlands. England would gain economically strategic towns of Walcheren, Cadzand and Sluys at the mouth of the Scheldt (once they had been captured), hopefully destroy Dutch naval power and in doing so, avenge the Medway and seize their trade. All very sound – leaving aside that both England and France were formally allies of the country they were plotting to attack. This would have been enough to make the treaty secret, but there were clauses that were so sensitive that they were to remain secret until 1826.[5] These clauses were that Charles would receive payment from Louis for making the treaty, would then announce his conversion to Catholicism at a suitable time, after which he would receive a further payment of two million crowns from Louis and 4,000 French troops if necessary to put down opposition to his conversion. Not in the treaty was the work Clifford was carrying out in preparation for returning the Anglican Church to Rome, finding resolutions to problems such as married clergy, and returning land to the Catholic Church.

That Charles agreed these secret terms is completely astounding. It could be argued that he was using it as a ploy to secure the treaty that would enable him to avenge the Dutch and he never intended to honour the agreement. If this was the case, it was a huge and dangerous gamble because public knowledge of the secret terms would have been ruinous. There is no doubt that foreign policy was regarded as a royal prerogative. Charles was, therefore, quite within his rights to make a treaty with a foreign power even though it would be sensible, and even polite, to get any such treaty agreed by parliament, especially as it was committing the country to war. On top of that, at the very time Charles was agreeing this draft treaty with France to jointly attack the United Provinces, he was actually asking parliament to vote on funding in preparation for war by the Triple Alliance against France. Parliament did indeed vote £300,000 per year for the purpose, to be raised as a wine tax. There is no doubt that parliament was difficult and fractious, but the king's action displayed his complete contempt for the institution.

The king had got his funding under false pretences, but it also came at a price. Although Charles wanted to promote religious toleration, parliament were still intent on stamping out dissent. Charles had therefore been obliged to agree to the renewal of the Conventicle Act. So began a renewed persecution of Nonconformists, with their chapels and meetings houses closed and fines for non-attendance at an Anglican church. Many Nonconformists resigned themselves to the situation and dutifully attended church but held their own services in private. The Quakers were not prepared to consider such a compromise and continued attending their meetings, as a result of which they were dragged before magistrates, fined and – on refusing to pay – thrust into prison. On eventual release they returned to their boarded-up places of worship and held their meetings in the street outside. On one of these occasions William Penn and a Quaker minister called William Mead were arrested at an open-air meeting in Gracechurch Street, in London in August 1670. Having been gaoled in Newgate they were brought before the Recorder for London, John Howell, and the Lord Mayor, Samuel Starling. There then began a classic case of how Dissenters could be denied justice in the courts.

When the trial began, Penn and Mead demanded to know under what law they were indicted. When the Recorder replied that it was the Common Law they asked to be shown it. The Recorder was furious and despite any amount of browbeating of the two prisoners, he could not get them to back down. In fact, Penn (the future founder of Pennsylvania) then gave the Recorder a lecture on the legal rights of prisoners as secured in the Acts of Henry III and Edwards I and III. This made Howell incandescent with rage. Howell had Penn and Mead removed from the court and began to charge the jury, with

Penn shouting out that it was illegal to charge the jury in the absence of prisoners. When the jury gave their verdict it was simply that the accused were guilty of speaking in Gracechurch Street. The Lord Mayor then said that he presumed that they meant speaking to a 'tumultuous assembly', but the jury replied that was not the case. As result, they were tersely sent out to amend their verdict. When they returned later, they again gave a verdict of not guilty of an offence; the Recorder ordered them to be locked up for the night without food, drink, fire or candle. The next day the jury stated in writing that they had no other verdict. There followed threats and intimidation of the jury with Penn protesting in the background, which resulted in him being put in chains; the jury stood firm and spent another bleak night locked up without food or drink. The next day, the jury stuck to their not guilty verdict and were all fined forty marks (approximately £25 or roughly £3,700 today) and committed to prison until the large sum could be paid. Penn and Mead were likewise also fined and imprisoned. Penn used his influence to lodge an appeal and have the case brought before Lord Chief Justice Vaughan when the whole proceedings were pronounced illegal; both the accused and the jury were released. It was a happy ending for English justice, but the case demonstrates that dissenters without the stature and determination of Penn could find themselves totally at the mercy of a biased judiciary. The case also gives an indication of the human cost of the king agreeing to renew the Conventicle Act to get the funds he needed.

Agreeing to take what amounted to a bribe from the king of France was a national humiliation even if, from Charles's point of view, it enabled him to rule without having to persuade an increasingly difficult parliament to grant him funds. To agree that he, as supreme Head of the Anglican Church, would announce his conversion to Rome and bring in foreign troops to suppress opposition amounted to treason. It is an interesting legal point whether a king could be guilty of treason. Clearly some had thought so, as Charles I had been convicted of treason for making arrangements for Irish soldiers to support his cause in the Civil War. If the use of Irish troops to put down rebellion was considered treason, how much more would be an invasion of French soldiers. Despite Clifford planning to transfer the Anglican Church back to Rome, the treaty did not expressly say that was Charles's intention. Indeed, everything points to him merely wanting to allow religious toleration to Catholics. Roman Catholics only represented a small minority in England and Scotland and the great majority of the population in the two countries were either Anglican or Nonconformist, who regarded the Church of Rome with at best, contempt, and at worst, downright hatred. In a devout age, the Pope was regarded by many as the Anti-Christ, and for the monarch to declare himself a Papist could well have sparked rebellion. In the secret treaty, Charles was agreeing to provisions that reeked of treason and if known, would have been a greater threat to the Crown than all the other plots and rebellions of his reign put together. Fortunately, the secret provisions were never to be implemented and they were to remain secret well beyond Charles's lifetime.

With the secret treaty now drafted, the next step was for it to be signed and Minette now came back into the picture. Although sharing the promiscuous nature of her brother, Minette was a devout Catholic and delighted with the secret terms of the treaty, which she had been instrumental in developing. She had given birth in August of that year but was very upset that it was another girl. She could console herself that at least the child was healthy and time was helping her to get over the loss of her mother. On the other hand, relations with her husband had not improved. He too was bitterly disappointed that she had not produced a boy and was continuing to be objectionable, egged on by the Chevalier de Lorraine. Minette had enough and complained to Louis about Lorraine. Louis was concerned about Lorraine's malign influence over his brother and ordered him to be imprisoned in Lyon, but that was soon changed to banishment to Rome. Orleans was in despair to lose the love of his life and pleaded with his brother for Lorraine's return but with no success. Meanwhile Louis had decided that Minette would be the best intermediary for taking the secret treaty to England for signing. She provided the perfect cover as the visit could be portrayed as being no more than a family reunion. Orleans, with characteristic vindictiveness, refused to consent to Minette travelling but after much argument and being over ruled by Louis, he reluctantly agreed that she could travel to England for a short time as long as she remained in Dover.

So it was that in May 1670 Charles at last set off for Dover to meet the beloved sister he had not seen for nine years, and sign the treaty he had worked for so long to achieve. As it happened he was travelling at the very time Nell was giving birth to her first son by him and Moll Davies was producing him another daughter. These ladies were probably far from his mind when he arrived in Dover and had a joyous reunion with Minette. When she arrived, Minette appeared pale, weak, and with little appetite, but being with her brother soon seemed to bring her back to normal. Charles had of course arranged entertainments but finding the facilities of Dover extremely limited, moved the royal party to Canterbury. Brother and sister had a magical time together during which the secret treaty was signed by Charles and witnessed by both Arlington and Clifford. An added pleasure of Minette's visit was that she had brought with her a maid of honour called Louise de Kéroüalle. She came from an ancient but impoverished noble Breton family but, more importantly, she was strikingly beautiful. Louise was also charmingly feminine in stark contrast to Barbara, who was developing into a bullying harridan. Charles was immediately captivated but she, like Minette, was to return to France all too soon. Minette and Charles found their parting very painful, but at least they had a wonderful fortnight together during which Minette's health seemed to have improved. Just a couple a weeks after returning to France she was to die in excruciating pain.

Minette returned first to Paris where we may assume Orleans was less than happy that he had been overruled about her visit, and annoyed that she had broken the agreement to remain in Dover. Minette and her husband then travelled to St Cloud to get away from the Paris summer heat. On 29 June she was looking tired but appeared reasonably well and for once had eaten a good meal at lunch. After lunch she had asked for a cup of chicory waters. The water and chicory were kept in jugs in a closet together with Minette's silver cup. The chicory water was mixed into the silver cup and brought to Minette. As she drank the chicory she cried out in pain and said she had been poisoned. Doctors were called and Orleans sat by her bedside and began to show genuine affection for his wife. As Orleans was concerned about the possibility of poison, two of Minette's ladies mixed chicory water themselves and drank it without any ill-effect. Following seemingly endless convulsions and appalling agony, the 26-year-old princess died the next day. The big question was whether she had been murdered, with obvious suspicion falling on the Chevalier de Lorraine and quite possibly even Orleans. Montagu, the ambassador, had rushed to be with her as she died and he was convinced that she had been poisoned by Lorraine. He sent Sir Thomas Armstrong to break the news to Charles and give his view that she had been poisoned. Needless to say, Charles was heart-broken to hear of her death and did not leave his room for four days. Still thinking that Orleans and Lorraine had caused his sister's death, Charles refused to see De Croissy when he came to officially offer Louis's condolences. Hearing the dangerous rumours of poisoning, Louis ordered a public autopsy to be conducted and the finding was that Minette had died of acute peritonitis following the perforation of a duodenal ulcer. This made perfect sense and explained Minette's lack of appetite and frail condition.

On the face of it the findings of the autopsy are completely plausible, but there are grounds for believing they should not be taken on face value. According to Madame de Lafayette, a friend of Minette, who was staying with her at the time, the murder was instigated by Lorraine. [6] Madame de Lafayette states that on hearing of Minette's death, Louis had called for Morel Simon, Orleans's Maitre d'hotel, to be brought to him under armed guard and asked him, under pain of death, whether Minette had been poisoned. Simon had said that he believed that Minette had been poisoned on Lorraine's instruction by two of his friends who were living in the household, d'Effiat and Beuvron. They had put poison on the rim of the cup that was used for the chicory water. Simon did, however, assure Louis that Orleans had no knowledge of the murder. Madame de Lafayette also relates that Minette's silver cup had gone missing and when it was eventually found it showed marks of having been put in a fire. Her account is to some extent supported by the Chronicle of the Duc de Saint-Simon, which recounts that the plot had been hatched in Italy by Lorraine with d'Effiat and Beuvron, but that Orleans had no knowledge of it.

Montagu stated that although the post mortem was very public, he was dissatisfied with the results. As English ambassador he had been allowed to nominate two English physicians, Hugh Chamberlain and Alexander Boscher, to be present. Both Chamberlain and Boscher expressed their dissatisfaction over the professionalism of the French physicians in the post-mortem and the fact that much of their work was hidden from view. Nevertheless they, agreed to sign the post-mortem for diplomatic purposes. Following the post-mortem Louis had decided to help kill the rumours of Lorraine's involvement by cancelling his banishment and allowing him to return to Orleans.

About a year after Minette's death, Orleans married Charlotte Elizabeth, Princess Palatine. She had heard the rumour of poisoning by Lorraine and was anxious that the same fate might await her now that Lorraine had returned as her husband's constant companion. She even asked Louis directly about the poisoning and was told that Orleans had not been involved. She accepted this but made her own enquiries over time. She records that a footman saw d'Effiat in the closet where the water and Chicory were kept and saw him wiping Minette's silver cup with some paper. When asked why he was there, d'Effiat said that he had been thirsty and noted that the cup was dirty so was cleaning it.

There is no doubt that Minette had been unwell for some time and it is quite possible that she died from that illness, but it is also quite possible that she was helped on her way by poison arranged by a vindictive Lorraine, but very probably without the knowledge of Orleans. If Minette had been murdered, it was in nobody's interest to say so officially. Neither Louis nor

THE SECRET TREATY

Charles wanted her death to destroy the secret treaty that had taken so long to achieve and was, in a way, a monument to Minette herself. Charles kept his personal suspicions about Minette's death to himself and pressed on with implementing the treaty. Buckingham was sent to represent the king at Minette's state funeral. He was also given the task of negotiating an official treaty with Louis that could be made public when the time was right and would provide a cover for the real secret treaty of which Buckingham still had no knowledge. Buckingham was delighted to be given the status of carrying out this task and was made to feel that he was the architect of an alliance with France. It was particularly gratifying to know that his lobbying for an alliance with France had prevailed over Arlington's for continued alliance with the United Provinces. Buckingham's spirits were also high over the fact that he had not only got his enemy Ormonde dismissed from Ireland, and Ormonde's son was married to Arlington's sister, but he had recently engineered the dismissal of Sir William Coventry, who had been Arlington's appointee as Treasurer of the Navy. Exactly how much Buckingham despised Arlington can be seen in this verse he wrote about his rival:

First draw an arrant fop, from top to toe,
Whose very looks at first dash shew him so:
Give him a mean, proud garb, a doper face,
A pert, dull grin, a blak patch on his face,
Two goggle-Eyes, so clear, tho' very dead,
That one may see, thro'em quite thro' his head.
Let every nod of his, and subtle wink
Declare the fool would talk, but cannot think.
Let him all other fools so far surpasse
That fools theselves point at him as an ass[7]

There is no record of Arlington producing a poetical reply commenting on Buckingham but a few years later, John Dryden produced this excellent description of Buckingham in his *Absalom and Achitophel*:

Stiff in opinions, always in the wrong,
Was nothing by starts and nothing long;
But in the course of one revolving moon
Was chymist, fiddler, statesman and buffoon;
Then all for women, painting, rhyming, drinking
Besides ten thousand freaks that died in thinking.

It might be thought that it was very annoying for the king to have his two principal members of government at daggers drawn. Quite the contrary, it suited the king to bolster Buckingham's apparent power and so play him off against Arlington. Arlington was becoming increasingly powerful and Charles had no wish for him to dominate government in the way that Clarendon had done. George Monck, the powerful Duke of Albemarle, had died in January leaving Buckingham and Arlington as the most important figures at court. Arlington had had setbacks over Ormonde and Coventry, but he had been very much a part of producing the treaty with France, which Buckingham now thought was his doing. In fact, probably as sweetener to reward Arlington for working on the secret treaty, it had been agreed that his daughter Isabella would be betrothed to Henry Fitzroy – Barbara's second son by Charles. It has to be said that this was not a love match as Henry was 9 years old and Isabella only 5, but to Arlington, it meant that the king would be his daughter's future father-in-law. Of perhaps greater importance was that he had managed to get his protégé, Sir John Terry, made secretary of state for the North and so was in fact controlling both secretary posts. Nevertheless, to all appearances, Buckingham was in the ascendancy and very pleased to be negotiating directly with the king of France. It was gratifying for Buckingham to find that his diplomacy had resulted in swift French agreement to the terms of the official treaty, which was virtually the same as the Minette treaty but without the secret provisions about Charles's conversion. The official treaty was signed in December and, although it could not yet be made public because of parliament's hostility to France, at least it could be revealed to the principal ministers. As a result, it was countersigned by Ashley and Lauderdale as well as Arlington and Clifford who had signed the secret treaty.

Buckingham was probably hoping that his cordial relations with Louis during the negotiations might make the French king suggest to Charles that he supplant Arlington. Whether or not that was the case, Buckingham decided to continue to influence Charles through his mistresses. He had fallen out with Barbara, but had found Nell Gwynn for Charles. The relationship between Charles and Nell was blossoming; she had produced him a baby boy and he had set her up in a house in Pall Mall. Following his visits to France, Buckingham thought it might be prudent to arrange another mistress as a backup. Nell would have influence over the king, but her background meant she was never going to be a potential *maitress en titre*. He therefore suggested to Charles that it would be a kindness to Minette's memory if he took on one of her former servants. The servant he recommended was none other than Louise de Kéroüalle whom he knew Charles had found so attractive.

Buckingham may have also felt that there was even an outside chance that Charles might divorce the barren Catherine and make Louise his queen, a thought probably not lost on Louise herself. Charles agreed to Louise joining his court, much to the pleasure of Louis who thought that Louise could take over Minette's role as an unofficial channel between the two monarchs. She would also have the potential to become a French intelligence source at the heart of English government. Unsurprisingly, Louis had several meetings with Louise before she left to prepare her for the task ahead. However, things were not to work out the way either Buckingham or Louis had anticipated.

Buckingham was supposed to be escorting Louise to England but in his typical, unreliable fashion, forgot to collect her and left her stranded at Dieppe. It was Arlington who eventually arranged her passage and had her to stay when she arrived; she never forgave Buckingham. Understandably, this 21-year-old girl, far from family in a foreign country, looked to Arlington as her protector. He realised her potential and become something of a father figure to whom she would become very attached. Louise took up her duties as a Maid of Honour to the queen and was rapidly accepted but as the English could not get their tongue around her surname, she was called 'Mademoiselle Carwell'. Louise's charming manners and the fact that she was a genuinely devout Catholic made her particularly liked by Catherine. The same could not be said of Charles who seemed to take little interest in her. Perhaps he was grieving for Minette and the sight of Louise reminded him of the loss. Also, Barbara was still dominating his life with exorbitant demands and threats to publish his letters if they were not met. She still retained some hold over him and the ability to make him jealous of her many new lovers, who included a nimble tightrope dancer called Jacob Hall. The relationship was getting quite unbearable. Charles had managed to put a distance between them by moving her out of the Palace of Whitehall to a Berkshire House – a magnificent mansion that, ironically, had been the London home of her enemy Clarendon. Charles had had to borrow £8,000 to buy it for her. [8] She was also receiving a new pension of £4,700 a year from Post Office revenues. Charles now added to her titles: Baroness Nonsuch, Countess of Northampton and Duchess of Cleveland, and gave her Elizabeth I's Nonsuch Palace with its 2,000 acres of land. A little later Charles also agreed to pay her enormous debts and provide a total income of £30,000 a year in the hope that she might depart abroad and leave him in peace. Despite Charles's efforts, Barbara was to remain in London as a continuing nuisance and embarrassment for another five years, but she had completely lost her place in his affections.

Having fallen out with Barbara, Buckingham would probably have been pleased to see her decline in influence, especially as he had a protégé in Nell Gwynn who had become Charles's current focus of affection. The king's actress friends also became a topic in parliament when it resumed in October. Parliament's main business was to consider the king's request to vote additional funds for the navy in view of the fact that both France and the United Provinces were increasing their navies. Parliament duly agreed to vote funds, but then had to decide what taxes should be used to raise the required sum. One proposal under consideration was a tax on theatres but when it was objected to because they contributed to the king's pleasure, one of the MPs, Sir John Coventry, asked sarcastically 'whether his majesty's pleasure lay amongst the men or women players.' Charles was furious when he heard about the remark and the obvious slur on his relationships with the likes of Nell Gwynn and Moll Davies. Monmouth, in his role of enforcing public order, sent a detachment of Guards consisting of two officers and thirteen soldiers to lie in wait for Coventry as he returned home from parliament. The detachment caught Coventry in the Haymarket and proceeded to attack him. Coventry put his back against a wall, drew his sword and – grabbing his servant's flaming torch – put up a good fight, wounding several of the soldiers. Eventually he was overpowered by sheer numbers and held down while his nose was slit to the bone with a penknife to teach him respect. The House of Commons was in uproar when it heard what had happened to one of its members and demanded that the offenders should give themselves up for punishment. It need hardly be said that no action was taken against Monmouth or anyone else involved. This was not to be the only piece of street violence to be engineered in high places during the month of December.

With Barbara side-lined, Buckingham still had other vendettas to pursue as well as his long running one with Arlington. Although he had been delighted with Ormonde's removal from the Lord Lieutenantship of Ireland, his triumph over him had not been complete. Ormonde had indeed been removed from his prestigious appointment but was not disgraced, in fact, as compensation, he had been made Lord High Steward and Chancellor of Oxford University. In some ways it must have been even more annoying for Buckingham to have Ormonde now living in London rather than far away Dublin and making his presence felt as a senior member of the Royal Household and Privy Councillor.

On 5 December there was a grand banquet at the Guildhall in honour of Prince William of Orange who was visiting London to see his uncle the king. Ormonde had attended the banquet and was making his way back home by coach in St James Street when a man on horseback shouted at his driver to stop as there was a dead man lying in the road. As the driver pulled to a halt the coach it was surrounded by six men. Pistols were put to the chests of the driver and footman and the duke was dragged from the coach and thrown on the back of the saddle of one of the horsemen. He was then tied to the rider who sped off into the night down Piccadilly with the other assailants following. While at full gallop Ormonde managed to get his foot under his rider's stirrup and dismount them both. While on the ground he grappled with the rider, pulled off the ropes and grabbed the man's sword. No mean feat for a 60-year-old man after a substantial dinner! Meanwhile, the coachman had raised the alarm and some of Ormonde's servants arrived at the scene and began fighting with the rest of the horsemen who were trying to secure Ormonde. One of the attackers was heard to cry 'kill the rogue' and two shots were fired but missed their target. The assailants now feared they would be overpowered and so made their escape to the Fulham Ferry and then to Southwark.[9]

Ormonde survived his ordeal with no broken bones and was soon fully recovered. The question everyone was asking was: who would carry out such an attack on so well respected a duke? In fact, the attack had been planned and carried out by Thomas Blood. He had been living in London under the name Allen and had been practising as a doctor, which gave him the perfect cover to come and go at odd times for his nefarious business. The rider who was thrown from his horse was Blood's 21-year-old son, also called Thomas, who had been using the alias Hunt. Blood junior was a chip off the old block and had recently been released from the Marshalsea Prison having been convicted of highway robbery. Other members of the gang who attacked Ormonde were a Fifth Monarchist man called Richard Halliwell and, just possibly, Roger Jones and Jeramiah Marsden. It is believed that Blood's purpose in the kidnapping was to take Ormonde to Tyburn where he would be hanged like a common criminal. Blood had a long running grudge against Ormonde because the Irish land settlement had not found in his favour and so his motive for the assault was clear. However, did anyone else have a motive to attack Ormonde and either sponsor or encourage Blood in the crime? Suspicion naturally fell on Buckingham, who was believed to be in contact with Blood through his Steward, Henry North. There is no conclusive evidence that Buckingham was behind the attack, but it would certainly have been in character for this completely unprincipled man, with a vicious streak, and who regarded himself above the law. Certainly Ormonde's son, the Earl of Ossory, was in no doubt. He went up to Buckingham as he was speaking to the king and said:

My lord, I know well that you are at the bottom of this late attempt of Blood upon my father; and therefore I give you fair warning: if my father come to a violent end by sword or pistol, if he dies by the hand of a ruffian, or by the more secret way of poison, I shall not be at a loss to know the first author of it; I shall consider you as the assassin; I shall treat you as such; and wherever I meet you I shall pistol you, through you stood behind the king's chair, and I tell you thus in his majesties presence that you may be sure I will keep my word.[10]

Buckingham made no reply.

The king gave his secretaries of state the high priority task of discovering who was responsible for the attack. Over fifty people were brought in for questioning and it was clear to Williamson that the attack had been led by Allen (Blood), with Hunt (Blood's son), Richard Halliwell, William More, and William Smith, as members of the gang. The investigation was very thorough and did not make its final report until February 1671. Unfortunately, despite the hard work of the secretaries and their staff, there was insufficient evidence to make prosecutions against any but the two Bloods and Halliwell. Naturally, all those involved had gone into hiding and could not be traced. Thomas Blood took on yet another alias but seems to have felt that his exploits made him deserve promotion so began calling himself 'Colonel Blood' in the Phanatick underground.

Although Williamson's investigations had not resulted in the arrest of Ormond's attackers, they did discover another plot thanks to an informer called Richard Wilkinson. Earlier in the year the Commons had reissued the Conventicle Act as the original Act had expired. The reissue of this Act had been one of the causes of the Bawdy House riots. The real problems for Nonconformists were to begin in the summer of 1670 when the strict enforcement of the Conventicle Act began. After the Act had expired, Nonconformists had begun slowly returning to worship openly in their chapels and meeting places without any official interference. Now it was suddenly back to the dark times of persecution with ministers arrested, fines imposed and Christopher Wren, the Surveyor General, told to seal up all Nonconformist meeting houses. The Trainbands militia were strengthened, and security in London and other major cities was tightened.

It was probably in response to this that Phanaticks decided to try to take up arms once again. According to Wilkinson, someone who was later identified as John Mason, was leading a plot to attack the gates of Whitehall with some 50 men.[11] Wilkinson and other informers implicated Blood,

Lockyer and Buller in the plot; all those involved in the Mason escape in fact. Assuming the information from Wilkinson and others was correct and an attack was being planned, it must have been in its early stages. Clearly, to break through the gates of Whitehall would have achieved little in itself. It must have been the first phase of a general uprising that would take place if, having stormed Whitehall, the king and other leaders had been taken prisoner or killed. Although we shall never know if a significant plot was being hatched, it was certainly disrupted by the rigorous investigations following the assault on Ormonde and the general crack-down on the activities of the Nonconformists. This may have been Blood's last attempt at organising a general uprising as he would soon be turning his hand to a quite different form of attack on the crown.

Chapter 9

Implementing a Secret Treaty
1671

Blood that wears treason in his face
Villain complete in parson's gown
How much he is at court in grace
For stealing Ormonde and the crown!
Attributed to John Wilmot, Earl of Rochester

As mentioned, the Duke of Ormonde had been attacked after attending the Guildhall banquet in honour of William of Orange. The reason for Prince William's visit had been to persuade his uncle to repay the considerable loans, amounting to £280,000, that the House of Orange had provided during the Commonwealth and Civil War. Given Charles's dire financial situation the visit was naturally doomed to failure. The visit also went badly in another way. The main political issue on the king's mind was implementing the secret and now semi-official treaty with France to invade the United Provinces. Charles was very family orientated and although hoping to destroy the Republican United Provinces, he was intent on looking after the interests of his sister's son. He thought the best way this could be done was by a three-way carve up of the United Provinces once they had been defeated. England would gain the promised ports and Louis would take the rest with the exception of Holland, which would be given to William to rule as a sovereign prince rather than Stadholder. William had only just turned 20 and Charles treated him in the kind but condescending manner that an uncle might adopt with a very young nephew. This was a mistake. The king had been considering letting William in on the secret terms of the treaty but soon decided against it when he discovered that William was his own man, implacably opposed to Louis and with a fervent hatred of Roman Catholicism.

Things were not going well in preparation for the war. Louis had promised £150,000 in accordance with the secret treaty, but that would not be nearly enough to re-equip the navy and pay for the sailors and soldiers needed for war.[1] At the end of the previous year parliament had voted £750,000, but not explained how it should be raised. When parliament met again in early 1672 they grudgingly agreed on the methods of collection, but this proved difficult as only half the sum actually entered the royal coffers. It had become clear there was little chance of parliament voting the Crown more funds so the king prorogued them. Funding may have been completely inadequate but at least there was now some money to spend on the navy, although it was going to take time before the fleet would be at war-readiness. As the king's forces were still far from being on a war-footing, Charles was instructing Sir William Temple, the ambassador in The Hague, to repeatedly reassure De Witt that England was his staunch ally in the Triple Alliance.

Fortunately for Charles, Louis was also facing delays. He needed time to conclude agreements with the Bishopric of Munster and Archbishopric of Cologne about an attack on the United Provinces. He also had to complete his negotiations with Leopold I of Austria, the Holy Roman Emperor, that the Emperor would not oppose an attack as long as French forces did not enter the Hapsburg Spanish Netherlands. This did not pose Louis a problem because there was a route for French troops to enter the United Provinces through the Bishopric of Liege, which was part of the Archbishopric of Cologne. Louis would be successful in all these agreements, but they took time to formalise. Charles might be plagued by lack of money for the war but he was still able to prepare himself in other ways for implementing the secret treaty. The Earl of Lauderdale had achieved his ambition of completely dominating the management of Scotland. The king had made him High Commissioner for Scotland and Lauderdale had appointed his protégé Lord Rothes as the Lord Chancellor to act as his man on the ground in Edinburgh. The previous year's crack down on Nonconformists had been even harsher in Scotland than in England, with the death penalty being introduced for attending open-air services. The Presbyterians of Scotland were sullen but submissive. Lauderdale had placed the forts and arsenals in the hands of officers he could trust but his greatest service to the king had been to induce the Scottish Parliament to pass the Militia Act. This Act agreed that 22,000 Scottish troops would be made available if required to support the king and that they could, if necessary, be deployed to England. Louis and Charles were currently thinking that Charles should announce his conversion to Roman Catholicism before the start of the war. If the king's conversion was announced, then a major reaction could be expected which might well include armed uprisings. In such a situation it would be very handy to be able to call on Scots troops to augment Charles's few regiments of Life Guards.

Two other stumbling blocks needed to be addressed before going to war. The first was parliament. Although most members of the Lords and Commons disliked the Dutch, they were overwhelmingly anti-Papist and would oppose allying with Catholic France against a Protestant nation. They would be even more suspicious of an alliance with an autocratic monarch like Louis who was trying to expand his empire. The solution to this was not to have a parliament sitting until the war was a *fait accompli*, at which time they would, hopefully, be presented with victory over the Dutch and the major commercial advantages that would bring. The second problem area was the Nonconformists, who were already seriously discontented over the imposition of the Conventicle Act. Another war with the United Provinces could result in them working with exiled Phanaticks and Republicans in Holland and making an alliance with De Witt. A Nonconformist uprising coordinated with a Dutch invasion had not happened in the last Dutch War, but there was always the danger that it might occur this time round, especially if Charles was to declare himself a Catholic. Measures were needed to neutralise this threat before any declaration of war.

In the chance way that things can happen in life, a visit to a tourist attraction was to lead to a way of dealing with the Nonconformist threat. In April 1671 a clergyman and his wife were visiting the Tower of London to see the Crown Jewels. They went to the Martin Tower where the Crown Jewels were held and paid their admission to Talbot Edwards, the Yeoman Warder responsible for the regalia. During the visit, the clergyman's wife was unwell and Mr Edwards was asked if she could lie down. Mr Edwards took the clergyman and his wife upstairs in the Martin Tower where he and his wife lived. Once the lady had rested she appeared much better and she and her husband left. A couple of days later the clergyman returned with three pairs of gloves as a thank-you present to Mrs Edwards for her kindness in letting his wife rest in their quarters. From this, a friendship blossomed between the two families during frequent visits to the Tower over the next weeks. In fact, the families got on so well that it was agreed that Edwards's daughter would be a good match for the clergyman's nephew who had 'two or three hundred a year in land'.[2] To progress this romance it was agreed that the nephew would be brought round to meet the daughter on the evening of 9 May and become betrothed.

The course of true love did not run smoothly because, as will have been guessed, the clergyman was Thomas Blood. On 9 May, Blood arrived with his 'nephew', in fact his son Thomas junior, and another man called Robert Perrot. Blood explained that his 'wife' was slightly delayed and suggested that Edwards show the visitors the Crown Jewels to pass the time. When Edwards took them to the room where the jewels were held a cloak was thrown over his head and he was gagged, hit several times with a mallet and then stabbed as he struggled to shout for help. Blood broke open the flimsy cross wired door protecting the Regalia, grabbed the king's state crown and put it in a bag under his cloak; meanwhile Perrot put the orb in his breeches and Thomas junior tried to saw the sceptre in half to make it less noticeable. All was going very well when Richard Halliwell, who had been waiting outside with the getaway horses, rushed in to say Edwards' son had unexpectedly returned and was about to discover the robbery. As Blood and the others ran out of the Martin Tower, Edwards was sufficiently recovered to shout 'Treason the crown is stolen!' At which his son raised the alarm. Blood junior had fled without the sceptre but Blood and Perrot still had the crown and orb. Edwards' son and others caught up with Blood and Perrot as they mounted their horses and in the melee that ensued, Blood fired both of his pistols but he and Perot were eventually overcome. Meanwhile Blood junior, Halliwell and another accomplice called William Smith, who had been holding the getaway horses, all managed to escape from the Tower. Blood junior was soon caught when he was thrown from his horse after crashing into a cart in nearby Gravel Lane, but Smith and Halliwell rode on and escaped completely. The two Bloods and Perrot were taken as prisoners to the dungeons of the White Tower. The crown and orb were recovered with a few jewels broken off but these were all soon found and restored to their former magnificence few weeks later.

Quite why Blood should have decided to steal the Crown Jewels is not known for sure. It was a dangerous operation that required considerable time and patience to gain Edwards's confidence. Also, even if the theft had been successful, selling the jewels would be no easy task. However, Blood was attracted to an adventure and may have thought that he could financially recompense himself for the loss of his Irish lands and at the same time show his contempt for the principal symbols of monarchy. Naturally, Blood and the other two were examined that evening by local justices and the Master of the Jewel House, but they revealed nothing. In fact Blood was bold enough to say that he would speak, but only if examined by the king himself. When Charles was told of this he was amused and decided that he would indeed question Blood himself. Blood was taken to the Palace of Whitehall in chains and brought before Charles, who had the Duke of York, Prince Rupert, Arlington, and Williamson, in attendance. Blood surprised all by speaking openly and confidently about the attack on Ormonde and the attempted theft of the Crown Jewels, saying that they were revenge for having lost his Irish lands. Although always refusing to implicate any accomplices, he also elaborated on other plots he had been involved in, including one to shoot the king with a carbine as he went for a swim in the Thames at Vauxhall. Blood said that he had been hiding in the reeds on the river bank but found himself unable to carry out the assassination as the king's 'life was better for them than his death, lest a worse succeed him'.[3] As there is no other evidence that this assassination plot took place, it is very probably a bit of blarney invented by Blood on the spot to impress his audience. And impress his audience he did, not only by his audacious manner, but by talking about the large number of Phanaticks yet unknown to the authorities and implying that as one of the principal leaders, he had considerable influence over them. At the end of the interview the king asked 'What if I should give you your life?' to which Blood replied 'I would endeavour to deserve it.' Blood was then returned to the Tower to await his fate.

Arlington and Williamson were clear that there was merit in turning Blood so that he could become a source on the Phanaticks. Charles also saw the merit in this, and of using Blood as an intermediary with the Nonconformists to try to keep them loyal in a war against the Dutch. Discreet negotiations with Blood showed that he was more than happy to change sides and become a Crown servant if his life was spared and he was given enough remuneration. It was part of the royal prerogative for the monarch to be able to grant a pardon. The pardon for the theft of the Crown Jewels might be fairly easily arranged, but to grant a pardon for the attack on Ormonde was more difficult. It was decided that Blood should write a letter of apology to Ormonde, which Arlington delivered to the duke along with the king's wish that Ormonde would accept it and forgive Blood for the outrage. Ever loyal, Ormonde immediately did as requested and on 14 July, Blood and Perrot were released from the Tower. Blood junior was not released, presumably being held as a hostage to ensure that Blood kept his side of the bargain.

A very favourable bargain it was too. Blood had his Irish land returned and was granted a pension of £500 a year from lands in County Kildare. To everyone's amazement he was seen about the court two weeks after his release in a new suit and periwig and looking happy and confident; as well he might. A little later Evelyn records that he attended a dinner at the home of Sir Thomas Clifford, Comptroller of the Royal Household, at which

'Colonel' Blood was a guest along with several French noblemen.[5] Blood had certainly risen in the world but he soon had to fulfil his side of the bargain. The well-publicised public pardon and his ostentatious behaviour around court made it clear that he was now in royal favour and therefore meant that he was blown as an agent against the Phanaticks before he started. Arlington had realised this and was hoping that the fact that someone as infamous as Blood could be pardoned might lead some Phanaticks and Republicans to also seek pardon. Blood's role was to be an intermediary with the radical Nonconformist leaders, to bring them into the loyal government fold before the onset of war.

No one should have expected Blood to make an easy transition from a notorious criminal to a Crown servant, and so it was the case. Things began quite well, with Blood working to Arlington through Williamson and beginning to approach his Phanatick and Radical contacts with a view to arranging their pardon in exchange for taking the oath of allegiance. Blood appears to have been instructed to have two partners in this task. These were a Mr Church, the Clerk of the Fleet Prison, and an Anglican clergyman, Dr Nicolas Butler, both of whom were Williamson's agents and had contacts with Nonconformists. Naturally enough most of Blood's erstwhile underworld associates were deeply suspicious of him. With time the suspicion reduced when they realised that he was not intending to give evidence against them or act as an informant. Nevertheless, many of his former accomplices, such as Captain Roger Jones, Captain John Mason and the Fifth Monarchist William Smith, continued their distrust and refused to even consider applying for a pardon. On the other hand, Blood did have his successes and organised pardons for Major John Gladman, Captain John Lockyer, a Dublin man called Captain William Low, and Major General Thomas Kelsey, who returned from the Netherlands in Nov 1671.[6] Blood was also in touch with James Innes, a Scots Nonconformist who wanted an audience with the king to plead for freedom of worship in Scotland. As the king was eager to build bridges with the Nonconformists he granted Innes an interview, which was arranged by Dr Butler, probably with some participation by Blood. At the interview Charles said that he sympathised with the Nonconformists, but was not in a position to change the law at the present time and suggested that they hold their services as discreetly as possible.

Blood was also making himself useful to the Post Office intercept operation by identifying some of the handwriting of Republican exiles in the Netherlands and being able to provide the key to some of the ciphers used by them. Unbeknown to Blood, Williamson had also instructed his Post

Office staff to intercept Blood's private correspondence. Williamson had every reason to be wary of Blood and kept a very close eye on him. He discovered that Blood had fallen out with Butler and Church who suspected him of still cooperating with the Phanaticks and also that Blood had begun reporting to the king through Lauderdale rather than through himself and Arlington, presumably because Lauderdale appeared to be in particular royal favour at the time. From intercepts, Williamson found out that Blood was carrying out correspondence with Innes but keeping it secret from the king. Blood must have realised that his nefarious activities could endanger his pension and new status in life so came back into line but with Blood, it would be unwise to place bets on how long his loyalty might last. Despite Williamson's deep suspicions about Blood, he was continuing to be of use in helping to improve knowledge of the Phanaticks and Republicans and the extent of the threat they might pose if war was declared.

While Blood was making his own form of contribution to neutralising the potential threat from Nonconformists, another important matter was being addressed in preparation for war. It would be very well to present parliament with the *fait accompli* of a successful war, but some credible reason would have to be found for going to war in the first place. Arlington came up with a plan to create a pretext for war, to which the king agreed. It was decided to send the *Merlin*, one of the many royal yachts to sail past the Dutch fleet anchored off Brill. The purpose of the journey was to bring back Lady Temple, the wife of the English ambassador who had recently been removed for being too accommodating with the Dutch – who he still believed to be England's allies. As the *Merlin* neared the Dutch ships they dutifully struck their colours but they did not fire the ceremonial white smoke due to an English man-of-war. The reason for not firing the salute was quite simply because the *Merlin* was to all appearances just a large yacht. However, like most royal yachts, the *Merlin* did carry a cannon and was, theoretically, a warship so not firing a salute was an insult to the honour of the king of England. When De Witt heard of the incident he sent profound apologies to Charles and imprisoned the officer who had failed to give the salute. Charles replied that he expected all the Dutch admirals who had been at sea off Brill to be imprisoned, which De Witt politely refused. A potential pretext to break with the Triple Alliance and declare war on the United Provinces had been achieved.

Relations with France continued to strengthen during the period with visits of nobles between the two countries and Charles asking Louis to send a Catholic priest to advise him on how he should carry out his promised announcement of conversion. Anglo–French relations were also blossoming romantically as Charles had finally begun to notice Louise de Kéroüalle and had fallen madly in love with her. The strength of his love can be demonstrated by the fact that he walked all the way from Whitehall to Hampton Court in cold weather accompanying her coach. Strong though this new love was, it did not of course mean that he had lost interest in Nell Gwynn who provided him with sex and amusing company. In Louise, Charles had found the same level of infatuation he had experienced with Frances Stewart and, like Frances, Louise had not yielded to the king's advances. This was much to the concern of both the French ambassador Colbert de Croissy, and Arlington. De Croissy had been imploring Louise to go to bed with the king but she had resisted, possibly because she was a proud and religious woman who did not want to be just another mistress. Also, she could have thought that there was the possibility that Charles might divorce the queen and be free to marry her. Lady Arlington eventually had a chat with Louise, which may have tipped the balance when she told her in a motherly way that if she did not go to bed with the king she would end up in a nunnery.

A plot was devised for the October race meeting at Newmarket, which was close to Arlington's Euston Hall estate. De Croissy, Louise and others were invited to stay at Euston for the meeting and the king was invited over for evening entertainment from his Newmarket house. For entertainment one evening Lady Arlington thought it would be a charming idea to hold a country wedding with the king playing the groom and Louise the bride. This type of entertainment had, of course, been done before for Frances Stewart without the desired result. This time would be different. The Arlingtons invited 200 guests to a party held with all the magnificence for which they had become so well known. The guests all enthusiastically joined in with the country wedding masque, which ended with the 'bride and groom' being put to bed by the assembled company. At that moment the guests all suddenly disappeared leaving the king and Louise to complete the entertainment themselves. The evening was a resounding success all round. It was an amusing and memorable event for all the guests, and the host and hostess could congratulate themselves on having brought the evening to a particularly enjoyable climax for their principal guest.

Louise was now well on her way to becoming *maitresse en titre*. She was soon to receive a pension of £10,000 a year, which was just the beginning of the vast amounts of public money that would eventually come her way. De Croissy was naturally delighted that Louise's relationship had blossomed as planned and King Louis sent Lady Arlington a diamond necklace as an expression of thanks. While an evening's entertainment had been sufficient to further enhance relations with the French there was still more to do regarding the other side of the coin. That is in engineering the further deterioration of relations with the Dutch. As the agreeable Temple had been withdrawn from being ambassador to The Hague, it was now necessary to find a replacement whom the Dutch would find truly obnoxious. This was easily done because the former ambassador, Sir George Downing, immediately came to mind. Downing was generally disliked by most people but was truly hated by the Dutch so was the ideal person to destroy what little goodwill there was between the United Provinces and its supposed ally England. Downing was therefore transferred from his current post, as Secretary to the Treasury Commissioners, back to The Hague.

Downing was both the perfect choice for upsetting the Dutch and a very skilled intelligencer, ideal for building up an intelligence network in preparation for war. Mention has already been made of his success in agent-handling and the kidnapping of regicides. The extent of his success can be indicated by what Samuel Pepys recorded that Downing had told him about his previous time as ambassador:

> *He told me that he had good spies, that he hath had the keys taken out of De Witt's pocket when he was a-bed, and his closet opened, and papers brought to him, and left in his hands for an hour, and carried back and laid in the place again, and the keys put into De Witt's pocket again. He says he hath always had their most private debates, that have been but between two and three of the chief of them, brought to him in an hour after, and an hour after that, hath sent word thereof to the King, but nobody here regarded him.[7]*

Even if Downing was exaggerating a bit to Pepys, there is no doubt that he had been running agents who had penetrated the government of the United Provinces at the highest level. It is very likely that the Dutch were well aware of this and so had another reason for disliking him so intensely. Certainly the king was expecting good intelligence from Downing as is shown by the following extract from a letter wrote to him when he had taken up his appointment in The Hague:

> *I must enjoin you to spare no cost in informing yourself exactly how ready those ships of war are in all their ports, how soon they are to put to sea, and to send what you learn of this kind hither with all speed.[8]*

We may assume that Downing went about his intelligence work with his normal energy and professionalism but it would come to an end only a few weeks after his arrival. The reason was that he had been working equally hard at his other task of annoying the Dutch by treating them with undisguised contempt and making impossibly extravagant demands for compensation for the *Merlin* incident. These included giving the English free access to the Dutch plantations in the East Indies and for the Dutch to dip their flags to English vessels even on their own coasts. Downing had overplayed his hand and had aroused so much hatred among the Dutch that he feared his life was in danger and so fled back to England. He did not receive a welcome home. The king was annoyed that he had left his post without permission and sent him to the Tower.

There was another reason the king was angry with Downing and that was because he had been over zealous in antagonising the Dutch. Charles wanted to create a slow deterioration in relations with the United Provinces that would provide a cause for war when the time was right. In a matter of weeks, Downing had succeeded in almost precipitating war single-handedly. Charles did not want war to break out until two outstanding issues had been resolved – more money to pay for the war and some confidence that Phanaticks and radicals would not be a fifth column supporting the Dutch. There was good news on the financial side when the first of the French subsidy of £50,000 arrived at Rye.[9] There had been trouble in the dockyards with contractors not being paid and the wages of workers in considerable arrears, so the money was timely. Unfortunately it was not nearly enough as the navy had unpaid debts of £50,000 for victualling alone. More money had to be obtained and with city financiers refusing further loans, some other way had to be found. At this point Sir Thomas Clifford came up with an imaginative idea that the king adopted with alacrity. On 2 January 1672, it was announced that the Exchequer would not pay back the capital sums of any loans that had been made to the Crown until 31 December, but would pay six per cent interest on the loan. This device was called the 'Stop of the Exchequer' and raised a much needed £1.3 million for the war. The downside was that interest was seldom paid and the repayment date was continually extended, with the result that many of those who had made loans to the Crown ended up bankrupt. As Bishop Burnet wrote: 'the bankers were broken, and multitudes who had put their money in their hands were ruined by this dishonorable and perfidious action.' This short term gain for royal finances brought an understandable backlash against the government, and by association, against the king himself.

Chapter 10

Indulgence for Tender Consciences 1672–3

'Give me liberty to know, to utter, and to argue freely according to conscience, above all liberties'

John Milton *Areopagitica*

The Blood initiative had brought some Phanaticks in from the cold, but there were still many who might rise up if there was war with the Dutch. The king decided on a means of ending the grievances of Nonconformists and at the same time giving a signal to Louis that he was moving towards Catholicism. On 15 March 1672 Charles issued the Declaration of Indulgence for Tender Consciences. This suspended penal laws against Nonconformists, who were allowed to worship publicly as long as their places of worship, and ministers, were registered. It also suspended the penal laws against Catholics and allowed them to worship freely, but only in their own houses. There had been debate in the Privy Council whether the king had the legal power to overturn parliament's legislation by issuing such a proclamation. It was eventually agreed that he had, although few were confident that parliament would see it that way. As far as its role in the preparations for the war was concerned, the Declaration was a success. Charles and Louis had agreed that Charles would announce his conversion before the outbreak of war. Charles had realised that such a move at the present time would put his throne at risk so the Declaration's tolerance of recusants at least offered some reassurance to Louis. With regard to Nonconformists, the Declaration achieved its end except for the Quakers, who refused to take part in the registration of meeting houses. Luckily, the Quakers had been moving towards pacifism and posed no threat to the Crown. As far as all other Nonconformists were concerned, there was a general uptake of the offer for licensed services and over the next year, more than 1,500 licenses were issued.[1] Thomas Blood was to demonstrate that he had moved from being a wanted criminal to an official Crown servant by becoming a leading figure in arranging for the distribution of the licences.

By early 1672, De Witt was under no illusions that England and France were planning war against him. Louis and Charles had agreed that Monmouth should command the English brigade to fight alongside the French Army against the United Provinces. Buckingham was furious at this because he had been given to understand that he would be made the commander. His bitterness in being notified of the decision did not extend to Monmouth with whom he remained friends, but further damaged his difficult relationship with the king. For his part, Monmouth began openly recruiting for his force and it was clear to the Dutch that this force would soon be used against them. If there had been any doubts in De Witt's mind that his ally England was about to go to war with him, this would have been dispelled by Admiral Holmes. On 12 March he carried out an unprovoked attack on the Dutch Smyrna Fleet returning past the Isle of Wight with its valuable cargo from the Levant. The attack was a failure and Holmes was beaten off by the Dutch but it served the king's purpose of showing that the Triple Alliance had ended. With the Declaration of Indulgence being put in place three days later, England declared war on 17 March. The official reason for the war was because of Dutch intransigence in providing suitable compensation for the insult received by the *Merlin* incident.

Louis declared war against the United Provinces almost simultaneously. The 130,000 strong French Army marched through Liege, took the six fortifications along the Rhine, invaded the United Provinces and, before the end of June, the Dutch province of Overjssel had capitulated. In order to come to an accommodation with the opposing Orangist party, De Witt had agreed that William of Orange should be the Dutch field commander. The 22-year-old William had only 9,000 troops and, being far outnumbered by the French, had to withdraw to Utrecht. When the Utrecht burgers decided to open the gates to the French to avoid a siege, William had to retreat back to the Water Line. In the event of an invasion the Dutch planned to open the dykes to flood the areas in front of an enemy advance, but at that time the flood defences were not yet ready. On 14 June the States of Holland felt they had no option but to sue for peace at almost any price. It looked to Louis that he had won and would obtain all he sought from the war.

For England the war had not gone so well. Charles's strategic aim was to quickly defeat the Dutch fleet in order to obtain command of the sea so that a force could be safely landed to invade Zeeland. It was hoped that the whole operation would be successfully completed and victory achieved before the end of the year's campaigning season. Unfortunately the implementation of his strategy did not go as planned. In June the Dutch fleet of seventy-five ships under Admiral De Ruyter surprised the combined English and French fleets of ninety-five ships as they was refitting in Sole Bay off the Suffolk coast. As the Dutch approached, the French ships sailed south and played little part in the battle apart from long range cannon fire. It was a particularly destructive engagement for both the English and Dutch fleets with no clear winner but, predictably, both fleets claimed victory. The English fleet had lost its flagship and was so badly mauled that there could be no question of invading Zeeland that year. Repairing the fleet and continuing a war into another year was obviously going to cost far more money than anticipated.

Negotiations for peace had begun with the Dutch when there was a surprising turn of events that was to rob Louis of his anticipated fruits of victory. First, the polders, those low lying lands protected from the sea by dykes, became ready and areas were flooded, which prevented any further French advance into Holland. Second, many Dutch blamed the De Witt government for the humiliating defeats and pro-Orangist riots took place. In June, Johann De Witt was wounded in an assassination attempt and resigned as Grand Pensionary. His brother Cornelis was arrested and when Johann visited him in prison on 15 August, both were murdered by the Orangist militia. William of Orange had already become Stadholder of Holland and Zeeland, and now became the Dutch leader. With his nephew having taken over as the ruler of the United Provinces, Charles naturally thought that he could arrange highly favorable peace terms and dispatched Arlington and Buckingham to negotiate them. The gist of the English proposals was the same as those offered by Louis. These were that the United Provinces should have William as its sovereign but be under the protection of France and England. For good measure Charles also proposed exorbitant sums of money and a variety of major trading concessions to enable William to reward his uncle for starting the war which had led to him becoming ruler! When Buckingham told William that if he did not accept the proposals he would lose all, William replied that he was prepared to die in the last dyke to protect Dutch liberty. Peace negations were put on hold. Inspired by the determination of their young leader from the illustrious House of Orange, the Dutch began to resist the invaders. Before the end of the campaign season, a French force had been repulsed before Aardenburg and the Bishop of Munster was forced to give up the siege of Groningen. Although the year ended with French troops still firmly on Dutch territory, Louis had lost the alliance of both the Elector of Brandenburg and the Emperor Leopold I, both of whom had become concerned about French territorial expansion. In fact, Brandenburg became allied with the Dutch and sent an army of 4,000 to the Rhine. The war against the United Provinces was not going to be the pushover that had been expected.

With the war in progress Williamson was busy obtaining military intelligence about the Dutch, particularly their naval strengths and dispositions. Indeed the king himself, always interested in naval matters, was also taking an active part in naval intelligence. An indication of his involvement is shown by the following two of his letters to his brother James in July:

> *I dispatched this bearer Skelton with what I know of the enemy's fleet, which you will find partly by the letters I received from Harwich this day which the Secretary does send you. and besides I have spoken with one I sent unto Holland, who tells me that one of the Admiralty of Rotterdam did assure him the fleet had orders to go out which if it be true cannot believe they intend to go directly to fight with you because their ships are too small, but will strive to slip by you if they can and join to the northward their East India Fleet, and then return all together, so as if they can by a running fight save their merchant ships with the loss some of their men-of-war they will think themselves happy.*[2]

And,

> *You will see by the note here enclosed the intelligence I have received this day from Plymouth by two East India ships newly arrived here by which I begin to believe that the Dutch East India fleet must have stopped on the way. And I can guess at no place but Fero [sic] because as they tell me here there is no good port, and if they had gone for Spain or Norway we should have heard of them.*[3]

Williamson was using every informant and agent he could muster to gather information on the Dutch, and Blood made his contribution to the intelligence war effort. In March 1672 he was sent to Amsterdam and then moved to Texel in North Holland to monitor ship movements and began reporting them back to Williamson along with anything else he could pick up. For example, he was able to report that Dutch propaganda pamphlets were being sent to the Spanish ambassador in London hidden in barrels of butter.[4] Sadly, despite the careful collection of intelligence, it had little effect on the war – it had not been able to give warning of De Ruyter's surprise attack on Sole Bay. After that, it was of little value because the English fleet was in no position to be able to attack the Dutch and De Ruyter was skillfully keeping his, equally damaged, fleet out of harm's way in the shallow waters off Holland.

Although Williamson and his intelligencers were putting considerable effort into intelligence on the enemy, they also had to keep a watchful eye on possible trouble from Republicans and Phanaticks. The Declaration of Indulgence had done a great deal to remove the threat from Nonconformists; their feelings were largely ones of relief and rejoicing. Relief that they were no longer being regarded as criminals for their beliefs, and rejoicing that many of their number were at last released from prison, including John Bunyon. Most Nonconformist leaders were concentrating on obtaining the necessary licences for their ministers and meeting houses so that they could legally resume open worship. The principal person responsible for administrating the issue of licences was Dr Nicolas Butler, but Blood was also very much involved in the task. With Butler, and particularly Blood, constantly liaising with the Nonconformist communities, including their Phanatick elements, they must have been able to provide Williamson with very good coverage of the radical scene and any potential threats that might be posed. In fact, largely thanks to the Declaration and the efforts of Blood and Butler there appear to have been no radical plots against the state during the war. Williamson's hard work and success as an intelligencer were given the recognition they deserved and the king granted him a knighthood.

Sir Joseph Williamson also had to carry out counter intelligence against Dutch agents in England. For example, he discovered that Pierre Du Moulin, who was a member of the Council of Trade, was thought to be passing information to the Dutch. Before this could be proved, Du Moulin fled to Holland in the summer and once there, entered the employment of William of Orange. From Holland, Du Moulin continued making contact with his London associates and established a Dutch intelligence network that included William Medley, William Howard, Richard Goodenough, John Ayloffe, William Carr and Robert Crouch. It would take Williamson another two years to uncover this network but he eventually did, when Carr and Crouch were enticed into becoming his informants.

The Dutch were not the only ones wanting to collect intelligence against England. Louis wanted to keep a close watch on his ally Charles, whom he knew from the past was not above double dealing. In particular, Louis needed to know if Charles might make a separate peace with the United Provinces despite the fact that France and England had signed an accord that they would not do so. Louis's best facility for obtaining inside intelligence on Charles had already been put in place in the form of Louise de Kéroüalle. The French ambassador, De Croissy, had been delighted to see Louise's spectacular rise in Charles's affections but had been puzzled to find that this had not as yet resulted in her passing him information on the king. Louise had remained on polite terms with De Croissy but appeared to show no inclination to advance French interests. It could have been that, as a young woman, she had not yet gained confidence in her position as the king's most favoured lover. In fact, she was just one of Charles's three principal mistresses to present him with a baby the year 1672. Nell Gwynn had given birth to a baby boy, James, at Christmas, and both Louise and Barbara produced babies in July. Barbara, now Duchess of Cleveland, was spending little time in Charles's bed but had been maintaining her high standards of sexual expertise by constant practice. Her many lovers had included the handsome playwright William Wycherley, but the sixth and last child she bore in July was fathered by John Churchill, the future Duke of Marlborough. Understandably, there was no question of Charles's acknowledging Barbara's baby girl as his own, so the child did not receive the titles and pensions of her other children, but eventually become prioress of a convent in France.

Despite Louise being Charles's current principal love, her new baby son, Charles, was not acknowledged by the king, although he was in no doubt that the child was his. It was perhaps understandable that much as he loved Louise, Charles may have felt that he already had rather too many royal bastards to maintain. About twelve had been recognised in fact, and there were a few others not officially recognised who also received royal funding. Louise was distraught and no amount of attention from Charles could make up for the fact that she was the mother of a bastard who had to give precedence to the Duchess of Cleveland and endure the public teasing of the former orange girl, Nell Gwynn. Status and precedence was important to everyone at court, but to Louise these were of paramount importance. Her friend Arlington realised that her lack of formal status made her of less value to either himself or De Croissy, so began to nudge the king into giving Louise the royal recognition for herself her son.

The king and Arlington had more pressing matters to concern them than Louise's status. What should have been a swift war to bring major economic advantages had no end in sight and had used up what money was left in the Treasury. After the Stopping of the Exchequer, there was little chance of raising more loans from the City. With insufficient money from French subsidies, the only options left were to make a dishonourable peace or to call parliament in the hope that it would vote enough funds to continue the war. In February 1673 parliament reassembled. Having been prorogued since April 1671 they would have a lot to talk about, not least the war and the suspension of penal laws, neither of which they had been consulted about. Parliament had been becoming increasingly difficult as the reign progressed and so this one would require careful management. The king's main instruments for trying to manage the Lords and Commons were Arlington and the unreliable Buckingham in the Lords, both of whom led factions opposing one another. The king's position in the Lords was now bolstered by the presence of Buckingham's friend, Anthony Ashley Cooper, who had been promoted to Lord Chancellor and created Earl of Shaftesbury. Short in stature but high in ambition, Shaftesbury had a brilliant mind and a gift for oratory, which made him an excellent advocate for Crown policy. The management of the Commons was left to Sir Thomas Clifford, who had been made Baron Clifford and was Lord Treasurer. Clifford was referred to as the king's 'bribe master general' because of the way he bought the support of members.[5] Clifford had two methods of obtaining the support of potential opposition MPs; one was to try to arrange for them to be given a remunerative position in government service, and the other was to quite simply bribe them using secret service funds. Patronage and bribery had been used in the past by Charles's ministers to manage parliament and if organised properly, worked quite well. Many MPs were happy to accept inducements for supporting relatively minor Crown policy, but were far less prepared to support something that was against their deeply held principles, such as religious belief. They might, for example, accept that the king had entered into an unpopular war with the United Provinces, but suspending parliament's penal laws was another matter.

The February session of parliament did respond to the king's plea to provide funds for the war. Shaftesbury gave a rousing speech against the Dutch and parliament agreed in principle to provide £70,000 a month for eighteen months to support the war. That was not to be the end of the matter however. Most members of both Houses disliked the Dutch so they could accept the war, but were wary of an alliance with the equally disliked French – who carried the additional odium of being Catholic. It was the religious issue that was foremost in their minds and was not to be removed by court bribery. The fact that the French king was rampaging through the Netherlands was bad enough, but that the Catholic mass was now being celebrated in places like Utrecht Cathedral was of real concern. Parliament's main quarrel with the king was over religion and specifically his Declaration of Indulgence. They were not happy about his unilateral suspension of penal laws against Nonconformists, but they were furious at its application to Papists. There was growing concern that the court was favoring Catholicism. After all, the queen was Catholic and had her many priests wandering the corridors of court; the king's two mistresses, Barbara and Louise, were Catholic; some of the king's ministers, such as Clifford, were suspected Catholics, and it was whispered that even the Duke of York had Catholic sympathies. Parliament made plain to the king that funding for continuation of the war would come at the price of the cancellation of the Declaration. The king felt he had no option but to agree, but worse was to come. Parliament did feel that there was merit in easing restrictions on Nonconformists and began considering a bill to achieve that, but were adamant in opposition to Popery. On 12 March 1673, parliament passed the Test Act, which required all office holders to take the oaths of allegiance and supremacy, together with a declaration against transubstantiation and a commitment to receive Anglican Communion at least once a year. Office holders were given until mid-summer to comply.

Anti-Catholic feeling was running high and being whipped up further by Dutch propaganda. The Dutch agent Pierre Du Moulin had written *England's Appeal from a Private Cabal in Whitehall* saying that the king's ministers were supporting a crusade by Louis against Protestant Europe. People began looking out for signs of popish inclination among the country's leadership. There was great interest over who was taking Easter Communion, and concern when neither the Duke of York nor Clifford did so. On 17 May, Clifford's closed coach overturned in the Strand and out he tumbled, together with a Catholic priest in full vestments; not an easy incident to explain. Then to everyone's amazement, on 15 June the Duke of York resigned as Lord High Admiral. Clifford resigned as Treasurer four days later. It showed that Catholicism was at the heart of government and that the childless king's heir was also a Catholic. Charles would have much preferred his brother had kept his religious inclinations to himself – then life could have gone on as normal, but now the cat was out of the bag.

Meanwhile the war was continuing. With new parliamentary funding Charles had recruited 8,000 troops for the attack on Zeeland and they had concentrated at Blackheath. Monmouth and his English brigade were with Louis, besieging Maastricht where he led a courageous assault and began winning a reputation for bravery and generalship. Prince Rupert replaced the

Duke of York as admiral commanding the joint Anglo–French fleet, with the French squadron commanded by Jean d'Estrees. On 11 August, following a number of inconclusive skirmishes, Rupert's fleet, and the Dutch under De Ruyter, closed for battle off Texel. As with the Battle of Sole Bay the previous year, the fighting was bloody and destructive for both sides with no clear winner. Once again the French squadron appears to have kept a healthy distance from the fighting, probably because Louis had ordered d'Estrees not to endanger his ships. The English fleet was so badly battered that a furious Rupert brought it home. Such was the damage that it was clear the fleet would not be strong enough to support a landing for the rest of the year. The 8,000 troops at Blackheath would be left kicking their heels. On returning to England, Prince Rupert was voluble in his condemnation of the French. News of this quickly spread around the country and, rightly or wrongly, the naval failure was blamed on the French.

One person in England who continued to support France was, of course, Louise. After many tears and entreaties Charles had at last decided to make her Duchess of Portsmouth, but as a French citizen this needed to be cleared with Louis. De Croissy made the request to Louis, but he was not happy as shown in this letter:

> *I own I find her on all occasions so ill-disposed for the service of the king, and showing such ill-humour against France (whether because she feels herself despised there or whether she is just capricious), that I really think she deserves no favour of His majesty. But as the King of England shows her much love, and so visibly likes to please her, his Majesty can judge whether it is best not to treat her according to her merits.*[6]

Louis did agree, and after some persuasion by Charles also gave her the French ducal estate of Aubigny, which had become free following the death of Frances Stuart's husband the Duke of Richmond. Louise was very grateful but the question was would she be grateful enough to Louis to act as an informant.

The Duke of York's wife Ann had died the previous year and as his only two legitimate children were daughters, he was in search of a new wife to provide a son. To the astonishment of all he decided upon Mary of Modena who was not only a Catholic, but Modena was a client state of France and she was the grandniece of Cardinal Mazarin, who had ruled France during Louis's minority. Given the increasing strength of public feeling against both

France and Catholicism this was not good choice. Unkind people started to refer to Mary as 'the Pope's daughter' – not a term of endearment among staunch Protestants. Unsurprisingly the 14-year-old princess received a cold welcome when she arrived in England; there were no celebratory bonfires. It could have been worse. At least arriving in late November had spared her witnessing Bonfire Night, when 1,000 drunken Londoners were burning effigies of the pope as the Whore of Babylon.

Although things were going badly for the king on most fronts, at least the Nonconformists had not become a threat following the cancellation of the Declaration of Indulgence. The reason for this was that no-one quite knew whether or not the licences for ministers and places of worship were still valid or not. Parliament had actually intended to allow at least some freedom of worship to Nonconformists, but had been prorogued before anything came of it. As a result, most Nonconformist congregations continued worshipping as before the cancellation of the Declaration and were seldom troubled by the authorities. Also, Blood, who had been so instrumental in issuing the licences, was becoming more trusted and able to get a feel for whether any seditious plots were afoot. Fortunately there were none and the Phanaticks were putting what disruptive energy they had into joining anti-papist demonstrations.

The king would have been relieved that he could expect no immediate threat from Nonconformists, but knew that a far greater threat to the outcome of the war was lack of money. Parliament had reconvened in October 1673 but instead of voting funds for the war, had railed against the war, the French, the standing army, Catholics, and the Duke of York's marriage. Charles prorogued them after nine days and sacked Shaftesbury as treasurer for not managing them better and even appearing to take the side of the opposition on the matter of the Modena marriage. The king had been becoming increasingly irritated with Shaftesbury, who had been pressing him to divorce the queen so he could marry a Protestant and produce an heir. The dismissal of Shaftesbury meant that Charles had not only lost a talented minister, but had turned him into a formidable opponent. The financial imperative meant that the king had to meet parliament again on 7 January 1674 and say that money was urgently needed to either complete the war or achieve an honourable peace. Charles even assured parliament that there was no secret treaty with France and conceded that Buckingham's official treaty should be seen by a small parliamentary committee. Commons and Lords united in aggressively raising grievances and attacking the king's main advisers: Buckingham, Arlington and Lauderdale. Shaftesbury led the attack with relish. Lauderdale was fortunate in being away in Edinburgh, so did not appear before the Lords. When Arlington had to defend himself before them, he naturally put any blame onto Buckingham and made such a good impression that they decided to take no further action against him. Buckingham received the Lords full wrath, both for making the treaty with the French, and for the scandals surrounding his affair with the Countess of Shrewsbury. These scandals included Buckingham having given their illegitimate child a title and when the boy died, arranging for him to be buried with full pomp in Westminster Abbey. The Lords directed that Buckingham and the Countess pay a bond of £10,000 to live apart and petitioned the king for Buckingham's dismissal. Charles readily agreed in the hope that it might lead to funding. The next month Charles concluded a hurried peace with Dutch envoys without consulting Louis, which become known as the Treaty of Westminster. This did not satisfy parliament who pressed for new safeguards against Catholicism, such as having royal children brought up in the Church of England. Having proved unmanageable, the king prorogued parliament on 13 February without it having voted the vital funds for the Crown.

In the Treaty of Westminster, the Dutch agreed to return the town of New York, which they had captured, salute English ships in the Channel, and pay reparation for the war. As the reparation was exactly the same sum as that owed by Charles to William of Orange, the Dutch merely transferred the money direct to their leader. At last there was peace, but few would have agreed that the terms of the peace had been worth the price of the many dead and wounded sailors, the loss of ships, and the general impact on the country's economy. Although England was at peace, the United Provinces and France were not, and the autocratic Louis was busy rampaging through the Rhineland. This, and the heir to the throne declaring himself a Catholic and marrying a Catholic from a client state of France, meant that there was little chance of a compliant parliament in the future. Charles would just have to muddle through as best he could.

Chapter 11

Muddling Through
1674–78

We have a pretty witty king,
Whose word no man relies on,
He never said a foolish thing,
And never did a wise one

Attributed to John Wilmot, Earl of Rochester

Arlington could rejoice that his arch-rival Buckingham had been removed from power, but he realised that he had nearly suffered the same fate. He began to lose his nerve. He was now 56, suffering from gout, and becoming weary of the pressures of office. The impecunious Harry Bennett had amassed a fortune, become an Earl, Knight of the Garter, and prominent member of the Privy Council so he probably felt it was time to enjoy his good fortune rather than fight to retain his position. He decided to buy the post of Lord Chamberlain from the current incumbent and sell his post of secretary of state to Williamson. For Arlington, the move would allow him to remain close to the king, have a former employee as secretary of state, and continue to influence government without being in the front line. This would all take some time to arrange and it was not until September that he resigned as secretary of state, having received a payment of £10,000 from Williamson. The change round had proved more complicated and ended up with Williamson becoming secretary for the North replacing the very experienced 56-year-old Henry Coventry, who then took over Arlington's Southern Department. As Lord Chamberlain, Arlington would continue to appear a major figure at court but he became yesterday's man. Real power had passed to another, and that was the Lord Treasurer, Thomas Osborne, who had been made Earl of Danby in June 1674.

The dynamics of power changed. Lauderdale was still supreme in Scotland, but Buckingham and Arlington were out of the picture. The king's highest priority was finance and so Lord Treasurer Danby became the most prominent minister. Williamson provided some continuity, having taken over as the senior secretary of state and retained his responsibilities for intelligence. He had achieved a position of power, but it would never be on the scale of the politically astute Arlington. The Danby regime would be different from what had gone before. He was a Cavalier by nature and wanted to strengthen royal authority, uphold the Anglican Church, give no tolerance to Nonconformists or Catholics, and ally with the Protestant United Provinces against Catholic France. Only some of these aims were shared by his royal master, but his efficiency as treasurer meant that his policies generally gained the king's support. During his time as Lord Treasurer, Danby would do a great deal to repair the king's finances by cutting government expenditure and making efficiency savings but this would take some time. The king decided to extend the prorogation of parliament from November 1674 to April 1675, in the hope that he might have time to win over some of the opposition, the influential Shaftesbury in particular.

Danby began a systematic attempt to create a court faction in both houses based on support for Anglicanism and traditional loyalty to the Crown. He used the usual method of bribery and patronage to great effect, but not always successfully. Approaches were made to Shaftesbury and it was even hinted that he would be offered the post of Lord Lieutenant of Ireland, but he declined and made it publicly known that 'All their places put together shall not buy me from my principles.'[1] Shaftesbury did agree with Danby on having friendly relations with the Dutch and opposition to both France and Catholicism, but he differed in wanting to curb royal power and allow religious toleration for Nonconformists. These differences were unbridgeable. The two men were rivals for power who disliked each other intensely. Shaftesbury once described Danby as 'an inveterate liar, proud, ambitious, revengeful, false, prodigal and covetous to the highest degree.' No doubt Danby held much the same opinion of Shaftesbury.

Under the Danby regime the agreeable Sir William Temple was sent back as ambassador to The Hague and trade was resumed between the United Provinces and Charles's three kingdoms. Although relations with France had officially cooled, Charles and Louis still kept close and amiable contact with each other and France was even allowed to continue recruiting for its army in Scotland and Ireland. In February 1675 and in accordance with Danby's aim of supporting Anglicanism, Charles issued a proclamation for the suppression of conventicles. This went hand-in-hand with measures against Catholics, such as ordering all Jesuits and Catholic priests out of the country unless they were part of the queen's household or a foreign embassy. Both these repressive moves were to some extent window dressing and their major purpose was to soften up the forthcoming parliament in the hope that it would at last vote supplies. Although it differed from one part of the country to another, conventicles were unofficially tolerated and so the official suppression did not result in an increase in Phanatick activity. Catholics, as always, remained loyal and kept their heads down in the hope of better times.

When parliament met in April 1675 the king spoke to them in an almost deferential manner, saying that he hoped for their advice on resolving religious and property issues. He did not even ask for money, other than saying that the fleet needed to be refitted. The king's smooth words and Danby's preparations did not have the desired result. Danby's court faction was led by Williamson as senior secretary of state in the Commons, and of course Danby himself in the Lords. Many years of life at Whitehall, and his rise to being a man of power and wealth, had changed Williamson from being the impoverished government clerk from Cumbria, to being an urbane courtier. He now dressed extravagantly and took full part in court social life, sometimes dancing till dawn. This more flamboyant lifestyle did not reduce his capacity for hard work but for all his many administrative talents, Williamson was no orator and so not an ideal advocate for the Crown in the Commons. He was opposed by the eloquent Shaftesbury and the Country faction, who were now joined by Buckingham, who had brought his own supporters with him. Members had a growing distrust of the king and Danby, and were more interested in raising grievances than agreeing taxation. Parliament became even more difficult when the two houses fell into a long squabble with each other about their privileges. This supposedly 'managed' parliament had become unmanageable and in June was prorogued once again until October. Charles's response to lack of funds was to make a secret agreement with Louis for an annual payment of £100,000 a year if the October parliament failed to vote money.

Danby was not aware of this arrangement and he and both secretaries of state put a great deal of effort into ensuring that the October parliament would be compliant. He mobilised the bishops to provide a block-vote for the court faction in the Lords. Personal contacts were used to the full; for example, Danby tried to get the support of MPs in his own home area of Yorkshire, and his wife's in Lincolnshire; and there were others, such as the Speaker, who could use their influence in local areas. Danby reckoned that 137 MPs could be relied upon to support the Crown through patronage, family, or regional connections. Over thirty of these had received bribes from Secret Service funds.[2] It was as well that the country was at peace and there were no immediate threats from Republicans or Phanaticks with Williamson being distracted from his intelligence work, and his Secret Service funds being used for other purposes.

Many MPs did not always attend parliament; in fact, of the 508 MPs, there were only about 300 with houses in London, and only about 180 were regular attenders.[3] Just before the October session, the secretaries of state wrote to the hundred or so MPs likely to support the court faction encouraging them to attend. When parliament did meet, Danby's careful preparations were in vain when the Commons voted 172 to 165 to refuse supply. Knowing that he could expect secret funding from Louis, the king prorogued parliament for fifteen months until April 1677. Both Lords and Commons blamed Danby for the prorogation and were incensed at his attempts to bribe members. It has to be said that Danby had few friends; he was disliked by Arlington, loathed by Buckingham, and hated by Shaftesbury. The only senior figure who was his ally was the equally hated Lauderdale who, despite his appalling manners and boundless avarice, always managed to retain the king's favour. The king himself had no natural affinity to his tall, pale and cold-blooded treasurer, but would increasingly rely on him for the efficient management of the royal finances. Danby did manage to make considerable savings on the expenditure of the royal household, but wisely ensured that they did not fall on Louise, Duchess of Portsmouth, as principal mistress. Louise's apartments in the Palace of Whitehall were considerably more sumptuous than those of the queen, largely because Danby always found money for the king to pay for them with. As a result, Louise was one of the few people who liked and supported him. Louise had further strengthened her position by finally having her son acknowledged by Charles and made Duke of Richmond. Barbara, Duchess of Cleveland, was put out by this and insisted that her second son was made Duke of Grafton. Charles agreed to this hoping for a quiet life, but then Louise and Barbara both pestered Charles to give their own son precedence over the other in the peerage. Charles attempted to have both patents signed simultaneously, but Louise manage to get hers signed by Danby at midnight just as he was leaving for Bath, which Barbara discovered to her fury when her patents were brought round for signature the next morning. Danby rose even further in Louise's affections.

Louise's success would soon receive a blow. Towards the end of the year

Charles II: charming, generous and unscrupulous. A man of considerable energy which was largely devoted to the pursuit of pleasure.

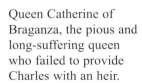

Queen Catherine of Braganza, the pious and long-suffering queen who failed to provide Charles with an heir.

James Duke of York, brother and heir to Charles whose unbending manner and open Catholicism caused all the trouble.

'Minette' Duchess d'Orleans, a delicate beauty much loved by her brother Charles.

Duke of Monmouth, the spoilt Royal bastard who opposed his father and plotted to seize the crown.

Barbara Villiers, Duchess of Cleveland with one of her royal bastards, posing rather unconvincingly as the Virgin Mary.

Louise, Duchess of Portsmouth, Charles' last principal mistress whose unbounded avarice may have even surpassed that of Barbara Villiers.

Nell Gwyn, described by Pepys as 'pretty witty Nelly'.

Duke of Buckingham: amusing and multi-talented, a boyhood friend of the king who was viciously vindictive to those he disliked – who were many.

Earl of Arlington: urbane, a schemer who made good use of intelligence. Here seen proudly wearing his habitual black nose plaster.

Sir Joseph Williamson, Secretary of State and architect of the Restoration intelligence organisation.

Sir Leoline Jenkins, a diligent Secretary of State and intelligencer.

Titus Oates, the skilful liar who invented the Popish Plot and was encouraged by Shaftesbury. Seen in the pillory – and not before time.

Earl of Shaftesbury, a brilliant and ambitious little man who plotted for liberal principles and his own advancement.

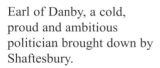

Earl of Danby, a cold, proud and ambitious politician brought down by Shaftesbury.

COLL: BLOOD

Thomas Blood, the rebel and inveterate plotter who turned government agent after stealing the Crown Jewels from the Tower.

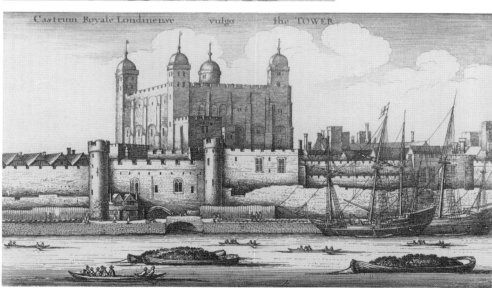

Tower of London – the temporary and sometimes final residence of many of the personalities of the period.

the most talked about woman in Europe arrived in London on horseback, wearing men's clothes. The beautiful Hortense Mancini was a niece of Cardinal Mazarin and had been married off to the incredibly rich Armand de la Meilleraye, who had been given the title Duke de Mazarin. The marriage was difficult to say the least. The Duke insisted on her spending at least a third of the day in prayer and was decidedly eccentric, ordering, for example, that the front teeth of all his female servants be knocked out so that they could not attract the attention of young men. Hortense was a free-spirited and bisexual lady who began to take varied lovers, which resulted in the duke confining her to a convent. At the convent she unmercifully teased the Sisters before escaping to the protection of the Duke of Savoy. When the duke died, his wife insisted that his mistress leave and so Hortense went to Paris. In Paris she met the English ambassador Ralph Montagu, who saw an opportunity to advance in royal favour. He persuaded Hortense to go to London with a view to becoming Charles's chief mistress. So it was that Hortense had arrived in London. She was immediately accepted at court, being a relation of the new Duchess of York who, like her, was a niece of the great Mazarin. Hortense was already known to Charles, in fact he had suggested marriage to her during his days in exile, but that had been dismissed by Mazarin because of his lack of prospects at the time. Charles was interested to renew his acquaintance with the woman whose wit and good looks were the talk of society. Before long the fascinating Hortense had captured the king's heart and had been taken on as his mistress with an annual pension of £4,000. Arlington had backed Barbara Cleveland, but the influence of both was on the wane. Buckingham had backed Nell Gwynn, but her background excluded her from being *maitresse en titre*. Now Hortense, backed by Montagu, and Louise, backed by Danby, were struggling for that title. The court would have to wait for a year-and-a-half to see which of 'the two French whores' would win, and which of the backers had made the best bet.

Those in the Lords and Commons who detested Popery and the arbitrary government of King Louis, feared that England was moving in the direction of both. With parliament prorogued for fifteen months they could not use it to voice their concern. Shaftesbury decided to continue his campaign through propaganda. Either Shaftesbury or his secretary John Locke had written *A Letter from a Person of Quality to his Friend in the Country*, which was published while parliament had been sitting but was now given far wider circulation. This document attacked Popery, the court generally, and the Bishops in particular, for being pretentious and supporting the divine right of kings. More anti-government pamphlets were to follow and were being eagerly read in the many coffee shops that had sprung up in London and in main towns throughout England. Shaftesbury and his followers were turning the underground press into a political weapon aimed at achieving a broad base of support. Williamson tried to suppress the subversive literature but with little effect. On New Year's Day 1676, Danby ordered that all coffee shops should be closed by royal proclamation but there was such uproar that he cancelled it ten days later. Instead he ordered that coffee shop owners had to take the oaths of allegiance and supremacy, and give bonds not to allow anti-government pamphlets or discussion on their premises. A reward of £20 was also offered to anyone who provided the identity of the author of printed or manuscript libels against the government. This too had little effect and only served to make Danby and the government more unpopular. L'Estrange was doing his best to stamp out Country Party propaganda and Williamson was granting him warrants to conduct searches and seize seditious material, but he only managed to make a few arrests and a couple of convictions.

In parliament an opposition group was coming together and beginning to organise itself around Shaftesbury and Buckingham. Buckingham had made a speech in the October parliament proposing the lifting of penal laws against Nonconformists. Despite Buckingham's notoriously moral laxity, he was seen as a hero to Nonconformists and was entering into discussions with many of their leaders, such as William Penn of the Quakers. Buckingham also had his more radical associates such as Wildman, with contacts among Phanaticks and Republicans. Naturally, Williamson was trying to gather any intelligence he could about opposition plots but there seemed to be none at this stage, although there was the mysterious letter from Buckingham's former employee Henry North. For some reason, North had been sacked by Buckingham and taken up highway robbery, but had been caught in Lincolnshire and condemned to be hanged. North wrote to Williamson saying he would make a confession about a conspiracy by 'divers eminent persons' against the king.[4] Unfortunately the letter was delayed and North was executed before Williamson could follow it up, but he would keep a close watch on Buckingham.

Someone who had prospered by Buckingham's fall had been Monmouth, who had been given Buckingham's two Crown appointments of Master of Horse and Lord Lieutenant of the East Riding. Following his success in the Dutch War, Monmouth was made effectively head of the army insofar as all army orders had to be sent to him for agreement. He also had the specific responsibility for the suppression of rioting but had no cause to carry out the role. Although there were many murmurings of discontent against the court, Danby, and the Bishops, there were no riots or even demonstrations at this time. All three kingdoms were having a period of stability and, in some areas, a return to prosperity resulting from improved trade following the end of the war.

At court, Hortense appeared to be eclipsing Louise. She had established a salon at St James's Palace to which the most fashionable flocked. Aphra Behn, the sometime spy and now famous authoress, dedicated her play *The History of the Nun or the Fair Vow-Breaker to Hortense* and was probably one of her lovers. Like many ladies of the court, Hortense was a keen gambler but, unlike other ladies, was also a crack shot, good swordswoman, and keen swimmer. Her many accomplishments included being able to perform a Spanish dance while accompanying herself on the guitar. Louise just could not compete. Few could accuse the king of being a prude, but even he began to be slightly concerned when his daughter by Barbara Cleveland, Anne, Countess of Suffolk, began having an affair with Hortense. Neither of the pair were discreet and incidents such as the two of them carrying out a pretend duel in their nightdresses in St James's Park certainly raised eyebrows. However, what really spoilt Hortense's close relations with Charles was when she openly took the visiting Prince of Monaco as her lover. Charles was very annoyed to be publicly humiliated in this way and even stopped her allowance. She was soon forgiven and the allowance restored as it was not in Charles's nature to abandon his ladies. Charles would remain friends with Hortense till the end of his life, but she ceased to be his mistress. Louise was back in her position as *maitresse en titre*, no doubt to the relief of Danby and consternation of Montagu. Her position was to become even stronger than before as Louise would soon have Nell Gwynn as the only other royal mistress about the court. Barbara Cleveland's endless extravagance had made her short of funds and she decided to move to Paris. True to form, she soon acquired a number of French lovers including, it was said, the Bishop of Paris. However, she did not neglect her own countrymen and began a strong relationship with Ralph Montagu, the English ambassador.

As the fifteen months prorogation of parliament came to an end, both court and Country factions were getting ready for the February 1677 session. Danby and the two secretaries of state were using whatever carrots and sticks they could find to induce MPs and Lords to support the court faction. In Danby's words (reported by Bishop Burnet): 'Nothing is more necessary than for the world to see that he (the king) will reward or punish.' For their part, Shaftesbury and Buckingham were rallying members of the Country faction.

As well as using coffee houses as opposition meeting places, a new way for dissidents to gather was coming into being. This was the 'club', such as the Green Ribbon Club at the King's Head Tavern on the junction of Fleet Street and Chancery Lane. As a club was an association of members it was not bound by any of the recent laws relating to coffee houses. Also, as clubs were for members only, they could ensure that only those who were known to share the same views could enter. These clubs took off with some becoming meeting places for followers of Buckingham, some for followers of Shaftesbury, or some of the other leading lights in the country faction. The clubs were merely locations for like-minded dissidents to meet, exchange views, and discuss ways of putting pressure on the government. Their gatherings were not seditious. Nevertheless, it was very much in government's interests to learn of their discussions but, unlike coffee houses, it was difficult to have them infiltrated by informants. As the clubs grew in number and influence, Williamson would be putting a major effort into trying to penetrate them.

When parliament at last reassembled in February 1667, Buckingham and Shaftesbury had cooked up a plan to try to have a fresh parliament called in the expectation that newly elected MPs would be more supportive of the Country faction. Buckingham made a speech saying that as parliament had not met for fifteen months, it was illegal and should be dissolved. Danby's cousin, Lord Frescheville, responded by demanding that Buckingham be called to the bar of the House for challenging its legitimacy. This occurred and the Lords sent Buckingham, Shaftesbury, and a few other Country faction leaders to the Tower of London. With them safely out of the way a more compliant parliament voted a land tax to provide funding for the navy. Although England had made peace with the Dutch, war was still raging on the continent between France and the United Provinces with their respective allies. To the mounting concern of all true protestants, Louis's army was again rampaging about the Netherlands. In April, St Omer had capitulated to the French and Charles took the opportunity to ask for more funding, implying it was for use against the French. Parliament was prepared to vote money, but did not trust the king to spend it on war with France. An impasse was reached. The next month, parliament actually petitioned the king to declare war on France. He was furious at this interference in his prerogative and prorogued it. Meanwhile, Nell Gwynn came to Buckingham's rescue from imprisonment. She had always liked Buckingham and found him amusing company, so pleaded with Charles for his release. It was always difficult for Charles to refuse the requests of his ladies and so he agreed. Buckingham was released and returned to both the court and the king's inner circle, much to the concern of his rival Danby. Shaftesbury had no mistress to plead for him and remained in the Tower despite attempts by him to apply for a writ of habeas corpus. One of the reasons Shaftesbury was opposing the king was because of what he believed was the growth of arbitrary government. One can only assume that his continued imprisonment without trial hardened him in this conviction. Although he was confined to the Tower, and so unable to attend the Lords, this did not mean that he was unable to continue scheming opposition to the government. Shaftesbury used trusted supporters such as Wildman and Locke to continue his influence among the Country faction. Even in prison, this small, aging man, suffering constant pain from a cyst on the liver, remained a danger to the government.

We have already seen the methods Danby was using to increase the king's authority over parliament. He had made his policy very clear to Charles from the beginning as he wrote in an early memorandum to the king: 'In all things to promote the Protestant interest both at home and abroad. To keep firm to the Triple Alliance, and endeavour to bring all Protestant princes into it … To suffer no diminution nor embezzlement either in England or Ireland.'[5] In practical terms this had two objectives. The first was to win the support of the majority of parliament by portraying the king as an ally of the Anglican Church, anti-French and anti-Papist. Related to this was to encourage Crown support by managing members who either naturally supported the king, or could be made to do so through inducements. The second thrust was the efficient management of royal finances so that the impoverished king could live on his £1.5 million annual revenue from excise, and not be so dependent on parliamentary funds. In this latter objective he was most successful through his own strict oversight of the Exchequer and because there had been a revival of trade since the end of the war, which resulted in a higher take in royal customs duties.

In the first objective his success was more mixed. Danby's management of parliament was becoming so effective that it was the reason Shaftesbury and Buckingham had started to press for new parliamentary elections. He had achieved a strong alliance with the Bishops and clamped down on both Papists and Nonconformists. The problem with the obvious alliance with the Bishops was that they now appeared the royal puppets in the Lords and so created something of a backlash against Anglicanism from supporters of the Country Party. Of course, the measures against Papists had been popular, but those against Nonconformists were less so. There was a growing feeling in parliament that Buckingham and Shaftesbury were right, and that the restrictions on Nonconformist services should be lifted. With the heir to the throne an avowed Catholic and now also married to a Catholic, and the king's principal mistress a Catholic, there was mounting concern that the country was sliding towards Popery. Nonconformists might be odious, but at least they were Protestant and might be firmer allies against the advance of Popery than some of the Anglican Bishops.

What Danby needed was the king's support for a break with France, and an alliance with the United Provinces to give the country confidence that the leanings towards Popery and absolute monarchy were being reversed. In this objective Danby was successful, up to a point. Danby had long been pressing for an alliance with William of Orange and wanted to cement it with his marriage to the Duke of York's Protestant daughter, Princess Mary. Informal negotiations about this had been going on using Temple, the ambassador at The Hague. This was done with the king's knowledge, but only lukewarm support. When parliament was prorogued in May without having voted funds, Charles decided once again to turn to Louis for money. A third secret treaty was made in which Louis agreed to provide Charles with £145,000 if this anti-French parliament was not recalled until May the following year, by which time he hoped to have won the war. Danby was not aware of this, or the previous secret treaties, and it was totally against the policy he had agreed with the king and indeed all that he stood for.

The king was coming round to agreeing with Danby that a marriage between William and Mary might well take the steam out of parliament's simmering anti-papist sentiment and make it more likely to grant supplies. He therefore authorised Danby to press ahead with negotiating the marriage. William was suffering a series of military setbacks and was only too happy to establish a marriage alliance with England. The 15-year-old Mary was less than enthusiastic about living in Holland and being married off to a dour Dutchman, with a hooked nose and lazy eye, who was little taller than a midget. Naturally her views were of little consequence and the marriage took place in November. As it happened, they would become a very devoted couple but there was no romantic joy between them that November. There was, however, great joy across the country at this Protestant alliance and celebratory bonfires were lit across London. The Duke of York might be Catholic, but at least his heir was a Protestant and married to the foremost Protestant leader in Europe.

Unsurprisingly, Louis did not join in the marital celebrations. He felt that Charles had deceived him by pretending to be his ally then, without any warning, making an alliance with his greatest enemy. He cancelled Charles's subsidy and sent his new ambassador in London, Paul Barrillon, to undermine Charles by bribing Country faction MPs to refuse to vote money to the king so that that there would be no funding for war with France. Barrillon was also instructed to begin secret discussions with opposition leaders to find common cause against Danby, who Louis blamed for making the Dutch alliance. One such was Algernon Sidney who had returned to England in September as his father, the Earl of Leicester, was dying. Abroad, Sidney had been a leading Republican who had unsuccessfully tried to persuade both De Witt and Louis to support a rising in England at the Second Dutch War. Despite his subversive background no action was taken against him when he returned and he soon took up residence in Leicester House in London. He was, after all, a cousin of the Earl of Essex, who had been Lord Lieutenant of Ireland, and the two rising stars at court, the Earl of Sunderland and Viscount Halifax, were his nephews. Once re-established back in England, Sidney began scheming to establish a Republic, taking any ally – even if it meant using the ambassador of a king he despised as a Papist and absolute monarch. Sidney was a talented man of high, even (in his own way) noble principles, but was also a danger to the Crown and would need to be kept under close scrutiny by Williamson and his intelligencers.

The previous couple of years had seen lots of political scheming but no actual plots against the king. Williamson's agents and informants must have been finding it hard to make ends meet. Then just before the royal wedding seditious activity began to pick up, but of a slightly different nature from before. Blood discovered a plot by an MP called Sir Robert Peynton, who was the chairman of the Green Ribbon Cub. Green was prominent in opposition to the Crown and had been removed as a magistrate the previous year for distributing seditious material. According to Blood, Peynton and a group of Fifth Monarchists were planning to seize power by capturing the Tower and assassinating the king and Duke of York either in Newmarket or London. Their aim was to make Richard Cromwell provisional ruler over the three kingdoms and then form a Republic based on parliamentary authority. The plotters were motivated by being against Catholicism, France, and arbitrary government. These conspirators included William Smith, who had been one of Blood's accomplices in the attempt on the Crown Jewels. Arrests were made and Peynton and others interrogated, but there was insufficient evidence to bring any cases to court and all were eventually released. The apparent involvement of their chairman in a conspiracy made the Green Ribbon Club forced Peynton to resign. Just how much truth there was in Blood's report of the plot is difficult to say, but the interesting thing about it was that this was not just a Phanatick or Republican plot, but had at least one member of the Country faction.[6]

Although there was plenty of scheming going on, particularly in London, the three kingdoms had seen no significant civil disturbance for some years. One reason was that despite cancellation of the Declaration of Indulgence, there had been little persecution of dissenters. This was not to be the case in Scotland where Archbishops Sharp and Burnet began insisting on full attendance at Anglican churches. Covenanters and other Presbyterians in the South West Scotland responded by continuing to hold conventicles in the open air, often guarded by armed supporters. Lauderdale decided to finally stamp out Presbyterian disobedience. He directed that landowners must give a bond that their tenants and servants would not attend conventicles. This was not well received by the lairds, many of whom were Presbyterians themselves and they took little notice of the edict. As punishment, Lauderdale ordered the Highland Host to Ayrshire to enforce obedience. The Host was a wild militia of about 6,000 Catholic Highlanders who hated Presbyterians. The Host was billeted on householders without agreement or payment. As well as enforcing fines and imprisonment for non-attendance at church, the Host looted and assaulted the local population at will. The situation was so desperate that the Duke of Hamilton travelled to London to complain to the king. Charles had no love of Scotland or the Scots and as usual, supported his trusty servant Lauderdale. He did, however, make the concession that billeting should be suspended. This concession helped to keep the lid on the situation, but with the continuing harassment from the authorities, the Presbyterians might not remain submissive indefinitely.

As the year ended, the king was paying little interest in faraway Scotland because his attention was focused south and the continuing war. Parliament was pressing for war with France but refusing to provide funding, and any war would go completely counter to what he had agreed with Louis. Charles's hope was that peace between Louis and William could be quickly achieved so the question of war would be irrelevant. As a cousin of Louis and uncle of William, Charles felt that he should be able to mediate a peace agreement. He formulated terms acceptable to William, but these were declined by Louis. Nevertheless, negotiations had begun. As Louis had withdrawn the promised secret subsidy, the king recalled parliament earlier than intended at the end of January 1674. Many members would have read a publication that had recently arrived from Amsterdam called *An Account of the Growth of Popery and Arbitrary Government*. This pamphlet was almost certainly the work of Andrew Marvell and said there was a plot to turn the government into 'absolute tyranny' and religion into 'downright popery'. Although some copies were seized and burned by the public hangman, it was widely read and did not put parliament in a mood to be compliant to royal demands. The king opened parliament by saying that he had committed to an alliance with the Dutch to provide ninety ships and 30-40,000 troops against France, but would need £100,000 to pay for it. The money for war was reluctantly agreed in principle, but not how it should be raised, because many members did not trust the king. Some MPs called it 'a pick pocket war', in other words, that the king would not go to war at all but just pocket the money. The Lords decided to release Shaftesbury from the Tower and he returned to parliament to add his voice to opposition to Danby and the court.

There now followed a confusing period of parliamentary attacks on Lauderdale and Danby, and demands for a formal treaty with the Dutch against France. Parliament was also maintaining the standoff over voting money for war, which some thought might even be used by the king to subdue his own subjects. Parliament would reach a peak of strident opposition to the Crown, only to be briefly prorogued by the king while he played for time hoping that peace would be signed. This process then repeated itself. While this was going on, unknown to Danby, Charles was having secret negotiations with Louis to be given some Flemish towns and £600,000 a year to rule without parliament. This fell through when, without consultation, Louis captured the major city of Ghent, despite peace negotiations being in progress. Charles felt that Louis had played him so responded by sending an advance guard of 1,600 men under Lord Howard of Escrick to Ostend, and mobilised troops on Hampstead Heath. Monmouth was then dispatched to Ostend with additional soldiers to take command of the expeditionary force. On 25 March Charles sent new proposals to Louis for six million livres not to call parliament. Danby was completely against this but carried out the wishes of his royal master and dutifully sent the proposal to Ralph Montagu in Paris to present to Louis. Danby felt so strongly that he refused to sign the subsequent treaty, so the signatures were left to Charles and Ambassador Barrillon. On 23 May, Charles told parliament that he needed money to either continue to pay the army until peace was concluded, or to simply pay the army off and disband it. He said he would leave it to parliament to decide, but made it quite clear that he supported the first option. So bad were the relations between parliament and the Crown that they voted £200,000 to be used for the army's disbandment. On 31 July, peace was at last agreed at Nijmegen.

Although the treaty was agreed it was not yet ratified, so Louis thought he would try to snatch one last gain by getting the Duke of Luxembourg to capture Mons. The English expeditionary force had risen to a strength of 20,000 men. It had seen little fighting as the protracted peace negotiations were in progress, but it joined up with William of Orange and his troops for the defence of Mons. William managed to save the town by winning the Battle of St Denis in which Monmouth acquitted himself with bravery and further enhanced his reputation as a general. Almost immediately after the battle, Louis and William finally signed peace terms in the Peace of Nijmegen in August. The outcome of the war was that the United Provinces had been saved, but Louis had won France-Comté and a number of towns in the Spanish Netherlands. There was nothing in it for England other than that Charles would claim credit for helping to bring the conflict to an end. Other associated peace agreements were made by the various allies of the two belligerents: Spain, Austria, Prussia, Munster, Sweden, and the rest. Europe was finally at peace.

Charles could at last relax, parliament was prorogued until October and he could congratulate himself that he had displayed some statesmanship in bringing about the peace. He had also allowed Danby to have his popular war against France, which had been mercifully short. There was, of course, the usual problem of money. Parliament had voted funds in May for the express purpose of disbanding the army, which many feared might be used as an instrument of royal subjection. Not only had those funds all been used up on Monmouth's expeditionary force, but also Charles wanted to keep this army in being until the ratifications of the various peace treaties were all in place. So 20,000 troops were still in existence, continuing to cost money that the Treasury did not possess, and there was obviously no money to pay off the troops when they eventually were disbanded. That was a problem that Charles could leave to Danby for the moment, in the hope that he could come up with a solution. In the meantime, the king could be more than content with his private life. He had a father's pride that his much-loved eldest son Monmouth, had acquitted himself so gallantly on the field of battle. As far as his ladies were concerned: Louise, his main love, was no longer having tearful outbursts about Hortense and was continuing to be respectful to the long suffering queen, and Nell was around for uncomplicated, bawdy, fun.

Earlier in the year the king's hopes of domestic calm had been briefly shattered by the return of an irate Barbara Cleveland to London on a visit. She had been living Paris with her wayward daughter Anne who, unsurprisingly, was now estranged from her husband, the Earl of Sussex. Barbara's affair with Ralph Montagu had ended messily with mutual recriminations when she had left him for the Marquis de Chatillon. Both Montagu and Barbara wanted to hurt each other, but Montagu got in first by writing to Charles that Barbara's lascivious behaviour was bringing shame on England. Barbara decided to come to London to see Charles and denounce Montagu by any means her spiteful and inventive mind could conceive. When she saw the king she accused Montagu of numerous offences and demanded his dismissal as ambassador. Charles had thrown off Barbara's spell over him and was weary of being harangued by her. He is thought to have brought the interview to an end by saying: 'Madam, all I ask of you, for your own sake, live so for the future as to make the least noise you can, and I care not who you love.'[7] Barbara returned to France only to discover that Montagu had had his own revenge in her absence by seducing her daughter, Anne. Barbara was furious and wrote to Charles saying that Montagu had bedded their daughter. She finally got her revenge when Charles immediately dismissed Montagu as ambassador. This private squabble would be of little interest if it were not for major political implications. Montagu came back to England and blamed Danby, rather than the king for his dismissal, and decided to become an MP so that he had a public platform from which to attack the Lord Treasurer and get his revenge. That would take a bit of time because first he had to win a by-election, but once he had done that – his revenge would be great indeed.

Montagu's revenge would have to be deferred until he had taken his seat a month after parliament reconvened in October, but in August, all was reasonably calm. There had been a long spell of sunny weather and those who could were keen to leave London for the country. With parliament prorogued, Danby was preparing to go off to his mansion in Wimbledon to supervise the arrangements for his daughter Bridget's wedding to Charles, Earl of Plymouth. The wedding would be a further mark of royal favour, as the Earl of Plymouth was one of Charles's illegitimate sons, the product of his dalliance with Catherine Pegge during his exile in Bruges. For his part, Charles was looking forward to going to Windsor Castle, which had just received a massive refurbishment and where a variety of lavish functions had been prepared for the court. He would probably have been also looking forward to having some peace and quiet to himself, as Windsor was where he went to enjoy his latest hobby of fishing. On the morning of 13 August, the day before he was to leave for Windsor, the king was preparing to go for his morning walk across St James's Park with his spaniels. Just as he was about to set out, Christopher Kirkby asked for a note to be handed to him, saying he was in danger. Charles knew Kirkby slightly because he had been helping him with chemical experiments in the royal laboratory and asked for him to come forward to speak to him. Kirkby said that there was a plot to shoot him. Charles had heard of so many stories of threats against him in the past that he was completely unconcerned and went off on his walk as normal, but did ask Kirkby to tell him more about it on his return. After the king had completed his walk he saw Kirkby and merely asked him to return that evening with whoever was the source of the information. That evening Kirkby arrived at the Palace of Whitehall with the person who had told him about the plot, an Anglican clergyman of Puritan persuasion called Dr Israel Tonge. Kirkby and Tonge were then taken to the king in the Red Chamber and told him that a Benedictine, Thomas Pickering, and a Jesuit lay-brother, John Grove, had vowed to shoot him and if that failed, he would be poisoned by Sir George Wakeman, the queen's physician. Tonge then began to read out some forty-three articles of related plots that he had received from a trusted source, but the king got so bored with this he stopped him and asked for a summary. Tonge's summary was simply that after the assassination, all three kingdoms would rise up with French help. By this time the king had heard quite enough of what he considered to be complete rubbish. He directed that the investigation should be referred to Danby and left for Windsor the next morning.

On the afternoon of the following day, Kirkby and Tonge went to Danby's lodgings at the Cockpit, Whitehall and repeated the story. Danby knew a thing or two about informants. He is recorded as running six informants himself as far back as 1662 when he was Sheriff for the North Riding.[8] Like the king, he quickly assessed that the report was rubbish and was annoyed that Tonge had refused to reveal who had been the source of the forty-three articles of plots. It was left that they would seek out more information from their unnamed, trusted source and report back. Danby would no doubt have asked Williamson to check on Tonge and Kirkby and found that both were rather suspect. It would have been swiftly established that Tonge was far more Puritan than Anglican. His church had been burned down in the Fire of London and, after two years as a chaplain in the Tangiers Garrison, he had returned to London where he had been working as a physician in the Barbican. More importantly, he was regarded as being insane with a persecution complex about Papists who he blamed for both the Fire and the Civil War. Kirkby, on the other hand, was an acquaintance of Tonge who was perfectly sane, but shared his passionate hatred of Popery.

Although Tonge's accusations would have to be investigated further as directed by the king, it would seem the whole matter could be put to rest and Danby could get on with the wedding preparations. So ended the first chapter of a plot that was to dominate public life for the next three years and would turn into by far the greatest threat to the Stuart monarchy of the whole reign.

Chapter 12

The Popish Plot
1678–9

That this House is of opinion that there hath been and still is a
damnable and hellish plot contrived and carried out by the
popish recusants for the assassinating and murdering the King.
House of Commons resolution, 31 October 1678.

In the late summer of 1678 an event would occur which put England into
such fear as to cause a state of near national hysteria that would last three
years. The fear was of Roman Catholicism. Of course, the majority of the
population in impoverished Ireland were Roman Catholics and there were a
significant number of Catholics far away in the Highlands of Scotland but
relatively few in England. It has been estimated that there were about 260,000
Roman Catholics in England at this time amounting to 4.7 per cent of the
country's total population of five million.[1] As has been mentioned, most
Roman Catholics were members of the gentry and their servants, living
quietly in the country. There were a few Catholic peers, but the Test Act and
the Penal Laws meant that Catholics were barred from any government office
and so had little power. Papist priests had been expelled from the country
and Catholics had gone into survival mode, worshipping discreetly and
praying for better times. In short, Roman Catholics posed absolutely no threat
to the Crown or anyone else. Although this is obvious to us looking back
from our modern perspective, it was not the case for our Protestant forefathers
in the 1670s. The reason was that for generations, Catholicism – often
branded the 'Whore of Babylon' – had been seen as the enemy of God and
man.

Catholic doctrine was regarded as a foul, superstitious and idolatrous
perversion of Christianity presided over by a worldly Pope whom many
thought was the 'Anti-Christ' foretold in Revelations. Papists were regarded

as cunning and scheming fanatics, always attempting to forcibly convert honest Protestants to their detestable beliefs. The memory of the savage persecution of Protestants by Catholics was high in people's consciousness. Protestants could never forget Bloody Mary's burnings at Smithfield; the French massacre of St Bartholomew's Day; the attempted invasion by the Armada from Spain, the home of the hated Inquisition; and of course the Gunpowder Plot. In living memory there had been the savage Catholic uprising against Protestants in Ireland in the 1640s. It was no surprise that Foxe's *Book of Martyrs* was the second most published book in England after the Bible. This latent fear of Catholicism among English Protestants had been stoked by the real concern that the king's mistress, and the queen, were both Catholic, as was his brother and heir. Given the deep-rooted fears of Popery, Protestant minds were open to unquestionably believing anything that confirmed their prejudices about Roman Catholics. It just needed a spark to convince Protestants that their worst fears were true to ignite a conflagration of irrational hatred of Popery. This spark would be made by the source of Tonge's plot, a down at heel cleric called Titus Oates.

Titus Oates was an extraordinary looking man with a chin so large that his mouth sat in the centre of his face. He had an annoyingly harsh, loud voice, and his appearance was dirty and unkempt. It would seem that nature had dealt Oates a bad hand but he had one attribute that completely made up for the un-prepossessing first impression. He had the gift of being an inventive and persuasive liar. Part of this ability was an extraordinary memory. It enabled him to recount in considerable detail his accusations and then remember them with complete accuracy when questioned about them days later. Strangely, his phenomenal memory does not seem to be have been present when engaged in academic study and it must be said that his career thus far had been less than successful. His father had been an Anabaptist preacher who had jumped on the Restoration bandwagon and become an Anglican only to obtain a living at a parish in Hastings.

Titus had gone to Cambridge but was thrown out of two colleges having been described by one tutor as 'a great dunce'. His lack of a degree was not a bar to a career in the Church of England; he was ordained and became curate to his father. While in Hastings he was sent to gaol for perjury, having falsely accused a local schoolmaster of sodomy. Luckily he escaped from gaol and became a chaplain on a Royal Naval warship. This did not last long because he was dismissed for reasons described by his acquaintance Bishop Burnet as: 'some unnatural practices, not to be named'. He then managed to become an Anglican chaplain to the Catholic Duke of Norfolk and around this time joined the Catholic Church. His motivation for this, if it can be believed, was to discover the secrets of Popery in general and Jesuits in particular with the intention of exposing them. He was sent to the English College at Valladolid to study as a novice but was dismissed because of his poor Latin; he was then sent to the Catholic college in St Omer but was again expelled in 1678, either for his lack of application or his homosexuality. With no money and few friends at the age of 28, he made his way to London and went to see Tonge whom he had met two years previously. Knowing Tonge's hatred of Catholics, Oates fabricated a tale that he had uncovered Papist conspiracies, probably in order to win Tonge's help. Once Tonge had enthusiastically swallowed these stories, Oates produced a document of forty-three articles making allegations against those whose names he had come across during his time with the Catholic Church. This had led Tonge to tell Kirby, who had in turn informed the king. Unfortunately for Tonge, neither the king nor Danby had been convinced of the plots and Tonge had been sent away to get more information.

Things got rather out of hand for Oates, who had made up his lies simply to ingratiate himself with Tonge, he had no idea they would reach the king. He went into hiding but Tonge, who had been tasked with finding more about the plot, eventually tracked him down. Oates agreed to feed Tonge with more information against the Jesuits, which Tonge then reported to Danby. As no information provided so far gave sufficient evidence to act upon, Danby said that he would arrange for the Post Office to intercept the mail of known Jesuits. This gave Oates the idea of forging five incriminating letters from various Jesuits to Thomas Bedingfield, the Duke of York's confessor. These he sent on 31 August, but the staff in the Post Office failed to intercept them so they arrived with Bedingfield at Windsor the next day. Bedingfield opened the letters and could see at once they were forgeries. Four of the letters were supposed to be from Jesuits called Whitbread, Fenwick, Ireland and Blundell, who were well known to Bedingfield, and he at once saw that this was not their writing. The fourth letter purported to be from a William Fogart, whom Bedingfield did not know. Bedingfield realised he was being set up and immediately showed the letters to the Duke of York who was furious that there had been an attempt to incriminate his confessor. The duke took the letters to the king and demanded that this outrage should be investigated by the council.

Meanwhile, Oates decided to rewrite and elaborate on his accusations, extending them from forty-three to eighty-one articles. He was careful not to include anything that could be disproved, and brought the Benedictines and Dominicans to join the Jesuits in the plot; amongst other things, he claimed that the plots included the assassination of the Duke of Ormonde, and uprisings in Ireland and Scotland. Tonge had wanted to cover himself by persuading Oates to give a deposition of his allegations to a magistrate. They went to Sir Edmund Berry Godfrey, the only magistrate they could get hold of, and he took an affidavit from Oates, where he swore that the articles were a true account and could therefore be used in court if necessary.

The forged letters had made Danby even more wary of Tonge and Danby refused to see him for several days, eventually seeing him on 20 September in the company of the Bishop of London, whom Tonge knew, and had prevailed upon to persuade Danby to attend. There had been a recent fire in Limehouse, and Tonge made the point that the fire had been one of the events predicted in the forty-two articles. There was still serious scepticism and Williamson commented to Danby that he thought Tonge was making it all up in the hope of getting himself a deanery. Nevertheless, the king chaired the Foreign Affairs Committee on 27 September, where the main subject was the letters to Bedingfield and the allegations brought by Tonge. When Tonge appeared before the committee, as had been expected, he made a very poor impression. At lunchtime, the king left for the higher priority of the Newmarket races, taking Monmouth with him and being followed soon after by the Duke of York.

Prince Rupert took the chair for the afternoon session in a rather grumpy mood, probably because of his syphilis. In the morning, Tonge had named Oates as his source and so Oates, at last, appeared before the committee. There was only one copy of Oates's long list of articles, which it is unlikely anyone had actually read, so Oates obligingly ran through the various allegations. These described a Jesuit plot to assassinate the king, uprisings in Scotland and Ireland, the slaughter of Protestants, and the re-establishment of the Catholic Church with the military support of the French. As Burnet records, Oates 'named persons, places and times almost without number to shoot, stab or poison the king.'[2] At this point the whole atmosphere changed as Oates spoke with such authority and amazing detail about the plots and their conspirators. Of the main members of the Committee, Rupert and Lauderdale were fiercely anti-Catholic, and Danby, never fond of Catholics, was prepared to be convinced by Oates's smooth performance. Williamson, rather junior to the rest, remained the only sceptic. The questioning then moved onto the Bedingfield letters. Oates was shown small extracts from each of the letters and amazed those present by attributing the correct authors to each of them – not really surprising as he had written them! The question then posed was: how he could tell whose handwriting it was when the writing bore no resemblance to the normal writing of the Jesuits concerned? Oates gave the masterful reply that it was well know that Jesuits disguised their handwriting when engaged in nefarious work. Having given this plausible reply, Oates had won over the majority of the committee. As Robert Southwell, the Clerk of the Privy Council, wrote: 'What looked ridiculous this morning, when alleged by Tonge, was transformed when Oates himself came this afternoon to tell his tale with all the particulars of it, the lords stood amazed and could do no more than send for those he had upon oath accused.'[3] Before the council broke up, warrants were issued for the arrest of Fogarty, Grove, Pickering, Conyers, and Fenwick, all of whom had been named by Oates as conspiring to assassinate the king at Windsor. All but Conyers were arrested that night. The Popish witch-hunt had begun.[4]

Oates was now on a roll. The next day he accused Edward Coleman of treason and said that this would be confirmed if his letters were examined. Coleman was the secretary of Mary of Modena, Duchess of York, and had previously been the duke's secretary. His correspondence was searched and some old letters were found to show that he had been in correspondence with Father Ferrier, the Confessor of King Louis. From a cursory glance at the correspondence, the letters did not appear seditious but, to be on the safe side, a warrant was issued for Coleman's arrest. In order to demonstrate his innocence, Coleman voluntarily gave himself up to Williamson on 30 September and later that day appeared before the council. Oates rather lost credibility with the council when he failed to recognise Coleman. As nothing treasonous came to light during the questioning of Coleman, the council decided to put him in the care of a king's messenger rather than commit him to prison.

That might have been the end of the matter had it not been for the discovery on 17 October, of the body of Sir Edmund Berry Godfrey in a ditch on Primrose Hill with a sword sticking out of him. Godfrey had been missing since he left his house five days earlier telling his servants he would be back later. On examination, it was found that he had been strangled and then later run through with his own sword. Godfrey was the magistrate to whom Oates had given his deposition and so there was an immediate assumption that he had been savagely silenced by Papists to prevent knowledge of their plot getting out. If any more proof was needed, it was clinched when a large amount of candle wax was found on the body. All good Protestants associated candles with the detestable rituals of Rome and so the hand of a Papist priest was clear to see. How Godfrey actually met his death still remains a mystery over 300 years after the event. One theory is that he sometimes suffered from depression so may have committed suicide by strangulation but that his relatives had moved the body to Primrose Hill and run him through to make it look like a robbery. In those days, the estate of a suicide victim would be confiscated by the Crown, so it would have been in the interests of his heirs to cover the fact.

There have been many theories to explain the death but none are compelling. What was important about the death was what the great majority of the population believed at the time, and they believed that Godfrey had been silenced by Papists to prevent Oates's allegations getting out. Although Oates's allegations had only been made to the council, garbled versions had leaked out and spread like wildfire. If, as was thought, Godfrey had been silenced by Papists, it proved by implication that the allegations of a plotted Catholic insurrection were true. There was an overwhelming and strident public demand for the extent of the plot to be revealed and action taken against the perpetrators.

An immediate result was that Coleman was consigned to Newgate Prison. There had now been sufficient time to read his correspondence and discover that much of it was about trying to bring England back to Catholicism. This had included suggesting that King Louis might provide Charles II with financial backing so that he could rule without parliament. This correspondence had all been on Coleman's own initiative and both the king and his brother were furious that it should have taken place. Although Oates had not at this stage implicated the Duke of York in a plot, the fact that his wife's secretary was up to nefarious pro-Catholic activities with the French brought the allegations worryingly close to the heart of the court. For Oates it had been a great stroke of luck that the Coleman letters had included some Papist scheming, even if none of it amounted to anything approaching treason.

With London in uproar over the Godfrey murder and the allegations of Oates, parliament returned on 21 October. The opposition Country group had been secretly negotiating with the French Ambassador, Barrillon, about getting financial support from Louis. In fact Buckingham had gone on a clandestine mission to Versailles to see Louis accompanied by John Wildman. It need hardly be said that a flamboyant and extravagant personality like Buckingham could not expect to travel unnoticed, even though he thought he had taken adequate precautions by donning a dark wig and not wearing his Garter star. He was trailed by Williamson's agents but although he had seen Louis, he was offered nothing and so what was potentially seditious activity turned out to be a non-event. On his return, Buckingham seems to have decided to re-establish himself in the king's favour, starting by inviting Louise to stay at his fine new mansion at Cliveden. Before long, Buckingham had returned to Charles's inner circle and, being the excellent mimic he was, had the king in tears of laughter over his impersonation of Lady Danby. When parliament reconvened there had been a cooling off between Buckingham and Shaftesbury because the former was no longer in direct opposition to the king. Nevertheless, Buckingham and Shaftesbury still had in common their hatred of Danby and deep concern that the king's heir was a Papist.

It is unlikely that any members of the Lords or Commons would have been aware that Buckingham and Shaftesbury were drifting apart because the only thing on their minds was the rumours they had heard of the Popish Plot, Coleman's compromising letters, and Godfrey's murder. With wild stories swirling about, members waited in anticipation for the opening addresses of the king and Lord Chancellor to provide a full account of the plot. They were to be disappointed, as only oblique reference was made to it in either speech. If the king was hoping to sweep the preposterous allegations under the carpet, it was not going to happen. The Commons response was to immediately establish a committee for 'the better preservation and safety of his Majesty's person'. The Lords set up their own committee, mainly looking into the Coleman letters. Lord William Russell, the opposition Country faction leader in the Commons, proposed that all Catholics should move themselves to no closer than a twenty-mile radius of London. Charles decided to try to appease the Commons by immediately issuing a proclamation for a twenty-mile restriction. The day before parliament met, the council's Committee of Intelligence had issued a reward of £500 (roughly £733,000 today) for information on Godfrey's murderers to show that the government was taking the plot seriously. Clearly more was needed to show progress was being made in finding the Papist plotters. As a suitable scapegoat was required, and it was discovered that a Catholic banker called William Staley had been overheard, when drunk, saying that he wanted to kill the king; he was arrested, quickly tried with scant evidence and, protesting his innocence, sent for execution. The execution of an unknown banker did not convince the Commons that the judicial process was moving fast enough so it decided to establish another committee to make its own investigation into the Godfrey murder.

Now the whole matter of the Oates's allegations, Coleman and the Godfrey murder were all to be examined in the full glare of the Lords and Commons. The council had lost control of events and there could be no dismissing even the wildest allegations because these would soon become known to the London public and rapidly disseminated by word of mouth, newsletters and pamphlets across the country. On 23 October, Oates began giving evidence at the bar of the House of Commons revelling in his new celebrity. His long and detailed account was received by MPs with something close to awe, and certainly without any challenge or question. Once he had finished his account, the Commons agreed to arrest all the Benedictines in the Savoy. When Oates returned to his next session at the bar of the House he added the new allegation that in the summer, he had seen a number of commissions, signed by the General of the Society of Jesus, bestowing appointments to prominent English Catholics following the murder of the king. Those receiving the commissions were to contribute money towards the cost of arranging the king's assassination and the subsequent uprisings. The most prominent Catholics he named together with their promised appointments were:

Lord Arundell of Wardour (Lord Chancellor)
Earl of Powis (Lord Treasurer)
Sir William Godolphin (Lord Privy Seal)
Viscount Stafford and Edward Coleman (Secretaries of State)
Baron Belasyse (Captain General)
Baron Petre (Lieutenant General)
Sir Francis Radcliffe (Major General)
Sir George Wakeham (Surgeon General)
Richard Langhorn (Adjutant General) [5]

To this list he added the names of numerous members of the Catholic gentry who were to expect reward for supporting the uprising. Once he had finished this all-embracing 'Who's Who' of English Catholics, the Commons immediately directed that the five peers named should be arrested. This was done and before long they were all in the Tower.

Pressing matters of state, such as how to feed the 20,000 strong army still in existence, had to wait as did virtually all other government business. Williamson and his staff were working flat out using Post Office intercept and agents/informants to investigate the ever-expanding allegations. But the allegations continued when Tonge took his place at the bar of the Commons and gave evidence that Papists had started the Fire of London, and that they were planning another Gunpowder Plot. Members had got so carried away with Oates's revelations that they were even receptive to the ravings of the unhinged Tonge and took action accordingly. The cellars of parliament were searched without success, but gunpowder was found in a nearby street causing great alarm until it was discovered that it belonged to the king's firework maker. A regiment of the London militia was mobilised and given the task of checking all funeral processions to ensure coffins were not concealing weapons. Christopher Wren was given the task of improving the security of the Palace of Whitehall and his priority task was the bricking up of entrances rather than rebuilding London.

If parliament was getting the whole situation out of proportion, that was nothing compared with the London public. Many took to arming themselves against the expected Papist attack, and preparing defences such as erecting chains across streets. When Godfrey was buried on the last day of October, his funeral procession was vast and included seventy-two clergymen. On the evening of the funeral the Commons read some of the more incriminating of the Coleman papers and resolved: 'That this House is of opinion that there hath been and still is a damnable and hellish plot contrived and carried out by the Popish recusants for the assassinating and murdering the King, and for subverting the government, and rooting out and destroying the Protestant religion.' [6] The existence of the Popish Plot was now officially recognised by the House of Commons. Anyone left to cast doubts on the validity of the accusations against Catholics ran the risk of being branded a Papist sympathiser.

For Shaftesbury and the Country faction in parliament, the revelations of Tonge and Oates, and the indiscreet letters of Coleman, had been a godsend in their campaign to stop James from inheriting the throne. Shaftesbury certainly did not invent the Popish Plot and probably did not even believe it, but he played it for all it was worth. With the population gripped by fears of a Papist uprising, Shaftesbury introduced a motion that the Duke of York should be removed from the king. This was quickly passed and Charles had little option but to announce that his brother would no longer attend the Privy Council. In order to reaffirm his Protestant credentials the king issued a proclamation that all Catholics should return to their homes and not travel further than five miles from there, on pain of the total confiscation of their property. None of this was enough to reduce the anti-Catholic hysteria, especially as it was occurring around the highly emotive period of 5 November. Just when it looked as though the situation could not get worse for the court faction, it did so.

For about a year prior to Oates's fictitious Popish Plot, there had been little subversive activity in the three kingdoms and so the many informants who had been gaining their living from reporting suspected sedition found themselves unemployed. The Popish Plot gave them an opportunity to report the slightest apparently-suspicious activity of any Catholic, or to merely make up credible stories in exchange for payment. There was also the attractive carrot of the huge reward that had been offered for information about Godfrey's murder. Williamson and his staff were not just inundated with reports from their own agents and informants, but also from others who had seen the success of Oates and decided to join the band of informants. Indeed, Oates was doing very nicely. He had been given lodgings in Whitehall and his own armed guard, as well as funding to support the lifestyle of someone who was being hailed a national hero. It was no surprise that others wanted to jump on the same bandwagon. The most prominent of these was a 28-year-old conman called William Bedloe.

Bedloe, who sometimes went under the names of Captain Williams or Lord Gerard or Lord Cornwallis, had been gaoled for fraud but was now free.[7] He wrote to secretary of state Coventry from Bristol to say that he had important information about the murder of Godfrey. Despite Bedloe's criminal background, such was the thoroughness of Williamson and Coventry's investigation into the plot that they paid for him to travel to London. Two days after the many well attended burnings of effigies of the Pope rather than Guy Fawkes on Bonfire Night, Bedloe came in front of the council and then appeared before first the Lords and then the Commons. His story was that he had converted to Catholicism two years earlier and Jesuits who he had come to know were responsible for the murder of Godfrey. He named the Jesuits as Berry, Green and Hill and said that their motive was to steal Oates's deposition papers and the mastermind behind the murder was Baron Belasyse. Bedloe explained that his criminal background gave him an advantage as it was because of that that the Jesuits had offered him £400 to help kill Godfrey. According to his story the Jesuits went ahead and carried out the murder themselves but, following a chance meeting with Bedloe on 14 October, they invited him along that night to see the body in the queen's residence, Somerset House. Also present near the body was Samuel Atkins, the secretary to Samuel Pepys, and another unidentified person. Godfrey's body was removed by sedan chair, then run through and thrown in to the ditch on Primrose Hill to make it look like a robbery.

Bedloe's tale became more and more complicated when he explained that he had acted as a Jesuit messenger during the previous winter and, when visiting Douai in Northern France, had heard about a plot to assassinate the king at Newmarket, followed by a Catholic uprising. The plan was not only to kill the king, but also Shaftesbury, Ormonde, Monmouth, and Buckingham, then to seize the arsenal at Hull in order to equip 10,000 men from Flanders, who would land at Bridlington. There would be a rising in the west led by Lords Powis and Petre, 20 to 30,000 Spanish would land at Milford Haven and Lord Stafford, together with Coleman, would raise 40,000 troops in the Home Counties. Bedloe ended by saying that the plot was all ready to be implemented, but had been thwarted by Oates's revelations. Bedloe's whole story was farfetched in the extreme, in fact Charles burst out laughing when he first heard Baron Belasyse was named as a rebel leader as he knew that the 62-year-old had severe gout and could barely get out of bed. Bedloe's story was no laughing matter to parliament, who immediately ordered the arrest of those named.

Among those arrested was Pepy's Secretary Samuel Atkins. It was soon established that he was nowhere near Somerset House on 14 October as alleged by Bedloe, but on a yacht at Greenwich. Despite Bedloe's implausible account and complete unreliability as a witness, his statement was implicitly believed by virtually the whole Lords and Commons and he was granted the £500 reward for exposing the perpetrators of Godfrey's murder. By now, the shocking allegations of Oates and Bedloe had swept the country and all sorts of events were being reported that indicated a Catholic uprising was imminent, including numerous reports of mysterious horsemen being seen riding at night in different parts of the country. Few could doubt the existence of the Popish Plot now Bedloe had corroborated Oates's deposition. This corroboration was also significant because two witnesses were required to prove an indictment of treason and so the many Catholics who had been named as conspirators could now progress to trial.

On 23 November, Coleman was arraigned for high treason and four days later appeared before Lord Chief Justice Scroggs, a judge who was totally convinced of the existence of the Popish Plot. The only true facts about Coleman was that he had written to the French court about furthering Catholicism in England and although this correspondence was indiscreet, it was in no way treasonous. The evidence fabricated by both Oates and Bedloe for the trial would soon change that. This can be summarised thus: Oates and Bedloe had seen treasonous correspondence from Coleman to the Rector of St Omer which consisted of a sealed envelope to Father La Chaise, containing information about £10,000 to arrange for hit men to kill the king or, alternatively, pay the queen's physician, Sir George Wakeham, to poison the king. Although Bedloe's evidence was muddled and contradictory, it was sufficient for Coleman's conviction. Coleman had had everything stacked against him. He had not been allowed a defending counsel or information on the prosecution charges or witnesses against him, could not subpoena witnesses for his defence, and had the hearsay evidence of the likes of Oates and Bedloe accepted by the court. Naturally, Coleman was shattered at being sentenced to the excruciating death of a traitor, but was able to draw comfort from the belief that he would be reprieved. He was innocent, his former employer the Duke of York knew he was innocent and the king would know he was innocent, so a reprieve was assured. It was only on 3 December, when he was bundled into the sledge to be dragged through the streets on his way to public dismembering at Tyburn, that he realised that he had been over-optimistic. The royal brothers knew him to be innocent of treason, but his letters had made him guilty of causing embarrassment to the Crown, and that could not be forgiven.

Chapter 13

Anti-Papist Hysteria
1679

The very cabinet of Hell has been opened
Roger North 1668

In the autumn of 1678, Parliament's rigorous investigation of the Popish Plot led them into examining many other matters related to Catholics. They unearthed the fact that army commissions had recently been issued to Catholic officers, and that the person signing the commissions was none other than the secretary of state for the North, Sir Joseph Williamson. Williamson was arrested on parliament's orders and sent to the Tower on 18 November. This was a coup for Salisbury and the Country faction as it enabled them to strike at the heart of the government they so disliked. The day after Williamson's arrest the king told parliament that the Catholic officers concerned had been withdrawn from service with France and were quite legitimately being re-commissioned into a new regiment in Ireland. Williamson was released on the king's orders but the experience had destroyed his confidence. It was clear that the Country faction in parliament had him in their sights and there was no telling where the hysteria of the Popish Plot might lead. He might be falsely accused of being in league with the Papists and be returned to the Tower or suffer a worse fate. Although Williamson was the government spokesman in the Commons, his brief spell in the Tower had made him so insecure that he did not dare take his seat in the chamber. The king and his ministers were completely on the back-foot.

With Bedloe's evidence that Godfrey's body had been seen at the queen's palace, and the Duchess of York's secretary convicted of treason, accusations were getting uncomfortably close to the royal family. Charles felt that the answer was more appeasement. He suggested that there might be a constitutional way of limiting the power of any future Catholic sovereign and

165

agreed to a second Test Act. The Act meant that virtually all Catholics had to leave, which meant that people like the queen's secretary and Master of Horse were dismissed, as were two French servants of the Duchess of Mazarin and five of Louise, Duchess of Portsmouth. Ambassadors were only permitted to retain four priests and Englishmen were debarred from attending the chapels of Catholic embassies. All other Catholic priests and all Jesuits were to be arrested. The Act required all MPs and members of the Lords to make a declaration against Catholic beliefs, such as transubstantiation, before they could take their seats, thus debarring them from parliament (this remained law until 1829). Despite these draconian measures the fears of Catholicism persisted with rumours of uprisings in several areas. In fact the whole country was put into great alarm when the unfounded rumour spread that the French had landed an invasion force on the Isle of Purbeck. All the time new accusations by the likes of Oates and Bedloe were being made to add fuel to the anti-Catholic hysteria.

The rewards given to Oates and Bedloe for revealing the alleged plot naturally led to numerous would-be informants coming forward to try their luck at fabricating accusations. Williamson and his intelligence staff had, of course, spent years encouraging informants, now they reaped the negative side of their efforts. It would be tedious to recount the many new informants on the plot, but two in particular stood out. These were Miles Prance and Stephen Dugdale who, rather to the annoyance of Oates and Bedloe, began to steal their thunder. Dugdale was different from Oates and Bedloe in that he was a minor member of the gentry. Although an opportunist rogue, jumping on the plot's bandwagon, his concocted evidence carried added validity coming from an apparent gentleman. Prance was a strange case of someone who was falsely named as one of the plotters and had to concoct allegations to save his neck.

Stephen Dugdale was a Catholic who had been steward to Lord Aston, a Catholic landowner in Staffordshire. The cost of Dugdale's debauched lifestyle and gambling debts had led him into stealing from his employer and once this was discovered he had been dismissed and sent to prison for debt. In order to extricate himself, Dugdale made it known that he had important evidence about the Popish Plot and before long appeared before the Privy Council. He came over well to the council and corroborated much of the evidence already given by Oates. To this, he added a Staffordshire sub-plot of his own invention in which he claimed that two months earlier, Viscount Stafford had offered him £500 to assassinate the king and also that he had been told of various Catholic Staffordshire gentry who would rise up once the king was killed. As a result of Dugdale's story, Viscount Stafford was arrested together with the named Staffordshire Catholics. Thereafter, Dugdale became a full time government agent, providing more concocted reports and giving evidence at trials as necessary. He joined Oates and Bedloe as popular heroes receiving many gifts and £475 pay in his first year alone as a government agent.[1] Quite a turnaround in fortunes for someone who had so recently been exposed as a thief and in a debtor's prison.

Miles Prance, the other late arrival as an exposer of the plot, took a more circuitous route to becoming a prominent denouncer of supposed Catholic conspirators. Prance was a Catholic silversmith who had once been employed as one of the queen's servants. He had first come to official notice when his lodger informed the authorities that he had been suspiciously unaccounted for on the supposed date of Godfrey's murder.[2] As the lodger owed Prance a lot of unpaid rent, this just might have been the motive for the denunciation. Be that as it may, Bedloe latched onto this malicious accusation and said that he now remembered seeing Prance at Somerset House standing close to Godfrey's body. This was sufficient to have a terrified Prance imprisoned in Newgate's notorious Little Ease cell, without heating in the depths of a particularly severe winter, and threatened with the rack. Under duress he broke but then recanted, was then broken again, and finally confessed that two Irish priests called Fitzgerald and Kelly had told him of a plot to kill Godfrey. He said that the murder was carried out by two workmen, Henry Berry and Robert Green, along with the queen's Chaplain Thomas Godden, and his servant Lawence Hill, who was responsible for the actual strangulation while Prance stood lookout. When Prance's accusations became known, Godden managed to escape but Green, Berry and Hill were all arrested and sentenced to death by Chief Justice Scroggs early the next year (1679). Prance was later to admit that he had invented the whole story but it served him well because it saved his life and even resulted in him being granted a reward. Prance became an accepted witness against Papist conspirators, having joined the ranks of Oates, Bedloe, and Dugdale and, like them, would provide testimony to bring more innocent people to their deaths.

The king and his court faction were at loggerheads with the Country faction of parliament. Charles was calling for money to pay the troops until the final peace treaties were ratified, while parliament was demanding the immediate disbandment of the army but offering no money to pay it off. Oates and Bedloe now began to overreach themselves with even wilder accusations. They both said they had heard the queen having a meeting with Coleman, and prominent Catholic Lords, including Belasyse and Powis, to discuss the murder of the king. Oates declared 'I do accuse the Queen of conspiring the death of the King,' and called for the queen to be banished from London. This turn of events was received with glee by Shaftesbury because if the queen was seen to have acted as a traitor, she could be disposed of and the king would be free to remarry and produce a Protestant heir. Anyone who knew the queen, as indeed Shaftesbury did, realised that this long-suffering pious lady was deeply in love with her wayward husband and would do nothing to harm him. Nevertheless, it suited Shaftesbury politically to believe in the queen's guilt. He wanted the king to divorce her and produce a Protestant heir with a new queen. Buckingham shared Shaftesbury's political objectives to preserve the Protestant succession, but he would not be party to believing these monstrously unfair allegations against the queen. The divide between the two men grew, with Shaftesbury becoming the dominant figure in the Country faction and Buckingham gradually fading out of opposition leadership.

Things are never so bad for a government that unexpected events can't make them considerably worse. And that is just what was about to happen when Montagu at last became an MP so had the forum to wreak his revenge on Danby for having him removed as ambassador in Paris after his affair with Barbara Cleveland's daughter. Danby, like the rest of the government, was already being severely buffeted by the Country faction. King Louis wanted Danby removed because of his anti-French policies and so his ambassador, Barrillon, gave his full financial backing to Danby in trying to gain support to achieve the Lord Treasurer's downfall. Montagu let Danby know that he held incriminating letters from him and may initially have tried to blackmail him into making him a secretary of state. Danby's response was robust and he had king's messengers sent to Montagu's lodgings to search for and remove all documents. This might have been the end of the matter had not Montagu already put the most important correspondence in a box and given it to a friend for safe keeping. On 22 December, Montagu produced two of Danby's letters in the House, which the Speaker then read out. By far the more incriminating of the two was Danby's letter of 25 March to Louis, written against his judgement at the direction of the king, asking for funding of £300,000 a year for three years to enable Charles to rule without parliament. Publicly, Danby had always been completely anti-French, but it now appeared that he had secretly been in league with the French in the subversion of the English constitution.

It must be said that Danby was generally disliked for his cold, aloof manner, and envied for his power. He had many enemies, and given the frenzied atmosphere of the Popish Plot and judicious bribery of certain MPs by Barrillon, it was no surprise that parliament called for Danby's impeachment. The king knew that Danby had been acting on his orders and decided to save him. This was probably motivated less by sentiment and more by the self-interest in retaining an effective Lord Treasurer. Charles prorogued Parliament on 30 December 1668 and then dissolved it on 24 January 1669, hoping that the first election in eighteen years would result in a more amenable group of MPs. While waiting for the new parliament to be opened in March, the king and Danby were in negotiations with Shaftesbury and the Country faction to try to find a manageable solution to government. Shaftesbury's proposal was that the king should nominate any heir he wished as long as he or she was Protestant, and get rid of both Danby and the Duchess of Portsmouth. In exchange, parliament would vote sufficient money to disband the army in Flanders. Unsurprisingly, neither Danby nor the king saw any merit in the proposal and the court and Country factions appeared to have no common ground on which to build an agreement.

The dissolution of parliament did nothing to quieten public fears about Catholicism and growing concerns that the king wanted to impose a French style arbitrary government. Rumours spread round London that the army in Flanders would be brought back and billeted on the city to enforce obedience. Meanwhile, Williamson was still working flat out to sift through the avalanche of reports and rumours to see which, if any, had substance. On top of this, he and Coventry were very busy contacting the Lords Lieutenant, and all others with local influence, to encourage them to ensure that it was only supporters of the court faction who were elected for the March parliament. The preparation for the impeachment of the great Danby showed Williamson that someone of his more junior status could easily be next. He decided to try to improve his relations with parliament by demonstrating his zeal in investigating the Popish Plot, although he well knew the whole thing was a fabrication. In February he instructed Somerset House to be searched for any incriminating evidence that might point to the queen's involvement in the plot. Naturally nothing was found, but the king was furious that his wife's apartments should have been searched without his permission. The king angrily dismissed Williamson as secretary of state with the words: 'I do not wish to be served by a man who fears anyone more than me'.[3]

It seems madness that, just at this time of government crisis, the king should divest himself of his highly experienced secretary and irreplaceable head of intelligence. However, the truth was that Williamson had lost his nerve and become a lame duck. There was no one of sufficient knowledge and expertise to replace him as head of intelligence, but the espionage and intercept apparatus Williamson had so painstakingly set up would survive. It may have been that Williamson was relieved to have the burdens of office removed. He had married Catherine O'Brien, the widow of Lord Ibrachen, the same month he was dismissed; although Catherine had many debts, she jumped her new husband up the social scale as she was a baroness in her own right, sister of the Duke of Richmond and a distant cousin of the king. Fortunately, Williamson had been careful to make as much money as possible out of his time as secretary and had amassed at least £40,000, not including the £6,000 he received as refund for his payment for the post in the first place. His experience would be called upon in a future reign, but for the present he could enjoy his money and social status from the comfort of his Cobham Hall estate in Kent.[4] Sir Joseph Williamson could congratulate himself on having come a long way from his early years as the orphan of an impoverished Cumberland clergyman.

The post of secretary of state for the North was passed to Robert Spencer, Earl of Sunderland. The handsome and charming Sunderland was a man of considerable talent and political acumen who, although only 38, had already been an army officer and then served as a diplomat in Paris and Madrid. As gentleman of the bedchamber, the king enjoyed his company and may have felt the appointment would be welcomed by parliament because Sunderland was known to be anti-French. Sunderland was an intensely ambitious man with many talents but, although appreciating the value of intelligence, had no interest whatsoever in the painstaking work involved in the management and assessment of intelligence. With Williamson gone and Coventry not interested in making a bid for intelligence management, the king no longer had a de facto head of intelligence. However, the management of intelligence continued under Williamson's secretaries, such as Robert Yard, but the flair, dedication and expertise that had been the hallmark of Williamson's eighteen years of service was gone.

While Danby and the secretaries of state were doing their best to secure a court majority in the forthcoming elections, Shaftesbury and the Country faction were pressing for their candidates. The Popish Plot provided the all-consuming background to the election with Oates, Bedloe and Dugdale providing more evidence and repeatedly perjuring themselves in court with the result that two Jesuits were executed in January, and a few weeks later Berry, Green and Hill were convicted. With the plot uppermost in people's minds, and Shaftesbury pushing the anti-Catholic propaganda for all it was worth, it was no surprise that the Court Party did badly in the election. It was about the time of this election that the Court and Country factions got new nicknames. The court faction began to be called 'Tories' after Irish brigands of that name, and the Country faction were equally insultingly referred to as 'Whigs,' after the Scottish Presbyterian rebels known as 'Whiggamores'. The use of these names is sometimes regarded as the very beginning of the party system.

There is something to be said for these early Whigs having a semblance of a party because of their organisation, but the same cannot yet be said for the Tories. Danby's parliamentary organisation had collapsed. With his own credibility severely damaged by Montagu's revelation of the 25 March letter, and a backlash against the use of patronage for court support, it was no match for the country-wide organisation and effective use of propaganda coming from Whig groups such as the Green Ribbon Club. When the election results were in the Tories had gained thirty seats, while the Whigs had 150.[5] It was clear that the new parliament would be no better for the king than the previous one, and probably much worse. With this in mind, Danby had recommended that the king offered some appeasement by sending the Duke of York out of the country just before parliament met. He went to his nephew and niece in Protestant Holland, but the gesture was rather undermined when he later moved on to stay in the Catholic Spanish Netherlands.

The king wanted to show the new parliament that he would not budge on changing the succession, but that he was prepared to consider any means for preserving the Protestant religion when the Crown passed to his Catholic brother. In the words of the Lord Chancellor: 'If anything else can occur to the Wisdom of Parliament which may further secure the Religion and Liberty against a Popish Successor, without defeating the Right of Succession itself, his Majesty will most readily consent to it.'[6] Parliament was not interested in this proposal and was becoming fixed on ensuring that the Crown passed into Protestant hands. When the House of Commons got down to work it decided that it should interview Oates and Bedloe so that newly elected members could hear their horrendous accusations for themselves. Both perjurers once again gave evidence at great length, and once again the House was completely taken in. Oates' allegations had been ever-widening, and not confined to England. The allegations had led already to the arrest for high treason of Peter Talbot, the completely innocent Archbishop of Dublin who had then died in gaol; and the arrest and imprisonment of the Archbishop of Armagh, Oliver Plunket on the same charge. Oates was now saying that James I had been murdered by Catholics and the Jesuits were responsible for bringing about the Civil War. He even accused the Duke of York of starting the Fire of London. However outlandish his accusations, they were believed because they were made while anti-Papist frenzy was sweeping the country. This extract from an anonymous tract at that time gives the context in which Oates's allegations appeared entirely credible: 'Imagine you see a whole town in a flame ... you behold troops of papists ravishing your wives and daughters, dashing your little children's brains against the walls, plundering your houses and cutting your throats by the name heretick dogs.'[7]

Enthused with anti-Papist zeal, parliament next turned its attention to the unfinished business of the impeachment of Danby for High Treason. It was passed by 179 to 116; so much for Danby's ability to manage parliament.[8] The Commons ordered Danby's arrest but he went into hiding and resigned as Lord Treasurer. The king came to his rescue by pardoning him, but that was not the end of the matter. Buckingham and Shaftesbury may have had their differences, but they were united in their hatred of Danby. They pressed the Lords for Danby to he sent to the Tower and, despite the pardon, parliament overwhelmingly agreed. Danby, who had spent his career supporting Protestantism and the United Province against France was now portrayed in Whig propaganda as a Popishly affected Francophile, who had taken a leading part in the Popish Plot. So disliked had Danby become that he was to spend the next five years imprisoned in the Tower. This might have been sufficient revenge for his opponents but Buckingham, with typical vindictiveness, was one of those who had refused to let Danby out of the Tower to visit his wife when she was thought to be dying. Danby had one thing in common with Buckingham, he could not rest until he had got revenge on his enemies. Although confined to the Tower, Danby would be calculating ways of destroying Buckingham.

The king had lost both his chief minister and experienced secretary of state. Henry Coventry, the secretary of state for the South, remained popular with parliament, but he was a complete believer in the Popish Plot and was becoming increasingly inactive as a result of gout. The new parliament had already turned its attention to the last two prominent minsters, giving the king their unswerving support: Ormonde and Lauderdale. Ormonde had returned to his old post of Lord Lieutenant of Ireland and was attacked by Shaftesbury for being too sympathetic to Catholics, and Lauderdale was attacked for his high-handed actions in Scotland. Shaftesbury even made the point that Lauderdale was reducing Scotland to slavery, after which Popery would follow, whereas England was threatened by Popery which would be followed by slavery. With these formidable attacks on his administration, Charles decided upon a new and conciliatory approach. He created a new Privy

Council of thirty members. It contained strong Royalists such as Lauderdale, but also Whig leaders as well as able young men who were not firmly allied to either Whigs or Tories. Shaftesbury was made Lord President, which carried an income of £4,000 a year and other prominent Whigs joined him, such as the efficient administrator, the Earl of Essex, who was put in charge of the Treasury. Other Whigs of note were Sir Henry Capel, brother of Essex, and Shaftesbury's nephew, George Savile, Viscount Halifax. The bright young men included Sunderland, the new secretary of state, Laurence Hyde, younger son of Clarendon, and Sidney Godolphin, who had been a special envoy to King Louis. Collectively they were known as the 'chits' because of their youth. The new council was a clever move by Charles because he expected he would be better able to control his opponents if they were inside his administration. Also, he believed that Shaftesbury was merely after power and, having received it, would become more compliant. For their part, the chits would help to balance extreme views in council and move members towards compromise. This experiment was excellent in theory, but was to fail in practice.

It was soon clear that Shaftesbury was not to be bought off by position or money. For some time he had been seeing how he could remove MPs who were likely to support the king. One of those he targeted was Samuel Pepys who had owed his promotion in the Naval Office to the Duke of York. Salisbury got Whig MPs to attack Pepys in the Commons and to accuse him of being a Catholic, assisting privateers to attack English shipping and, most serious of all, treacherously passing Naval information to the French Government. The charge of treachery was levied by the highly disreputable 'Colonel' John Scott, who seems to have been paid for his accusations by Buckingham.[9] Pepys was imprisoned in the Tower but was released a month later on bail of £25,000. Friends put up a total of £15,000 but Pepys had to pay £10,000 and sell many of his possessions, including his house. He was obliged to resign as secretary of the Admiralty and found himself homeless, unemployed, and with the treat of trial hanging over him. Such was the misery that ordinary innocent people could find themselves in when the Whigs used the fear of Popery to further their political ends.

Salisbury had more important people in his sights than the likes of Pepys. On 13 May he got one of his supporters, Lord William Russell, to introduce a bill to exclude the Duke of York from inheriting the crown. There had been talk of this in the past, but now it was out in the open and became a full frontal attack on the royal prerogative and the status of hereditary monarchy itself. Charles was an easy-going man in his fiftieth year and could have done without a major political crisis at this stage of his life. In some ways his requirements were fairly simple. He needed the love of Louise and Nell, the company of his many children, particularly Monmouth, a few amusing friends, some tennis and buck-hunting, racing at Newmarket of course, and some quiet time to himself for walking or fishing. The proposal to exclude the Duke of York from succession could be easily resolved in one of two ways. He could divorce his barren queen, re-marry, and produce a legitimate heir, or alternatively, he could sacrifice his brother and nominate a Protestant successor.

Charles knew that, much as Queen Catherine was liked, few would blame him from divorcing someone who had failed in the first duty of a queen. Although Charles must have considered this option at some stage, he was now completely against it. He was fond of Catherine and protective towards her, but most of all he knew he had done her much wrong and could not do the ultimate wrong of divorce against this pious lady. As for sacrificing his brother, Charles was well aware of James's stubborn and unbending nature, which had led him into publicly declaring himself a Catholic when he could have worshipped in secret and avoided the whole problem. For Charles, family was everything, as was defence of his royal prerogative. Despite his brother's many faults, and general unsuitability for the Crown, there was no question that he would allow another to succeed. Charles, who was often inconsistent and opportunistic, was to be completely steadfast in refusing to abandon his wife or his brother. Indeed, the relaxed, pleasure-loving, and indolent monarch was to summon his hidden steely determination to ensure that Catherine and James retained their lawful status as queen and heir presumptive.

In order to counter the Exclusion Bill the king decided to prorogue parliament, and a little later, to dissolve it for a new parliament in October. He knew that this would not stop the Exclusion Bill, but it might buy time to find a compromise solution. Although the Exclusion Bill had been progressing through the Commons, it was negative in nature. It said that the Duke of York should be excluded from succession, but it did not say who should succeed. This was because there was absolutely no consensus among the Whigs over the matter, in fact few had thought that far ahead. Shaftesbury favoured the king remarrying. But if a divorce did not take place, or a new queen failed to provide an heir, what next? There was the Duke of York's two daughters, but Ann was only 13 years old, and her elder sister Mary was married to William of Orange. Although many Whigs admired William's Protestant credentials for standing up to Louis, they knew him to be strong-minded and did not relish the thought of having a determined Dutchman and his cronies running the country. The last option, which few thought of at this stage, was 'The Protestant Duke', Monmouth. Of course Monmouth was illegitimate, but a bastard Protestant might be preferable to a legitimate Catholic as king.

Meanwhile, Scotland was getting out of control. The Covenanters had continued their resentment about being forced by fines and imprisonment to worship by the rites of the Church of England. One of the main people enforcing Anglicanism was James Sharp, the Archbishop of St Andrews and primate of Scotland. Sharp was a former Covenanter who had decided to support the Restoration and had been made Archbishop for his service. In that position, he carried out his pious repression of his former Covenanter brethren. It had been he who had condemned eleven Covenanter prisoners to death following their capture at Rullion Green in 1666 with the words: 'You are pardoned as soldiers but you are not acquitted as subjects.'[10] On 3 May 1679, nine Covenanters had been lying in wait at Magnus Muir outside Aberdeen to attack the coach of the Sheriff of Cupar when they heard that Sharp's was in front of it. This was too good an opportunity to miss. They stopped Sharp's coach, shot the postilion and hacked the Archbishop to pieces with true Covenanter zeal, in front of his blood soaked daughter who was travelling with him. The murder was the spark for a Covenanter uprising. By the end of the month, eighty well-armed horsemen were proclaiming the Covenant and saying that Charles was a usurper. Their numbers grew to 1,500 and they defeated the government dragoons of John Graham of Claverhouse, who had to fall back to Edinburgh while the Covenanter force rose to 8,000 and soon occupied Glasgow. With royal forces in Scotland unable to cope with the rebellion, Charles appointed his son Monmouth as Captain General to lead a force to restore order in his Scottish kingdom.

Monmouth was strikingly good looking and had the charm and approachability of his father. He had also proved himself a brave military leader, but for all his attributes, he was a young man of many flaws. He had been thoroughly spoilt, first by Henrietta Maria and then by the king, which had made him headstrong and impetuous. His licentious conduct mirrored the worst excesses of the times. His privileged quasi-royal position made him feel above the law, which in some ways he was when, for example, he had been pardoned for killing a beadle in a drunken brawl. He had poor judgement, especially when it came to choosing his friends, as they tended to be libertines or adventurers. On the face of it, giving Monmouth the job of subduing Scotland did not look a very promising choice, but this was to be his finest hour. The militia was called out and Monmouth marched to Scotland where he joined forces with Claverhouse. The Covenanters were concentrated near Hamilton and holding Bothwell Bridge across the Clyde. The Covenanters numbered 6,000 but had a divided leadership, were largely untrained, poorly armed and without cannon. Monmouth's force was only 5,000 strong but reasonably well trained, properly armed and had cannon. Under these circumstances it was no surprise that on 22 June, Monmouth's men soon took the bridge and had the Covenanters in flight, killing about 1,000 of them.[11]

Where Monmouth really proved himself was his statesmanlike clemency after the battle. Naturally there were some reprisals. Of those captured, 1,200 were sent to prison in Edinburgh and later transported to the colonies. Torture was used to induce some of the captured to reveal who had been responsible for Sharp's murder. The torture methods used were varied and included the traditional boot, as well as simple ad hoc methods, such as hanging a small boy up by his thumbs, or using a pistol butt to tighten a cord around another suspect's head until it cut through to the skull. When none of the torture techniques provided results, those suspected of withholding information were executed in any case and their rotting bodies were to hang in chains at Magnus Muir for many years to come. However, there were a total of only about sixteen executions after the battle, which was very lenient by Scottish standards of the time. Monmouth then requested the king to authorise a declaration of indulgence, allowing a measure of toleration to Presbyterians. This removed the major grievances that had caused the rebellion and provided the potential for a lasting peace. Monmouth had done well in his short Scottish expedition. Naturally, anyone defeating Scots rebels was bound to be a hero in England and that was the case for Monmouth. His former, youthful peccadillos were forgotten. Monmouth was now regarded as a brave and victorious general who was displaying the best attributes of his royal blood. The 'Protestant Duke' had suddenly become a serious contender for the succession. A fact that was not lost on Shaftesbury.

Chapter 14

The Crisis Deepens
1679–80

'That Plot must be handled as if it were true, whether it were so or not.'

George Savile, Marquis of Halifax

Events in Scotland had not affected the tempo of the anti-Catholicism witch-hunt in England. Three Catholic priests were executed in various parts of the country, but London remained the focus of Protestant vengeance against the imagined plots. The five innocent peers, Powis, Stafford, Arundell, Petre and Belasyse, who had been sent to the Tower following the accusations of Oates and Bedloe, had been arraigned for High Treason but were still prisoners awaiting trial. In June 1679, five Jesuits were brought to trial for the murder of Godfrey on the evidence of Dugdale and Oates. Dugdale appeared in court suffering from venereal disease and very obviously drunk, so did not come across as an ideal witness. Oates saved the day for the prosecution by providing his perjured evidence with his customary confidence, as a result of which all five defendants ended their lives by a traitor's death at Tyburn. The continued Popish Plot hysteria served Shaftesbury and his Whig friends well; and they played it for all it was worth. The king had had enough of this difficult parliament and dissolved it in July but with the end of that parliament came the expiry of the Licensing Act. If Williamson had still been secretary of state, action would probably have been taken to prevent it, but as it was, the demise of the Act went unnoticed at court. It was not unnoticed by Shaftesbury however, who encouraged his Whig followers to exploit this new freedom of the press to the full.

Before the expiry of the Licensing Act, there had been officially authorised anti-Catholic publications, such as when Oates published his bestselling 'A True Narrative of the Horrid and Hellish Popish Plot' in April 1679 but few illegal anti-government pamphlets and handwritten broadsheets.

Now there was a deluge of Whig and anti-Catholic propaganda touching on the succession. Within a month of the Licensing Act expiring, Benjamin Harris had published the first edition of his newspaper *'The Domestic Intelligence*, a little later it was followed by *'True Protestant Mercury'*, and *'Protestant Intelligence'*.[1] This was just the start of an explosion of newspapers, books and pamphlets, the great majority of which were attacking arbitrary royal authority, Catholics and their supposed plots and the Duke of York as successor to the throne. Shaftesbury and Monmouth had become allies and there now began a new theme to Whig propaganda. The completely unfounded rumour was encouraged that the king had secretly married Monmouth's mother, Lucy Walter, which of course made him the true heir. Over the months, this story would be enlarged upon to include supporting details such as that the marriage had been witnessed by the Bishop of London, now conveniently dead, and that the marriage certificate had been placed in a casket which unfortunately no one could locate for the present.

The next major trial of someone implicated in the plot was that of the queen's physician Sir George Wakeman, who had been accused of wanting to poison the king. Oates and Bedloe gave their evidence before Chief Justice Scroggs. Oates was not only a celebrity as the 'saviour of the nation' but also acting like one. He had free lodging in Whitehall State Apartments, received £10 a week from the Committee of Examinations, was accompanied by his bodyguard, and took to wearing a 'silk gown and cassock, great hat, satin hat band and long rose scarf'. People began to think he might be getting above himself.[2] Although Scroggs had been a complete believer in the Popish Plot, the quality of evidence from Oates and Bedloe was so poor that the lawyer in him could not accept it. On 18 July Wakeman was acquitted, together with three Benedictines who were on trial with him. This was the first time that Oates's evidence had been officially challenged and was an indication that the juggernaut of mindless anti-Popery was at last slowing. Unfortunately, it still retained momentum for some time to come. Those who believed in the plot were scandalised by the verdict and blamed Scroggs for pro-Papist injustice. He was fortunate that he received no more reprisals than verbal abuse, vitriolic lampoons, and having a dead dog thrown into his coach. The jury were so scared that they went into hiding and Sir George Wakeman fled to Brussels.

Throughout these difficult times the king was still trying his best to enjoy life. Sport was always important to him and his state of physical fitness even suggested that he could well out-live his brother who was three years his junior and not in such good shape. On 21 August Charles was at Windsor where he played tennis in the morning and went hawking in the afternoon.

In the late afternoon he developed a fever. The unthinkable had occurred; it seemed that the heathy, energetic, 50-year-old king might die. Suddenly the worries about the succession passing to the Duke of York were brought home to everyone. For Shaftesbury this was a fear he would emphasise again and again in the months to come. However, Shaftesbury did not wholly benefit from the situation. The Whigs were divided amongst themselves about the succession, and Essex and Halifax became worried that with the Duke of York out of the country, Shaftesbury might use the king's death to mount a coup to place Monmouth on the throne. They therefore contacted the Duke of York who hastened back from Brussels in disguise. When he arrived on 2 September Charles had almost recovered, was eating well and talking about going to Newmarket. James's trip was not in vain as it had strengthened his position as heir presumptive in the eyes of many and more importantly, enabled Charles to re-emphasise his support. The Duke of York waited a couple of weeks until Charles was fully recovered and then returned to Brussels. In order to put Monmouth in his place, Charles relieved him of the post of Captain General and sent him to the United Provinces where he stayed with his cousins, William and Mary.

The new parliament of October was prorogued until January the next year. By doing this, the king denied the Whigs the opportunity of publicly attacking the government but, of course, this did not prevent the continued onslaught of their propaganda. Charles felt confident enough to allow James back, but still at a distance. The Duke of York was sent to replace Lauderdale in Scotland. Lauderdale was in no way disgraced by his career ending. His health was failing and the next year he was to be incapacitated by a stroke. Although a Catholic, James was well received in Scotland where the presence of a member of the royal family was appreciated. He took up golf and his pretty young Italian wife charmed Edinburgh society. The Covenanters seemed pacified and the duration of his stay was to be a welcome period of peace.

With the king away at Newmarket, Shaftesbury decided, as Lord President, to call the Privy Council to discuss the implications of the Duke of York's appointment in Scotland. Shaftesbury had obviously over-reached himself and was dismissed on 14 October by a furious monarch. Essex, the other prominent Whig in the Council, was removed from the Treasury and the post given to Laurence Hyde. A couple of months later, the remaining Whigs: Cavendish, Russell and Capel resigned from the council. Halifax had felt Shaftesbury had gone too far and remained in the council hoping to find a middle way between the Whig and Tory factions. The experiment of having a Privy Council for national unity had failed. Shaftesbury had followed his own agenda from the beginning and it is only surprising that Charles had let him continue for so long. With the dismissals came another blow from the king: parliament was further prorogued until November 1680.

Shaftesbury and his supporters were now firmly in opposition but without the forum of parliament. Their policy seems to have been to do all possible to inflame anti-Popery and to obtain mass public support for a return of parliament. In November there would be the normal Guy Fawkes Night bonfires but the Whigs were getting the taste for bigger bonfires. Earlier in the year the fervent anti-papist magistrate Sir William Waller had a public bonfire of four wagon-loads of Catholic books and articles he had confiscated. The Whigs decided to also celebrate the 17 November, which was the anniversary of the accession of Queen Elizabeth I. By celebrating the great Protestant queen, the Whigs were drawing comparisons with the present king and his Papist orientated court. What better way to celebrate the blessed memory of Queen Elizabeth than by burning an effigy of the Pope to represent his consignment to Hell. The Pope-burning was organised through the Green Ribbon Club in Chancery Lane on a scale that totally eclipsed normal bonfire nights. The theme selected was of a mock papal coronation ending with the climax of the burning of the Pope's effigy, inside of which were stitched fireworks and live cats to provide Hellish screeching as they caught fire. It was a grand show as Bishop Burnet describes:

> *Over the gate [at Temple Bar] Queen Elizabeth was decked with the Magna Carta and the Protestant religion; there was a devil in the pageant and four boys in surplices under him, six Jesuits, four bishops, four archbishops, two patriarchs of Jerusalem and Constantinople, several cardinals, besides Franciscans, black and grey monks in all habits; there was also a large crucifix, wax candles and a bell and 200 porters.... to carry lights along the show.... and Sir Edmund Godfrey, on horseback with ... behind him one of the murderers.*

The vitriol against Catholics was displayed in the banners in the procession, such as a Jesuit with a bloody sword and the legend 'Our Religion is, Murder, Rapine and Rebellion,' and people dressed as nuns declaring themselves 'The Popes Whores' and 'Courtesans in Ordinary'.[3] The whole show, including wine for the spectators cost the vast sum of almost £2,500 (approximately £370,000 today) and was attended by 100,000 people.[4] Shaftesbury was very skilfully mobilising mass support against the Duke of York's succession.

During this time the intelligencers in the offices of the secretaries of state had remained worked off their feet. They had the thankless task of investigating the numerous fictitious reports of Popish plots. Fortunately, unlike earlier in the reign, there were no real plots against the king, apart from the political skulduggery of Shaftesbury and his followers. Nevertheless, all the informants' reports of plots had to be scrupulously examined in case they might be genuine. Among those working alongside the secretariat was Thomas Blood, although operating independently and sometimes reporting direct to the king. Two cases in which Blood was involved show the difficulty of investigating the accusations being reported. The first concerned a Catholic Irishman called James Netterville, who had once been one of Danby's informers. He had become involved in a Catholic-sponsored scheme to turn the tables on the Whigs and discredit them by proving that they had invented the Popish Plot. Netterville had been sent to the Marshalsea for debt and while there had become acquainted with a fellow Irishman called Captain Bury. Netterville offered Bury £400 to help create evidence that the Popish Plot had been concocted by the Whigs and Bedloe. Bury managed to report this to Blood, who told him to pretend to go along with Netterville and find out who was behind the plot. Once Bury had won Netterville's confidence, he found out who was supplying money for the plan. Bury was able to report to Blood that the money was being offered by a man called Russell, who was a servant of the French ambassador, Barrillion.[5] Not much could be done about that, but it showed that it was not just Whigs and opportunist informants who were coming up with bogus plots.

At about this time there was the report of another plot of this type in which Shaftesbury, Buckingham and Monmouth were planning an uprising, and Thomas Blood was to be one of their Major Generals. This was reported by Thomas Dangerfield, who had decided to take up the lucrative business of Oates and Bedloe, but with a pro-Catholic twist. Dangerfield was a conman and seasoned criminal who had already spent time in various prisons for theft and counterfeiting coins. He had managed to contact the Duke of York, who paid him to find out more about the plot then passed him on to Secretary of State Coventry. Dangerfield's complete unreliability was soon discovered by Coventry and his story was dismissed. Undaunted, Dangerfield changed his whole story to make it one in which the Catholics wanted to spread untrue allegations of a Whig uprising but were, at the same time, planning to kill the king. Dangerfield told his new story to a former MP, Thomas Curtis, who mentioned it to the barmaid of the Heaven Tavern in Old Palace Yard. Fortunately, the barmaid was one of Blood's informants and reported it to him, who in turn reported it to the king.

Dangerfield was trying to obtain credibility for his stories so managed to bluff his way into the house of Buckingham's Steward, Colonel Mansell. Once inside he planted incriminating documents, which he had forged, behind the Colonel's bedstead. Dangerfield then informed customs officers that smuggled goods were being hidden in Mansell's house. He accompanied them for their search of the house and, when they had found nothing, 'discovered' the hidden papers with the cry 'Here is treason!' This might have given Dangerfield the credibility he wanted had it not been that Mansell brought his case to the Privy Council. Once Dangerfied was in front of the Privy Council, he found it prudent to change his story again. The story he now spun was that a well-known Catholic midwife called Elizabeth Cellier, and Lady Powis – whose husband was one of the Catholic lords in the Tower – had arranged for him to be released from prison. Their price had been that he would murder the king and Shaftesbury, and also falsely accuse the Whigs of plotting against the Crown. By way of proof, Dangerfied said that documents denouncing the Whigs could be found in a meal tub at the home of Elizabeth Cellier. The house was searched, the documents discovered, and Cellier and Lady Powis arrested and charged with treason. The truth of the matter was that Cellier and Lady Powis had been concerned with the plight of prisoners and befriended Dangerfield when he was in gaol – posing to them as a Catholic. They had later discovered that he was entirely untrustworthy and dropped him. It seems his revenge for their loss of support was to denounce them and then hide an incriminating document he had forged in Cellier's house.

It is difficult, with this distance of time, to know whether there was any truth at all in what became named the 'Meal Tub Plot'. It was equally difficult for those responsible for investigating the case. Given that Lady Powis's husband had been falsely imprisoned in the Tower for involvement in the Popish Plot, she may have decided to help him by trying to fabricate evidence that the plot was a Whig conspiracy. We shall never know for sure but Elizabeth Cellier was to remain in gaol until tried in June the next year when she and Lady Powis were acquitted on lack of reliable evidence. Dangerfield's revelations turned him into another star witness to join the growing number of Oates, Bedloe and the like, who Shaftesbury could call upon to give perjured evidence in the future trials of Catholics.

In late November, Monmouth returned to England without his father's permission and was greeted in London with bonfires and bell ringing. This was almost certainly on the advice of Shaftesbury with the intention of placing pressure on the king over the succession. Up to this time Monmouth may have had his dreams about being made a royal heir but he had been completely loyal to the king. Now he had returned in open defiance of his father. The excuse Monmouth made for his return was to defend himself against the allegations of the Meal Tub Plot. This did not wash with the king. Much as Charles loved his son he was furious about this open disobedience. Nell Gwynn, who was fond of Monmouth as a friend and fellow Protestant, pleaded for him to the king, but to no avail. Monmouth was dismissed as Master of Horse, stripped of his remaining appointments and ordered to immediately return abroad. Monmouth refused, took up residence in the Cockpit and built even stronger ties with Shaftesbury. To Shaftesbury, Monmouth was a puppet who he intended to manipulate in order to achieve an alternative route to power.

Shaftesbury and his followers needed a parliament in order to proceed with the Exclusions Bill but the king had prorogued it until November 1680 The Whigs therefore began raising public petitions to the king to recall parliament. This was done on an unprecedented scale. The Whigs were not a party as such, but a group with members having differing, and often changing, objectives. What united them was strong anti-Catholicism and a fear that if the Duke of York became king, the country would return to the Protestant persecutions of Mary Tudor, coupled with the arbitrary government of Louis XIV. Although Shaftesbury was a prime mover of the Whigs, there was no leader as such. They were organised around clubs based in taverns; there were about twenty such clubs in London alone such as the Swan in Fish Street and the Angel at the Old Exchange, which was used by Shaftesbury and his supporters, and the Salutation Tavern in Lombard Street, used by supporters of Buckingham. There were similar clubs in towns around the country, for example, the Presbyterian dominated Green Ribbon Club at the King's Head in Chancery Lane had sister clubs at taverns in Oxford, Taunton and Bristol.[6] Good courier communications were established between the clubs to facilitate the distribution of Whig propaganda and to co-ordinate activity. Shaftesbury's main activity as the year ended was organising petitions for the recall of parliament.

Early in 1680, Shaftesbury visited the king in secret and offered to call off the petitions if Charles would divorce the queen and marry a Protestant. Naturally Charles refused. A few days later Shaftesbury demonstrated his formidable ability to organise opposition by presenting the king with a 300ft long roll containing well over 16,000 signatures asking for parliament to sit.[7] Far from changing the king's mind, Charles regarded the petition as impudent in the extreme. His annoyance would increase as further Whig-sponsored petitions were presented from different parts of the country. Charles responded by dismissing some of the judges and JPs who had been instrumental in organising the petitions. Although this must have given him some personal satisfaction, it did nothing to stop the tide of popular support for parliament's return.

Meanwhile, Charles was still trying to persuade his wayward son to return abroad. After repeated requests, Monmouth sent word that he would only go abroad if the king would also banish Lauderdale, Sunderland and Louise, Duchess of Portsmouth. This so annoyed Charles that he decided to recall the Duke of York from Scotland. James duly returned, but remained Commissioner for Scotland. Charles still tried to reach out to Monmouth by saying that if he asked for pardon and promised to live well with the Duke of York, he would be restored to his appointments. Monmouth again spurned his father's overtures by replying that he would submit to the king but not to York or Portsmouth. Monmouth was now completely under Salisbury's influence and being egged-on by Sir Thomas Armstrong. Monmouth had complete trust in Armstrong after the two of them had served together, first with the Dutch and then in Scotland. Unfortunately, Armstrong was an ambitious, impetuous soldier who had killed a man with his sword in a London theatre and was highly unsuitable as an adviser. Any reconciliation with the king was becoming ever more unlikely.

Charles was not only wrapped up in the exclusion crisis and his soured relationship with his son, but with the ever-present problem of lack of money. Although Sunderland had been hoping to make a defence agreement with the United Provinces to boost the government's Protestant credentials, the king was getting him to negotiate money from Louis for not calling parliament. The negotiations were being done through Barrillon, who was dragging his feet and seemed to be getting nowhere. Shaftesbury also felt he was getting nowhere after all the effort of organising the petitions for the recall of parliament. He was now becoming more desperate and prepared to use any means to obtain his objectives. He waited until the king was at Newmarket and then appeared before the Privy Council on 24 March 1680 to tell them about a plot that had been reported to him of a Catholic revolt in Ireland, which would be supported by the French. This was, of course, a complete fabrication, but the story served two purposes. First, it kept alive the threat of a Popish Plot and second, it was an opportunity to attack his and Buckingham's old enemy, Ormonde the Lord Lieutenant. Shaftesbury's source for this Irish plot was an ex-Franciscan Friar called John Fitzgerald. Fitzgerald had gone to London having heard that Shaftesbury would pay for any information confirming the plot. Shaftesbury had heard his fabricated story and encouraged him to widen it to include the Duke of York and Ormonde. Fitzgerald obliged and, having concocted a plot that was suitably damaging to York and Ormonde, was sent to Ireland to recruit persons prepared to provide suitable perjured evidence.

In May, Shaftesbury's motley crew of bog Irish witnesses, some without shoes, arrived in London and began giving evidence. It soon became clear from their confused, contradictory and inarticulate statements that they could not be trusted and their evidence was dismissed. This did not stop many people still believing that a planned Catholic uprising in Ireland was true. Also, despite the king publicly announcing in the *London Gazette* that he had never been married to Monmouth's mother, the rumour would not go away. Indeed the belief in Monmouth's legitimacy continued to grow, helped by the invention of new 'evidence' such as the involvement of the Bishop of Durham in the wedding, and the black box containing the marriage certificate that was to be opened only on the king's death.

The king had been briefly ill again in May. Shaftesbury told Monmouth that Armstrong and Lords Grey and Russell were making preparations to have an uprising in the city if the king died and declare for a free parliament to decide the succession. As Charles swiftly recovered nothing came of this plan, but the fact that it could be considered showed that political opposition to the Crown was moving towards sedition and even outright treason.

At this time the king had no dominant minister. His government was mainly in the hands of Sidney Godolphin, Laurence Hyde and Sunderland, the secretary of state for the North. In February the honest and reliable Henry Coventry, secretary of state for the South, retired. He was 61 and was suffering from that great affliction of the time – gout. Sunderland was moved to replace him, leaving his own secretaryship for the more senior one of the South. Sunderland sold his old post for £6,500 to a new figure, Sir Leoline Jenkins. Jenkins had been Principal of Jesus College Oxford and then made a judge in the Admiralty Division where Pepy's wrote about his ability and integrity. Jenkins was a rather dour 55-year-old Welshman, whose sombre clothes and character must have made him almost invisible alongside the likes of the charming and extravagant Sunderland who adorned the colourful Restoration court. On the other hand, Jenkins was an intelligent, loyal, hardworking, safe pair of hands. In time he would channel his hard working and thorough approach to intelligence matters. Joseph Williamson had been de facto head of intelligence and Coventry had dutifully provided some coverage of this after Williamson's dismissal, but had done little in the way of intelligence management. Sunderland was interested in high politics and not at all in the mundane activity of intelligence management and so Jenkins was able to fill the gap. It would be foolish to suggest that Jenkins would become an intelligencer of the stature of Williamson, but he was to take intelligence management seriously and provide the focal point which had been lacking since Williamson's departure.

In April Shaftesbury tried another tactic, more to be irritating than with any hope of success. He got the Middlesex Grand Jury to consider trying the Duke of York for being a Popish recusant and Louise, Duchess of Portsmouth, for being a common whore. The trial failed, but had it gone ahead and achieved convictions, the Duke of York would have merely been fined whereas Louise would have been branded as a whore and placed in the stocks. For the highly sensitive Louise, proud of being from an ancient noble family and a duchess in her own right, the thought of this outcome would have be her worst nightmare. Fortunately, Lord Chief Justice Scroggs came to the rescue and dismissed the case, but in doing so made an enemy of Shaftesbury. Louise had been severely shaken by the whole event. She detested Shaftesbury, but she now also feared him and began to wonder if there was a way to stop him attacking her in the future. She also took the precaution of transferring large sums of her money to France, just in case she might have to make a quick exit from England.

Shaftesbury decided to burnish Monmouth's credibility as a successor by getting him to carry out a journey of stately progress throughout the West Country. Monmouth had the coat of arms on his carriage altered to remove the heraldic silver baton sinister of illegitimacy. The progress was a resounding success with the 'Protestant Duke' receiving a warm welcome wherever he went and crowds turning out in the thousands. Although probably an exaggeration, it was said that when Monmouth arrived in Exeter the crowd was estimated as 10,000 on foot and 1,500 on horseback.[8] Monmouth's immediate entourage were also encouraging those who met him to use the title 'Your Highness'. Not something that he ever corrected. To top it all, Monmouth began touching sufferers of scrofula to provide the regal cure for 'the king's sickness'. The king had occasionally carried out the ceremony of touching sufferers of the king's sickness at the Banqueting House, Whitehall. These events had been staged to emphasise Charles's God given royal status. For Monmouth to assume royal healing powers was quite intolerable. In order to distract from Monmouth's growing popularity, the king decided to remove one of the grievances against his government. He issued a proclamation that parliament would be brought forward to October. It had taken a long time, but Shaftesbury now found things moving his way.

Chapter 15

The Whigs Begin to Mobilise
1680

'Of these false Achitophel (Shaftesbury) was first,
A name to all succeeding ages cursed.'
John Dryden *Absolom and Achitophel*

Buckingham had never liked the Duke of York and certainly did not relish the idea of a Popish king succeeding Charles. On the other hand, he did not like Monmouth and knew that there was no doubt that he was a bastard and was just being manipulated for Shaftesbury's own ends. However, Buckingham had been distracted from politics by an issue that was to be the talk of London and beyond for many months to come. He was accused of buggery. Under the Buggery Act of 1533, the act of buggery was a capital offence. Given Buckingham's well-known record of debauchery, a jury might well be prepared to believe that the allegations were true. If found guilty, the penalty was the total confiscation of property as well as death. Given the hot and cold relationship Buckingham had with the king there could be no guarantee of a pardon. The situation was very dangerous. The question was, who put him in that danger? Buckingham had so many enemies, such as Ormonde and his son Lord Ossory, that there was a large field of suspects. Of these, the most likely was Danby, whose confinement in the Tower gave him ample time to plot his revenge on the man who had helped to put him there.

It is improbable that the truth of how the allegations occurred will ever be known for certain as the whole case is obscured by the fog of secrecy and deception that accompanied the activities of the London underworld at that time. The complex story appears to be as follows. Edward Christian had been one of Buckingham's stewards but had been dismissed for theft. Christian then later went to work for Danby. It appears that Danby may have used

187

Christian to provide evidence against Buckingham on two cases of buggery. The first was the allegation that he had buggered a London woman called Sarah Harwood, who had subsequently been sent to France in order to prevent her reporting it. The second allegation was that of a certain Philip Le Mar; his mother, Frances, would state that Buckingham had sodomised Philip six years previously. There was a story at the time that Lady Danby had offered Philip Le Mar £300 if he would testify to this in court, but that was never proved. Having been given the job of bringing Buckingham to court, Christian now needed some help. It seems that the person he turned to was Thomas Blood. The day job of Blood was as a government intelligence employee but he was also a 'gun for hire'. He made himself available to anyone who would pay enough to carry out a seedy operation which could not be linked back to the employer. We know next to nothing of these operations because they were, by their nature, secret but it is certain that Blood undertook such tasks for a number of important people, including the Duke of York. Blood had done such unconventional work for Buckingham in the past, but it may have been that the two later fell out for reasons unknown. As Danby had been the senior member of government employing Blood, it would be no surprise if he had selected Blood to assist Christian in bribing witnesses against Buckingham.

As well as the Le Mars, two other people had been identified to give perjured evidence against Buckingham. They were Samuel Ryther and Philemon Codden, both Irishmen. It seems Blood was to be the go-between for these two and Christian, and he met them at the St John's Head in Old Palace Yard, where they told him that Buckingham owed them both money and they would be prepared to accuse him of buggery in revenge – and for the right money. The idea was that Ryther would swear that Sarah Harwood had told him of Buckingham's buggery and that this would be corroborated by Codden. For some reason, Ryther began to have cold feet and decided to back out of the arrangement. Blood then got an associate, Thomas Curtis, who had been involved in the Meal Tub Plot, to try to persuade Ryther to change his mind for a larger bribe. The situation then turned on its head when Codden and Ryther decided to go and see Buckingham's lawyer, Mr Whitacker, and tell him about the plot. There can be little doubt that money changed hands at this point because Codden and Ryther were suddenly walking around with new suits, swords and periwigs. Whitacker then reported the matter to the magistrate Sir William Waller, an old enemy of Blood.

On 20 January 1680, Blood was asked to meet the magistrate in a tavern. Although Blood and Waller disliked each other intensely, Blood decided to go. When he arrived he found Waller in the company of Codden, Ryther and Whitacker. After a few glasses of wine, Waller suddenly accused Blood of attempting to suborn witnesses against Buckingham. Blood denied all allegations, saying that he knew nothing of the buggery accusation, was, in any case, a friend of Buckingham and clearly being framed.[1] Waller replied that he was satisfied with Codden and Ryther's story and told Blood to find bail. A few days later, Blood was arrested and taken to the Gatehouse Prison. Blood soon found himself on trial before a jury of the king's Bench Bar with Waller presiding. Blood's co-defendants were Christian, Curtis and La Mar, and a few others supposedly involved in the plot against Buckingham. At the trial, Blood denied everything and put up a stout defence providing, for example, witnesses who stated he was never present at the times and locations he was accused of suborning Codden and Ryther. The information Blood gave in his defence may have been entirely true, but it has to be said that he was not noted for scrupulous veracity. Naturally, Buckingham denied the accusations against him and did so in his usual urbane manner with the words: 'God knows I have much to answer for with the plain way but I am not so great a virtuoso in my lusts.'[2] With Waller presiding, the result of the trial was a forgone conclusion. The jury found Blood, Christian and Curtis guilty of blasphemy, confederacy and subornation, and all were fined and imprisoned. Le Mar had died under mysterious circumstance before giving evidence but his mother was placed in the pillory where she was harshly treated.

As if Blood's sentence was not bad enough, he then faced a charge of defamation by a vengeful Buckingham. The case was won by Buckingham and the duke was awarded £10,000 damages. This was a huge sum of money (approximately £1,467,000 today) which it would be completely impossible for Blood to pay. Blood remained in gaol, desperately trying to get someone to stand him bail so that he could contest the findings of the defamation suit. He tried many powerful people such as the Duke of York and Secretary Jenkins but to no avail; the months rolled on and he became weakened by fever. Clearly, no-one wanted to incur Buckingham's wrath by being seen to help the man who had attempted to destroy him. Then in June, the money for Blood's bail appeared anonymously, quite possibly from the Secret Intelligence Fund. For Blood it came too late. He was 62, his health had deteriorated badly in prison and his spirit had been crushed by the enormous fine hanging over him. On returning home his illness grew worse and he died on 24 August 1680.

Blood's body was buried the day after his death, but such was his notoriety that many believed that his death was a pretence to allow him to escape his debts and start a new life. This belief became so widely held that his body was disinterred by the coroner, attended by a number of people who had known him. The body was so decomposed by this stage that Blood could not be identified with any certainty, although one person thought that they recognised his thumb, which had always been very large. The coroner concluded that the body was very probably that of Blood, but there was sufficient doubt among the credulous that rumours of him being alive continued for some time.[3]

The death of Blood came at an unfortunate time for Jenkins and his intelligencers. The Whigs consisted of many types of people, from aristocrats to artisans, but they all shared deep concern about the king being succeeded by his Catholic brother. The fear and hatred of the Church of Rome made many feel that Protestants of all types should unite against the common enemy of Popery. For some time, Buckingham and Shaftesbury had been advocating toleration for Nonconformists, now this was extended to actively supporting them. Whig sheriffs in London began ignoring the penal laws against un-licensed preaching and conventicles. It was no surprise that the Whig ranks contained a large proportion of Nonconformists of all types from Presbyterians, to Baptists to Independents such as Congregationalists. Blood himself had been a Nonconformist who had spent most of his life either plotting with them, or working amongst them in the king's service. With sections of the Whigs becoming increasingly militant, Blood's detailed knowledge of their activities would be greatly missed.

Through their clubs and associated taverns and coffee houses, the Whigs were continuing to gain support. Their propaganda reached everywhere and there was little the government could do to stop it. In December the previous year, proclamations had been issued against seditious books and pamphlets and tumultuous petitions, then in May, for the suppression and printing and publishing of unlicensed books.[4] These had little effect and there were very few convictions. When the publisher Benjamin Harris was convicted and placed in the pillory, his supporters prevented anything from being thrown at him. The Whigs were also attracting good writers who were developing the old themes of fear of Popery and exclusion of the Duke of York into a doctrine that would be even more dangerous for the Crown.

One of these authors was Thomas Hunt, who had been one of Buckingham's many former Stewards. Probably his most influential document had the catchy title of '*Great and Weighty Considerations Relating to the Duke of York or Succession of the Crown....Considered.*' In this he disputed the divine appointment of kings, the unalterable succession and the obligation of subjects to obey their sovereign in all things. This was completely contrary to the prevailing beliefs of the day supported by the Church and all true Royalists. The Royalist writer, Sir Robert Filmer, had proclaimed the Royalist belief in the divine right of kings by providing a succinct and persuasive case based on indisputable biblical evidence. Filmer pointed out that God had made Adam monarch of the earth and, by primogeniture, Adam's descendants had inherited this divinely bestowed power. Absolute monarchy and primogeniture had been established by God himself and should be the model followed by all true Christians. Although many were convinced by this compelling argument, Hunt was not one of them. In '*Great and Weighty*', Hunt said that Filmer was spouting Popish ideas and that: 'The succession of the Crown is the right of the whole community, their appointment, their constitution…. and [is] unalterable.' He went on to say that parliament should choose the succession. His final blast was that it was acceptable to have popular resistance to stop Popery and 'all the authority of all the legislation in the world cannot make unlawful any act that is done in self-preservation'.[5] The Whigs had been challenging the royal prerogative in different ways for some time. Indeed, the Whig-dominated Commons had ruled that the king's pardon for Danby was unlawful. They had been trying to persuade the king to nominate a Protestant successor. Now at least some of them were denying the king's prerogative to nominate his successor at all, and even saying it was right to resist a Catholic monarch. The Whigs were moving from being an irritating opposition to being a potentially seditious movement.

The court's only effective means of countering this dangerous Whig propaganda was to create propaganda of their own. In this, L'Estrange eagerly took the lead using his *Observer* newspaper to rebut the Whigs' claims, and the court found a new persuasive pamphleteer in Nathaniel Thompson. According to Bishop Burnet, one of the court's most influential pieces of propaganda was not a written document, but a broadsheet engraving produced by L'Estrange and entitled '*The Committee or Popery in Masquerade*'. It showed rebels and dissenters, who had caused the Civil War in the past, being urged on by the Pope who wanted to introduce tyranny in order to bring Popery.[6] Time would tell whether this argument would gain any traction, but it at least showed court propaganda was fighting back.

Meanwhile the king must have been dismayed to discover there were unwelcome manoeuvrings in his court. Sunderland had struck up an alliance with Louise, which was reasonable enough. Louise had been so alarmed by

Shaftesbury's accusation of being a whore that she felt it best to try to work with him. She began to talk with Shaftesbury about the succession. After some meetings she agreed with Shaftesbury that it would be in everyone's interests if Charles abandoned his brother and Shaftesbury said that if this occurred, parliament would vote £600,000 in return for naming his successor. Sunderland supported this proposal and seems to have believed that Charles would be quite content to give up his brother if pressed to do so. This was a complete misreading of the situation. The king would stand by his family and prerogative no matter what. With the October resumption of parliament getting closer, Charles was prepared to give in to Louise and Sunderland on one matter. They persuaded him that parliament might be more compliant if the Duke of York was not at court. As a result, James was packed off back to Scotland.

Despite the 'banishment' of the Duke of York, there could be no grounds for optimism about the October parliament. Monmouth had been doing another of his popularity-seeking tours of the country and, the day before the opening, Shaftesbury and Monmouth had dinner with a hundred MPs in the Sun Tavern in the city. When the king addressed parliament, he called for good relations between him and them to resolve the problems of the Duke of York's succession and pleaded for troops to defend Tangier. By now Tangier was in a very perilous state. In March it had been attacked by a force of 7,000 Berbers, who had overrun some of the outer defences, but the garrison had just managed to hold out. Reinforcements were sent in the form of the newly raised Royal Scots and the Second Tangier Regiment and they had carried out a successful counter attack a few months later. The Berber force was beaten back and the garrison showed it had learned something from Moorish warfare by beheading and mutilating the dead. There was an uneasy truce, but for how long? The great warrior Sultan, Moulay Ismail, was determined to control the whole of Morocco and his ferocious Berber army could be expected to return to Tangier with reinforcements at any time. None of this was of the slightest interest to parliament, who regarded Tangier as a major drain on the exchequer and were wary of voting money for a larger army, which might be used to enforce arbitrary government at home.

With the Tangier question left unanswered, the Commons returned to the matter that was their greatest concern. Lord William Russell revived the bill to exclude James from the throne and it soon passed its third reading. The Bill then went to the Lords, where it could not expect so easy a passage because the court had a majority in the Lords and in any case, there was continued bad feeling between the two Houses over their respective rights.

The bill that had gone to the Lords had a final amendment from the Commons stating that the Crown should pass to the heirs of the Duke of York as though he was dead. This would make Princess Mary of Orange heir, so was not a welcome development for Monmouth. As it happened, the bill was defeated by the Lords following a ten-hour debate dominated by Salisbury for the Whigs, and his nephew Halifax for the court, in which Halifax's oratory triumphed. Although it did not affect the outcome, there was a surprise speaker in support of Exclusion, Sunderland. The king was present in the Lords at the time and was amazed, describing it as 'the kiss of Judas'.[7] When the vote was taken, of the 100 peers present, thirty voted for exclusion and sixty-three against.[8]

It would seem that the king had won the day, but that was by no means the end of the matter. Shaftesbury was in no mood to retire to his West Country estates; in fact, the day after the vote, he proposed in the Lords for the banishment of the Duke of York for five years and a royal divorce. It was now November, and Shaftesbury was taken up with organising Popish Plot trials. The trials had received a setback when Bedloe, a prime witness, had died in the summer. Nevertheless, it was decided to start putting the five Catholic peers in the Tower on trial. The one chosen to start the proceeding was Viscount Stafford because he was old and frail, and there were sufficient perjured witnesses to obtain a conviction. Oates, Dugdale and Turberville all concocted stories such as, for example, that Stafford had offered £500 for them to kill the king, and that he had been given a patent to be Postmaster General after a Papist coup. The show trial took place in a packed Westminster Hall with a disorientated and barely audible Stafford unable to counter the torrent of absurd accusations hurled at him. On top of everything, evidence against him was provided by his kinsman, the Anabaptist Lord Howard of Escrick a man unencumbered by moral principles. On 7 December, Stafford was found guilty of High Treason and sentenced to be hanged, drawn and quartered.

To many, the guilt of someone as eminent as a peer was proof positive that the Popish Plot was true. The king was in no position to pardon someone who the law said was planning his assassination, but he did commute the execution to beheading, which was carried out at the end of the month. A few days later the Commons offered the king what they considered a compromise. It was to provide funding for the fleet and Tangier in exchange for the king excluding his brother but nominating a Protestant successor of his choice. This got nowhere. Charles was becoming irritated by the Commons disregarding his express wishes that his brother should remain his heir. The

Commons were also being difficult in other ways. They had challenged his right to commute Stafford's sentence to beheading and had begun impeachment proceedings against Lord Chief Justice Scroggs for acquitting Sir George Wakeman, and dismissing the case against the Duke of York and Louise. The Commons was again getting out of hand. In January 1681 the king first prorogued and then dissolved parliament, saying that the next parliament would meet at Oxford rather than Westminster on 1 March. The Whigs were furious, firstly about the unexpected dissolution and secondly, about holding parliament in Oxford. The choice of Oxford by the king was a shrewd one because it meant that parliament would be held in a traditionally Royalist city and far away from the London mob, which the November Pope-Burnings had proven that the Whigs were so good at mobilising.

The first two months of 1681 were therefore taken up by frantic electioneering by Whigs and the court. Someone who would normally have been taking a leading part in this was Sunderland, but the king had waited until the end of the parliament before dismissing him for supporting the Exclusion Bill. Sunderland was replaced by Sir Leoline Jenkins, who was moved to the more senior appointment of secretary for the southern department and so placed in a stronger position to manage government intelligence. Edward Conway, a 58-year-old who had given long service to the Crown, replaced Jenkins as secretary of state for the North. He had served in the Irish Privy Council under Ormonde, and then the English Privy Council. Conway, a viscount by birth, had recently been made an earl, for which it was rumoured he had paid Louise £10,000.[9] Both secretaries and their staff would be working flat out to encourage the election of court-sympathising Tory MPs. As the country had not been so divided since the outbreak of the Civil War, the election would be hard fought. The king had called a new parliament because he hoped that it would be more tractable than the one he had just dissolved. Indeed, there were some grounds for believing that would be the case. Doubts were beginning to form in the minds of the public about the veracity of Oates and his co-witnesses. When the head of old Viscount Stafford had been held up by his executioner the crowds had not responded with the usual cheer, but with a deep sigh. Also, court propaganda was starting to draw people to the Tory cause and the court still had the ability of mobilising support by giving or withdrawing Crown patronage. Balanced against this there was the general fear of Popery, and the Whigs had a formidable party machine to activate supporters, distribute propaganda, and buy influence with money from its City backers. Both sides would have to wait a couple of months to see which could dominate the new parliament and by so doing, probably resolve the question of the succession in their favour.

The person most interested in the succession was far from the electioneering in Edinburgh. Scotland had changed since the Duke of York had left almost a year before. The tolerance that had been expected by Monmouth's Declaration of Indulgence was gradually being brushed aside by the Church of Scotland bishops and in May 1680, they persuaded the king to cancel it. The next month a small breakaway group of Covenanters came into being, regarding themselves to be true Presbyterians. They were led by Richard Cameron, who had been ordained in the ultra-strict Calvinist kirk of Rotterdam and had returned to Scotland after Bothwell Bridge. He and about twenty followers made a declaration at the village of Sanquhar in Dumfries, in which they vowed to take up arms against the king and levy 'war with such a tyrant and usurper and the men of his practices, as enemies to our Lord Jesus Christ, and his cause and Covenants'.[10] Cameron and his group became known as 'Cameronians' and moved on from Sanquhar, singing psalms and being joined by a trickle of supporters. This little band of religious extremists posed no real threat, but they had stated that they were at war with the king. Dragoons were sent after them and caught up with the 'rebels' at Airds Moss in Ayrshire, by which time their numbers had grown to sixty. Many of the Cameronians were cut down and killed in the skirmish, including Richard Cameron. They were the lucky ones. Twenty of those who were caught were hanged, drawn and quartered after first being tortured with the boot. One of the captured was David Hackston, who was convicted of having been involved in Sharp's murder. In his case, his hands were slowly cut off, with pauses between each cut, before the rest of his dismembering took place.

The Cameronians could have become a minor historical footnote if it had not been for one of their number escaping. This was a preacher called Donald Cargill, who kept the movement alive after the government had inadvertently helped recruitment by providing it with Covenanter martyrs. Although in years to come the Cameronians would form the basis for the famous Regiment of that name, at the time they were just a small group of fanatical Covenanters opposed to the king and his Catholic brother. Their real significance was that they gave the Church of Scotland an excuse to persecute Presbyterians. Archbishop Burnet had been moved from Glasgow to Aberdeen to replace the murdered Sharp as Primate of Scotland and was even more determined than Sharp to destroy what was left of Presbyterianism. Preaching licences were revoked and prosecutions for conventicles resumed. The Covenanter movement had been broken, but Cameronians and ordinary

Presbyterians who had been pushed too far by repression would remain a tiny group of extremists capable of carrying out small attacks such as assassination.

Back in England, the hard work of the secretaries of state had not been enough to prevent the Whigs gaining about two thirds of the 522 seats in the election. The only silver lining was that the whole process had made the secretaries learn a great deal about the candidates. For example, John Wildman, former Leveller and serial conspirator, was one of those to be elected. It was no bad thing for Leoline Jenkins to become familiar with such people who, although now respectable MPs, might not be above a bit of sedition in the future. On top of the disappointing election results, the government was unexpectedly faced with a major problem just before parliament was to meet. This was the case of Edward Fitzharris, an Irish gentleman down on his luck who decided to see if he could make his fortune out of the Popish Plot. Fitzharris was the second son of Sir Edward Fitzharris and had spent a short time in the French army then moved to an English regiment but had to resign his commission under the Test Act. He had a relative called Mrs Wall who was a maid of Louise, Duchess of Portsmouth. It seems that Louise was still trying to ingratiate herself with the Whigs and through Wall, employed Fitzharris to try to bribe the leading Whig, Lord Howard of Escrick, to support her. Nothing came of this, but Fitzharris then hit on the idea of writing a fake pamphlet which advocated deposing the king and murdering the Duke of York. His plan was to plant the pamphlet in the house of a senior Whig, such as Lord Howard, where it could be discovered and thus provide 'proof' that the Whigs were inciting treason. If the plan worked, Fitzharris could expect a substantial reward from Louise who was very probably privy to the plot. Fitzharris decided he needed an accomplice and asked a fellow Irishman of his acquaintance called Edmund Everard to help him. Everard was an equally shady character whom had been a junior secretary to Monmouth, but would work for any cause that paid him.[19] Everard reported Fitzharris to the arch anti-papist Sir William Waller then arranged to entrap Fitzharris by getting him to discuss the plot in a room where Waller was hidden behind a curtain. Having heard Fitzharris describing the plot, Waller had him arrested and committed to Newgate for treason.

While in Newgate, Fitzharris was visited by Henry Cornish and Slingsby Bethel, both Whig sheriffs of London and Middlesex respectively, who persuaded him to change sides to save himself from prosecution. He readily agreed to turn king's evidence and as a bonus, concoct with them more anti-Catholic allegations. The new story was that he had first heard of the Popish

Plot when he was in Paris in 1677. Sometime later he had been offered £10,000 by the Duke of Modena to kill the king in a plot to which the Duke of York was privy. Fitzharris's story also improved on the evidence of Oates and Bedloe, not only by confirming their statements about how Sir Edmund Bury Godfrey was murdered, but also claiming that Danby had been involved.[11] News of the Fitzharris allegations soon spread. The last thing the king wanted was the Whigs to come up with new Papist plots just as parliament was about to sit, especially one allegedly involving both Louise and his brother. Charles ordered Fitzharris to be transferred from Newgate to the Tower to place him under royal control. With a Whig majority of MPs and new allegations of Popish scheming against James and Louise, things did not look at all promising for the king at the forthcoming new parliament.

Chapter 16

Rebellion in the Air
1681

'41 is come again'
Popular saying in 1681

With the Oxford parliament likely to be a crisis point, the king had taken a few precautionary measures. He removed three lord lieutenants who had voted for Exclusion, and then began to purge deputy lord lieutenants and individual militia officers whom had been revealed to be potentially disloyal by the scrutiny of the secretaries of state. He also drafted 500 troops to Oxford in readiness for the parliament while leaving Lord Craven the responsibility for the security of London.[1] Although these measures showed that the king was ready to meet the worst situation if necessary, it did not explain his relaxed attitude. He travelled to Oxford with the queen, Louise and Nell a week early, going first to Burford to attend the races and spend time hawking before arriving in Oxford and making the royal party comfortable in Christ Church and Merton Colleges.[2]

The Whigs set off to Oxford from London in a grand procession led by Shaftesbury and Monmouth, attended by 200 well-armed horsemen. They were wearing ribbons in their hats woven with the words 'No Popery No Slavery'. Shaftesbury's secretary, John Locke, had arranged for him to be accommodated at Balliol with the government cryptologist, Dr John Wallis, and that college became the Whig headquarters. It was as though there were two armies in the city and people began to say '41 is come again', referring to the events of 1641 that had resulted in the Civil War. Despite posturing and scuffles in Oxford, there was no violence. That said, the supporters of either side could be menacing; when Nell Gwynn's coach was mistaken for that of Louise, a mob surrounded it shouting 'Papist whore!' Fortunately,

198

Nell had the presence of mind to open her window and shout 'I'm the Protestant whore!' at which she was cheered on her way.

The king opened parliament in the cramped circumstances of the Bodleian Library. In his speech he said that he ruled out Exclusion, but was prepared to consider any expedient by which the administration of the government remained in Protestant hands. The speech cut little ice with the Whigs and parliament launched with the usual bickering between the two Houses over their privileges. The Commons decided to impeach Fitzharris and in doing so, expose Louise's supposed intrigue with him against the Whigs and the claim that the Duke of York had been privy to a plot to kill the king. The Lords blocked this as a breach of their privileges but it would only be a matter of time before Fitzharris gave evidence to either the Commons or the Lords. In a final attempt to negotiate with the Whigs, Charles offered to make the Duke of York's Protestant daughter Mary, Regent during his brother's reign but this initiative was rejected by Shaftesbury. There seemed to be no room for compromise and the Commons began the first reading of a new Exclusion bill.

The king attended the temporary House of Lords, left his sedan chair outside and then summoned the Commons to the chamber. While the MPs were arriving, Charles went to his sedan chair where he had his crown and robes of state, which he hurriedly put on. When the whole parliament was present, the king entered the hall and dissolved them. This came as a complete shock. Naturally the dissolution did not go down well with the tradesmen of Oxford; they had been expecting a financial bonanza with the country's richest people crowded into their city. It was certainly not well received by the MPs and peers who had travelled from all parts of the country on appalling roads to attend a parliament that had lasted just seven days. Most of all it was a major blow to Shaftesbury and the Whigs. Without parliament they were deprived of a focus for their opposition and no longer had a public forum to press their case for excluding the Duke of York from the throne.

To most it was a mystery why the king should have dissolved parliament so quickly when he was known to be desperately short of money. But Charles had a secret. For some months he had been conducting clandestine negotiations with Ambassador Barrillon about a subsidy from Louis, but without success. By January, Louis had come to realise that there was a real chance that parliament would force Charles into the Exclusion and so decided that it would be in his interests to stop parliament operating. An agreement was reached that Charles would receive £380,000 over three years if he did not help Spain against France, or call parliament for that purpose. Louis also undertook not to attack Flanders in that time. The king left Oxford the morning after dissolving parliament and travelled to Windsor in the knowledge that his financial situation was to be alleviated by French money, the first instalment of which would be arriving in Rochester that very day.

At the short lived parliament the king had publicly shown himself prepared to make concessions and left the Whigs to discredit themselves by refusing to negotiate. It would seem that the king's cunning had won the day, but it wasn't quite as straightforward as that. The Whigs had received a setback but the movement still had strong support. When the Whigs returned to London they were met at the Crown Tavern by the Lord Mayor who made a speech stating that the dissolution might be fatal to the nation and 'and that unless prevented the whole community in the country would be in arms'.[3] Clearly the dissolution had not ended the matter and the fact that Monmouth was greeted with shouts of 'the Lord defend the Protestant Duke' foretold that a showdown with the king had merely been postponed.

On 8 April, almost immediately after arriving at Windsor, the king issued a declaration, which must have been written before the Oxford parliament had taken place. It was ordered to be read aloud in all churches; its title was: *Declaration to all His Loving Subjects. Touching the Causes and reasons that Moved him to Dissolve the two last Parliaments.* It ended with the words:

> *We do still declare that no irregularities in Parliaments shall ever make us out of love with Parliaments, which we look upon as the best method of healing the distempers of the kingdom, and the only means to preserve the monarchy in that due credit and respect which it ought to have at home and abroad. And for this cause we are resolved, by the blessing of God, to have frequent parliaments, and both in and out of Parliament to use our utmost endeavours to extirpate popery, and redress all the grievances of our good subjects, and in all things to govern according to the laws of the kingdom.*[4]

The king had taken the moral high ground. What was there not to like about these words? However, it did not go down well with everyone, especially those who had learned not to believe the king's promises. The Whigs were furious at this effective royal propaganda, and the Earl of Essex sacked his chaplain on the spot when he began reading it. Whigs apart, the king's declaration was very well received and it resulted in about 200 loyal addresses from justices of the peace, corporations and militia around the country. Although not realised at the time, we now know that the king was not to call another parliament and that Rochester's careful handling of the Exchequer and Louis's gold would mean that he would never have to rely on parliament for funding again.

Shaftesbury probably realised what had happened and was in a quandary. Although the Whigs had many supporters, including probably the City Trainbands militia, they were not strong enough to consider challenging the king militarily now that the army and militia had been purged to ensure their loyalty to the Crown. Propaganda could continue, but unless there was another parliament, there was little else that could be done for the moment. The king, on the other hand, began pressing home his advantage and attacking Whigs wherever he could; he prevented, for example, a Whig being appointed head of the Honourable Artillery Company. The king, who had once championed tolerance against the Cavalier parliament's unbending Anglicanism, turned against Nonconformists who had moved to supporting the Whigs. Prosecution of dissenters was encouraged and Nonconformists began to be removed from government posts in departments such as Excise and the Navy Office. Some Whigs saw the way things were going and decided to make their peace with the court. Some of these were immediately rewarded; Lord Townsend, for example, was made a viscount.

In June a minor Whig activist called Stephen College was arrested. He was the carpenter at the Green Ribbon Club and the person who had built the effigy of the Pope for the November burning. He had also written rude poems about the king and his mistresses, and had been one of those in the armed group who had accompanied Shaftesbury to Oxford. He was charged with treason, but a Whig Grand Jury in London pronounced the case *ignoramus* (we are ignorant), which was the legal term for finding that the accusations were groundless. The king had College transferred to the more suitable surroundings of Oxford for a retrial. It was important to get the right jury for the trial and Jenkins wrote to the Lord Lieutenant, 'to have all the care you possibly can that there be good, honest substantial grand jury consisting of men rightly principled for the Church and the King'.[5] There was not much of a case against him, the main evidence was that he had distributed a cartoon showing the Duke of York as the Devil riding to Rome. Nevertheless, this was enough for an 'honest' jury to convict him and he was hanged, drawn and quartered a few days later. The case was of interest because it saw a falling out between Oates and Dugdale, with Oates as a witness for the defence, and Dugdale for the prosecution. With two celebrity witnesses giving conflicting evidence, they both lost credibility.

It was a time of trials. Fitzharris was put on trial and his damaging accusations against the Duke of York and Louise were disbelieved by the court and, to the king's relief, he was sentenced to death. At the same time there was a more traditional Popish Plot trial. This was of Oliver Plunket, the Catholic Archbishop of Armagh. He was falsely accused of conspiring to bring over a French army to massacre the Protestants in Ireland. People were prepared to believe the worst of an Irish Catholic and it took five minutes deliberation to decide a verdict. The absurd accusations were believed and he was sentenced to death. It was ironic that Plunket and Fitzgerald, such entirely different men, shared the same scaffold on 1 July 1681.

The day after the executions, the king made a bolder move by having Shaftesbury arrested and making him appear before the council, of which he had once been President, on a charge of treason. His erstwhile colleagues sent him to the Tower to await trial. Ormonde was appointed to preside over the trial, which would be by thirty peers chosen for their dislike of Shaftesbury. As Ormonde detested Shaftesbury for once attempting to charge him for treason based on fabricated evidence, the verdict would be a forgone conclusion. It looked as though Shaftesbury would soon cease to be. The only problem was that in order for the trial to take place, Shaftesbury had to first appear before a grand jury nominated by the Whig sheriffs of Middlesex. Shaftesbury was accused of conspiring to have fifty armed men at Oxford to capture the king and force him to accept Exclusion. The evidence was slim and provided by perjured witnesses, so it was no surprise that the already biased jury gave a finding of *ignoramus*. Shaftesbury, old, sick, hunched, and walking with the aid of a stick, was released on bail amid much rejoicing in the city. Despite his frailty Shaftesbury had lost none of his fighting spirit and fully exploited this boost to his support. The city decided to celebrate Shaftesbury's release by minting a medal with Shaftesbury on one side and the Tower on the other, bearing the inscription *Laetamur* (let us rejoice). There was certainly no cause for the king to rejoice as he had acted too precipitously against Shaftesbury and so allowed him to regain the moral high ground. He was aided at this time by Louis, authorising the *dragonnades,* that is the brutal billeting of troops on Huguenot families for free. This enabled Shaftesbury to repeatedly declare that Popery and slavery were like two sisters walking hand in hand.

The king had gone to the trouble of replacing Scroggs as Lord Chief Justice because he was not confident of his loyalty to the Shaftesbury trial. His replacement, Pemberton, had done his best to obtain a verdict acceptable to the Crown but that was only half of the equation. There was also the matter of the jury and as they had been chosen by Whig sheriffs, Thomas Pilkington and Sir Samuel Barnardiston, the outcome was never in doubt. It was clear that the king's writ did not extend into the city, indeed the city was almost a state within a state. With a population of 550,000, London was the largest city in Europe, with its own treasury, military force of Trainbands, and courts that could defy the monarch.[6] What was more, most corporations in the kingdom were also dominated by Whigs and so could defy the king and ensure both the law courts and elections for MPs were biased against the Tories. Fortunately, Charles had a means of dealing with this by the process of *quo warranto* (by what warrant). As the monarch had granted corporations their rights in the first place, the monarch could also remove them if he felt they had been misused under the *quo warranto* process. Charles began the long process of challenging corporation charters. During the next five years, over thirty boroughs and other corporations surrendered their charters. New charters might mean new privileges such as additional markets. What the new charters did state, was that key figures in the corporation, such as the mayor and town clerk, had to be approved by the king, which was usually delegated to a loyal member of the local gentry. As these key posts in the corporations were able to influence the appointment of juries and the election of MPs, four fifths of which were returned by boroughs, having them on side would greatly extend royal influence.[7]

The king began the *quo warranto* process against the City of London in December, but it was fiercely resisted and would take two and a half years to see whether or not the charter would be renewed. As this delay meant that the Whig sheriffs would be able to go on selecting Whig juries, the king began investigating whether he could intervene in the elections of the sheriffs, but this too would take many months. In the meantime he had another go at bringing a leading Whig to court. This time it was the disreputable Lord Howard of Escrick, but, as with Shaftesbury, it was done too early. During the last Dutch War, Howard had been an agent for Williamson in Holland, but had played a double game and also provided information to the Dutch. William Carr, the English Consul in the United Provinces, reported this back to London but there was insufficient evidence so Howard was arrested on the trumped-up charge of writing the seditious pamphlet the *True Englishman*. The long standing Republican, Algernon Sidney, successfully defended Howard in court and he was acquitted, despite the perjured evidence against him. The only encouraging aspect of this unsatisfactory outcome for the king was that several of the low-level Irish and other perjured witnesses now felt it was in their best interests to provide invented evidence for the Crown rather than for the Whigs.

For the king, the main crisis appeared to be over and he turned his attention to the things he enjoyed and found interesting. The secretaries of state were left with the priority task of keeping a close eye on the Whigs and scratching their heads to come up with a scheme on how to get London sheriffs appointed who would support the Crown. The Whigs were still pouring out propaganda and much of it, like Robert Ferguson's, was of high quality. This was being countered by Tory propaganda by L'Estrange and others. Given that it had been estimated that thirty per cent of Englishmen were literate, and in London seventy to eighty per cent of tradesmen and artisans could read, the propaganda war was an important one to win.[8]

With the lapse of the Licensing Act, the Crown had tried to re-impose censorship. As long ago as October 1679, Tory judges had ruled that the government could seize seditious papers and jail those responsible but, despite issuing proclamations offering rewards to informants, very few prosecutions took place. If they did, there was a good chance that the defendant would be acquitted by a Whig jury. There were no demonstrations in London and all appeared quiet, but many citizens had taken to wearing different coloured ribbons in their hats, red to denote support for the Duke of York and blue for Monmouth. The major public issue of whether the succession should pass to a Protestant or a Catholic had not gone away. Both the Whigs and the court were preparing themselves for a final showdown.

While there was an eerie calm in England before the expected storm about the succession, the situation was rather different in the other two kingdoms. In Ireland the population was predominantly Catholic and so the heir to the throne being a Catholic was not a problem. There were of course Protestants, especially in Ulster, who would not relish a Papist king, but they caused little problem. The severe treatment of Covenanters in Scotland had led to some of their leaders moving to Ulster and they no doubt schemed and plotted to help their kinsmen back home. As it happened, there were no public demonstrations against Popery and if there were any plots, they came to nothing. The reasons for this was that local magistrates kept a good lookout for signs of sedition through their informants, and stamped on any indication of its existence. The overall credit for this reasonably peaceful time in Ireland must go to the Duke of Ormonde. As the highly experienced Lord Lieutenant of Ireland, who had been brought up as a Protestant but came from a Catholic family, he ensured as much tolerance as was possible in the circumstances. He had been obliged to go along with the restrictions following the Popish Plot, such as measures against Catholic priests, the introduction of licences to carry arms, and the shameful arrest of Oliver Plunket, the Archbishop of

Armagh. For all that, he was not gratuitously repressive to Catholics or Nonconformists and as a result, had no backlash from either.

In Scotland, the Duke of York was also using a measure of restraint. He was generally popular, introduced sound administration, and ended many of Lauderdale's embezzlements. As James was a Catholic himself, he did not discriminate against them. It was another matter with the Covenanters who had so recently been in rebellion, but even with them he was not vindictive as long as they kept the peace and attended church. Donald Cargill, the leader of the remnants of the Cameronians, had been captured and hanged in July, and the few remaining followers posed no threat. James made one particular error, which spoilt an otherwise successful period of government. Unfortunately, it was a serious one and concerned the Scottish Test Act. The Act meant that all office-holders had to swear their support for the Protestant faith and accept the king's supremacy of the Church. James made himself exempt, and as Catholics were already denied office, the Act made little difference to them. Presbyterians on the other hand could not, in conscience, regard the monarch as their spiritual head and so would find themselves deprived of any public appointment if they did not take the oath.

Between thirty to eighty Church of Scotland ministers refused to take the oath and were removed from their livings.[9] Several members of the council also refused to subscribe to the Act and Lord Stair made the point that he thought the purpose of the Test Act was to protect the Protestant succession, rather than penalise Nonconformists. That did not go down well with James who had him imprisoned in Edinburgh Castle. More importantly, the Earl of Argyll, Chief of Clan Campbell and one of the most powerful magnates in Scotland, expressed his reluctance to swear to the Act. He later agreed but added to his oath: 'as far as it was consistent with itself and the Protestant religion'. That seemed a good compromise and should have been the end of the matter. Indeed, for the next couple of council meetings James appeared to be on friendly terms with Argyll, then without warning, had him charged with treason and imprisoned in Edinburgh Castle. He was put on trial for treason in December and James appointed the Marquis of Montrose as foreman of the jury. As Montrose's grandfather had been hanged by Argyll's father, a guilty verdict was certain.

Montrose would be denied his revenge because Argyll escaped from the castle thanks to his stepdaughter-in-law, Lady Sophia Lindsay, who paid him a visit and had got him out disguised as her page. Argyll fled first to England, where he made contact with Shaftesbury, and then onto the safety of the United Provinces. The escape was more than an embarrassment for the Duke of York. He had turned an important potential ally into an implacable enemy of the Crown who could scheme revenge from the safety of the United Provinces. James then made matters even worse by getting the Scottish parliament to pass an act requiring office holders to swear to uphold his right to succession, and denial of his right would be treason. The two acts naturally resulted in protests from the Presbyterians and put new life into the Cameronians but although this presented no threat to law and order, James responded with a new bout of repression.

Graham of Claverhouse had become Sheriff of Wigton when his predecessor refused to take the Test. He was given the task of prosecuting all persons in Galloway who had broken bonds since the uprising of 1678 by, for example, not attending church. Claverhouse carried out his duties with enthusiasm and in his own words: 'rifled so their houses, ruined their goods ... that their wyfes and schildring were brought to starving'.[10] In March 1682, similar commissions were given in other shires and were executed with vigour. At the end of May, the king felt his position strong enough to instruct his brother to return to London. James left ardent Royalists to govern Scotland in his absence in the form of Sir George Gordon as Chancellor, the Marquis of Queensbury as Treasurer, and the Earls of Moray and Middleton as secretaries of state.[11] The repression of Presbyterians continued, and indeed escalated under them, in a period that has been named 'the killing times'.

Chapter 17

The Road to Rye House
1682–83

'Had it (the plot) taken effect, it would, to all appearance, have exposed the Government to unknown and dangerous events; which God avert!'

John Evelyn *Diary*

When the Duke of York finally left Scotland with his wife in June, their return journey to England was not uneventful. The dangers of travelling in those days are borne out by the fact that they were shipwrecked on a sandbank off Yarmouth. The duke and duchess were saved, but 200 were drowned although, as James later remarked, 'none of quality'.[1] It is pleasing to be able to report that the duke's dog was saved. An indication of how sentiment was begging to turn in favour of the Crown was that the duke and duchess were very well received in the towns they passed through as they progressed from Norwich to London. As a pleasant change from Pope-burning, there were signs of an anti-Nonconformist backlash with burnings of effigies of 'John Presbyter'.[2] The king was gradually winning the initiative through his *quo warranto* procedures and crackdown of the Nonconformists, who made up a significant proportion of the Whigs. In May, the king had found another way of attacking the Whigs in the form of one John Hilton. He had come to London from Westmoreland, was then gaoled for forgery, after which he ran an alehouse in Fetter Lane, while also engaged in counterfeit coining. Hilton's legal and illegal business interests did not prosper and he ran up debts, which made him decide on a new venture. Rather surprisingly, he managed to have an audience with the king at Windsor and received verbal consent to 'supress and disturb' dissenters.

From then on, Hilton applied to Leoline Jenkins for about twenty warrants a week to disturb conventicles anywhere in London. Some dissenters were brought to court, but most had their goods confiscated by Hilton and his gang, which came to number about fifty, at least fifteen of whom were women. Fines and confiscations were levied on the basis of one third going to Hilton and two thirds going to the Crown and poor relief. Given Hilton's criminal record it would be very surprising if the Crown received its full due. As a sideline, Hilton also compounded, that is threatened, someone with the law, but took bribes for taking no action. The confiscations were very lucrative for the gang, for example, a shoemaker was relieved of eighty-one pairs of shoes, and a cheeseman had £7 worth of cheddar removed. The gang's methods of operation were unconventional for Crown agents. It is recorded that on one occasion they broke into the house of a dissident carpenter, demanded £20, stayed all night, making merry on his brandy and rum, and in the morning took away several cartloads of timber.[3] Hilton and his gang became the scourge of dissenters and even established a weekly newspaper, *The Conventicle Courant,* to boast of their exploits and encourage more informants. Hilton thus provided two services: he spread fear among the Nonconformist allies of the Whigs, and provided a welcome addition to Jenkins's already sizable army of informants.

Ironically, the fact that events were moving in the king's favour against the Whigs made the situation more dangerous for the Crown. Shaftesbury and the other Whig leaders were deprived of parliament and constitutional means of opposition to a Catholic succession. They had to watch while the king was gnawing away at their power base in the corporations, and support among Nonconformists. The conduct of the Duke of York in Scotland had shown the Whigs the way he would run England if he became king and further strengthened their resolve to prevent his succession. Earlier in the year, Charles had been taken ill. Monmouth and Russell had a meeting with Shaftesbury at his London residence, Thanet House, in which they discussed an uprising. In fact these were merely exploratory talks and were almost immediately abandoned when the king recovered a few days later. What it did show was a determined opposition who, if pushed much further, were prepared to take up arms against the Crown.

The secretaries' skulduggery had resulted in the Lord Mayor of London becoming a Tory. This was Sir John Moore, who was a Nonconformist but seeing an opportunity for advancement, swore to support the rights of the Church of England and more importantly, informally agreed to support the Crown. In a related move, the ardent Tory Sir George Jeffreys was appointed Chairman of Middlesex Justices, and Whig aldermen were replaced in June when two Tories were nominated as sheriffs after their predecessors were convicted of riot by Jeffreys. John Hilton managed to dominate the city constables by ensuring that those who did not follow his direction were named in his newspaper for dereliction of duty and threatened with prosecution. In August, all constables were summoned by Sir John Moore, with Hilton present, and those who were deemed derelict were passed to Jenkins and indicted before the Court of King's Bench.

In August 1682, with so much going the king's way, Shaftesbury got Monmouth to go on one of his tours but this time to the North. Leoline Jenkins ordered local dignitaries at the stops on the progress route not to receive him, but although this worked in some places, such as Tory Litchfield, it did not work in Cheshire, where he got a warm welcome and was royally entertained by the Earl of Macclesfield. The king was so irritated by Monmouth's popularity-seeking progress as a self-appointed Protestant heir that he had him arrested at Stafford for disturbing the peace. Monmouth was brought back to London a free man, but banished from the court. In September, following three months of ballot rigging, challenges, and downright dishonesty, two Tory sheriffs were finally elected. The following month a new Lord Mayor was also elected, after a considerable amount of work by the secretaries. This had included arranging for the Bishop of London to direct all clergy to instruct their congregations to vote Tory, making the votes of potential Whig voters such as Quakers invalid; threatening to withdraw the licences of all keepers of ale and coffee shops if they failed to vote Tory; using threats, and offers of patronage, to members of the Common Council; and having the Trainbands stationed at the Guildhall to exclude known Whigs.[4] The exercise had aroused considerable resentment, but it had all been worthwhile. There was now a genuine Tory, Sir William Pritchard, as Lord Mayor and so at last, the king could be confident of having juries to his liking.

It seemed that the Whigs had no legitimate way forward other than to consider bringing about a Protestant succession by force. The Whigs' leaders began to actively plan an uprising. During the sheriff elections, Shaftesbury had proposed seizing the Tower but had been dissuaded by Essex, Russell and Monmouth, who felt that a rabble would not stand up to Trainbands. Now the plan for an uprising became more ambitious. Shaftesbury would be responsible for raising London, Lord William Russell the West, and Lord Grey of Werke and the Earl of Essex would be given other areas. It was proposed that Lord Howard of Escrick would also be a leader of the revolt, but he was still undecided about taking part. Also undecided was Monmouth, who completely rejected a plan that John Wildman put forward to assassinate the king as he returned from the races. The conspiratorial group also included the staunch republican Algernon Sidney, and Robert Ferguson, a Presbyterian minister, who would be the man on the ground responsible for organising the London uprising. The capital would be divided into twenty sections, in which one leader would recruit ten assistants each of whom would recruit a score or more.[5] Shaftesbury expected that several thousand Londoners would rise up if he gave the word. The plan being formulated was to launch the uprisings on 19 November, the anniversary of Queen Elizabeth's succession, but this was postponed when it was realised that the government would have placed troops in readiness to prevent any Pope-burning demonstrations.

Shaftesbury had been pleading with his fellow leaders to launch a rebellion, but their discussions had been all talk and no action; Salisbury is reported as saying in exasperation, 'Patience will be our destruction.' Their understandable hesitation to rebel, differing views on how it should be carried out, and whether the king should be replaced by Monmouth, Princess Mary of Orange, or a Republic, had prevented any unity of purpose. As it was, time for rebellion had run out for Shaftesbury. He realised that with the sheriffs in his pocket, the king would soon have him in court for treason, which was bound to result in his execution. In November, Shaftesbury went into hiding, then travelled to Harwich disguised as a clergyman and sailed to the United Provinces. Two months later his kidney disease and frail constitution caught up with him and he died in Amsterdam. Future generations would regard Shaftesbury as the founder of the Whigs and a semi-martyr to the causes of freedom and the Protestant faith. In fact, he was a talented leader with lofty ideals, but also an unscrupulous politician who had caused the death and misery of many innocent people by exploiting the Popish Pot for his own self-seeking purposes.

The Whig conspirators had been few in number and very careful about the security of their meetings. Between October and November 1682 three government informants had told Jenkins of preparations for a rising in the City. These reports had been unspecific and were probably regarded as referring to the expected demonstrations leading up to the banned Pope-burning event. In fact there was a massing of apprentices from the East End on 6 November shouting 'a Monmouth', but it had been a peaceful demonstration and the ringleaders had been arrested. As a result, Jenkins, for all his informants, had no knowledge of the planned uprising. For the king it appeared that the principal Whig leader was dead and the threat from them was virtually over. There is no doubt that the Whigs had lost a brilliant and charismatic leader, but the rest of the conspirators remained, as did their determination, to prevent the Duke of York becoming king.

Although the loss of Shaftesbury had resulted in some Whigs deciding that the time had come to get back into royal favour, there was still plenty of support for a Protestant succession, especially in London where there was considerable resentment over the Crown's flagrant interference in the municipal elections. Robert Ferguson, who was the only one who had the right contacts for organising a London uprising, had gone to Amsterdam with Shaftesbury. When Shaftesbury died, Ferguson returned together with Colonel Rumsey who had also accompanied the Whig leader. Conspiracy for an uprising could begin again. There was now a tight group of aristocrats getting together discreetly to consider an uprising. This strategic-level group had much the same leaders as before. They were Essex, Russell, Grey, Howard, Algernon Sidney and John Hampden junior, as well as Monmouth and his mentor, Sir Thomas Armstrong. Related to this group was a more tactical-level group consisting of people such as Ferguson and Wildman, together with Robert West, a barrister, and Colonel Romsey, a tax collector in Bristol who was a former Cromwellian officer. Again, there was a fair amount of talking but little action, however, Monmouth persuaded the others to widen any rebellion to include Scotland. It was therefore decided to involve the Earl of Argyll, and he sent over representatives from Holland to discuss how the two uprisings might be coordinated. A secret meeting was held under the guise of purchasing land in Carolina and the coordination of rebellions in both countries was agreed in principle.

Unfortunately coordination does not appear to have been a strong point among the Whig leadership. There seems to have been little cooperation between, or even within, the two Whig groups. Robert Ferguson was busying himself organising a London uprising almost independently from the others. By April 1683 the sense of outrage about the fixing of the London elections had still not died down. The City Coroner used his authority to arrest Pritchard, the Lord Mayor, and one of his sheriffs, for refusing to allow any more legal challenges about irregularities in the sheriff elections. Ferguson decided that this would provide a good flash point to start an insurrection. He made his plans in conjunction with Thomas Shepherd and Richard Goodenough. Shepherd had previously hosted meetings between Russell, Grey, Monmouth and Ferguson about raising London in rebellion. Goodenough was a member of Green Ribbon Club and Whig under-sheriff, who had worked with Robert West on planning to find leaders for the twenty areas of London to be raised. Their plans came to nothing because before many supporters got out onto the streets, the militia quickly restored order, so that was that.

While the Whigs had been plotting there had been a change to the government. The main members of the government were Halifax, Laurence Hyde, who had been made Earl of Rochester, and Jenkins and Conway, the secretaries of state. In January 1683 Conway had resigned after being accused of mismanagement of ambassadors and Sunderland replaced him as Secretary for the North. The rather surprising return of Sunderland to favour was largely through the good offices of Louise who knew that Charles retained a liking for him despite voting for Exclusion. The ambitious Sunderland was delighted to be back in government, not least to help pay his gambling debts. He enjoyed high politics and in the words of Burnet 'naturally loved craft and a double game, that so he might have proper instruments to work on which way soever he had turned himself in that affair'. [6] Fortunately, the restoration of Sunderland did not result in him getting involved in intelligence matters, which became the sole domain of Leoline Jenkins.

In fact Sunderland and the diligent Jenkins could hardly have had more different management styles. It is thought that Sunderland never actually visited his offices and the clerks of the Northern Department would bring papers to his London residence, which he would sign unread before returning to the card table. This suited Jenkins well, who merely got on with both his job and the other ministers. The same happy relationship did not exist between the other ministers. Halifax hated the indolent Sunderland, although he was married to his sister, and also hated Rochester, who was a firm supporter of his brother-in-law, the Duke of York. The bad feelings were reciprocated and further inflamed when Halifax attempted to charge Rochester with bribery. None of this made for a good atmosphere around the council table. Instead of the king being dismayed at the bitter rivalry of his principal ministers, he found it both amusing and a relief that no one person became so powerful that they turned into another Clarendon. Also, with the crisis apparently over, Charles was turning his attention to other things, most notably his plans for a huge palace at Winchester, intended to become the English equivalent of his cousin's Versailles.

Meanwhile, the Whigs continued their plotting, led by a council of six consisting of Monmouth, Russell, Essex, Howard, Sidney and Hampden. These leaders continued to be split in their purpose with Essex, Sidney and Hampden favouring a Commonwealth, and the rest, who wanted to come to terms with the king. They decided that despite the differences, they should try to agree on a declaration that could be used for the rebellion. Sidney began to formulate a declaration and brought in Wildman to help with the drafting. The resulting document demanded religious toleration for Nonconformists, the establishment of annual parliaments, placing the militia in the hands of parliament, and restoring the free election of sheriffs. So far so good, but whether this should be achieved through forcing terms on the king, or replacing him with parliament, Monmouth, or Princess Mary, was left undecided.

The more tactical-level group of Whig leaders such as Robert West, John Wildman and Nathaniel Wade were in no doubt over this – they wanted the king removed. While the Whig aristocrats were concentrating their endless debates on an uprising, the tactical group was planning that the king should be assassinated, and then there should be an uprising. Related to such a uprising would be the taking of the Tower of London, which was being planned by John Rouse, and a rebellion in Scotland, which was being coordinated by Wildman.[7] The plan for a Scottish uprising was not going well because the Earl of Argyll sent word that he needed money for ammunition and ships and none was readily available. Plans for raising London continued under a fairly low-level leadership. Zachary Bourne, a brewer and Independent, felt he could raise Cripplegate, Clerkenwell, Bloomsbury and Soho; Charles Bateman, a Baptist, would try to raise Barbican where he had influence; and fellow Baptists, one a brewer and another a tobacconist, believed they could raise Westminster, Cheapside and Newgate.[8]

Among the numerous, rather vague, seditious discussions taking place, a firm plan was being formulated to assassinate the king and the Duke of York as they returned from the March Newmarket race meeting on 1 April. Robert West led this conspiracy with Wildman, and they decided that the best location to carry out the assassination was at Rye House at Hoddesdon in Hertfordshire. This was a location where the road from Newmarket was very narrow, and leased by a loyal Whig and former Roundhead, the one-eyed Colonel Rumbold, who had been one of the guards at Charles I's execution. Most of those chosen to carry out the murders seem to have been Phanaticks. They included William Hone, a dissenting joiner, John Patchell, a Fifth Monarchist brewer's clerk, Josiah Keeling, a Baptist from East Smithfield, as well as a weaver and a shoemaker, who were both Congregationalists. Colonel Rumsey and Captain Walcot would lead the gang; the former would have a group to stop the coach and kill the king and his brother, and the latter would lead the party to take on the guards. It seems that the whole plan was ready to be put into operation when an unforeseen event resulted in it having to be abandoned. On 22 March there was a fire at the king's residence in Newmarket and the two royal brothers returned several days early before the assassins had got into position.

The plot had come to nothing; indeed, we do not have enough reliable information to know whether it really would have gone ahead if there had not been the Newmarket fire. It might have been that the conspirators would have called it off at the last moment, either from having cold feet or because the planned subsequent uprising was not sufficiently prepared. In any event, the conspirators met at the Dolphin tavern behind the Exchange and began considering other plans to carry out the assassination. It is very likely that the aristocratic wing of the Whig leadership was well aware that Robert West and others thought that the king should be assassinated, but whether any of them actually knew of the Rye House plot is far from certain. Lord William Russell is said to have been at Shepherd's wine shop and overheard talk of a plot to assassinate the king, but does not seem to have been engaged in the discussion. Lord Howard of Escrick seems to have been actually present when some of the conspirators, such as Walcot, Rumsey, Ferguson and Goodenough, were discussing their hopes of assassinating the king. That said, he does not appear to have been involved in any planning. The aborted assassination plot probably seemed like just another setback for those involved and it could be that most, if not all the Whig aristocratic group, were unaware that the plot even existed. They continued their discussions about an uprising and in May, Louise even tried to reconcile Monmouth with his father.[9] The loss of Monmouth to any uprising plans would have been a serious blow, but the headstrong duke found the acclaim he received as the 'Protestant Duke' too intoxicating to give up. The secret meetings and talk about an insurrection continued.

Rather surprisingly, Leoline Jenkins does not seem to have been aware of the existence of the Rye House Plot. Naturally, he knew from informants that the Whigs were carrying out secret meetings and were obviously up to no good. However, despite the tactical-level Whig leaders often having meetings in taverns, and the increasing numbers of those needing to be approached to take part in an uprising or assassination, the plots did not reach the ears of the secretary of state. This was about to change. On 1 June, the Mayor of Newcastle informed Jenkins that he had arrested a man named Pringle carrying seditious papers, some of which were in cipher. On decryption, it was revealed that the documents were probably meant for the Earl of Argyll in Holland and gave details of how an uprising in Scotland might be coordinated with one in England.

At about the same time, Josiah Keeling betrayed the Whig plots. Keeling had been employed by Goodenough to see what support there might be in the city for an uprising, and also to take part in the planned assassination, but it seems he became squeamish about assassinating the king. He was a salter who had gone bankrupt and, in the hope of restoring his financial position, had turned informant. He decided to report his knowledge of the Rye House Plot to the naval commander Lord Dartmouth, who he had heard was close to the Duke of York. Dartmouth referred the matter to Jenkins, who took a deposition but said that more witnesses were needed. Keeling decided to introduce his brother John to Goodenough, saying that he could be trusted and Goodenough outlined the plot to him. Keeling then took John to Jenkins' office and tricked him into repeating what Goodenough had told him. Jenkins sent them both away and as the king was at Windsor, immediately informed members of the council and began making arrests and gaining more information. John Keeling realised that he had been duped into betraying the plot and told Goodenough what had happened and advised him to flee. Word spread rapidly among the tactical-level Whig leaders that their plot was known to the government. Nathaniel Wade proposed an immediate muster for a rising, but Colonel Rumsey argued that the situation was hopeless and it was now every man for himself. Rumbold, Rumsey, Wade and several others directly involved in the Rye House Plot went into hiding.

West felt the best way of saving himself was to voluntarily surrender and seek a pardon in return for giving evidence against his accomplices.[10] Rumsey was arrested but wrote to Jenkins from prison also offering to give evidence in return for a pardon. Soon, Goodenough and others decided to cooperate with Jenkins for their lives. Their testaments corroborated the information from the Keeling brothers and implicated Lord William Russell, who was arrested and sent to the Tower. They soon implicated others and the arrests of Essex, Howard, Sidney, Hampden and Wildman soon followed, but Lord Grey of Werke and Sir Thomas Armstrong and Robert Ferguson eluded arrest and escaped to the continent. When the king heard of the Rye House Plot he found it very hard to believe that anyone would want to kill him. That his son Monmouth appeared to be involved in some way was an additional blow. He decided to lead the investigation himself. Meanwhile, Monmouth had gone into hiding and although searches were being made for him, this was done largely for show and Charles hoped that Monmouth would give himself up and reveal his knowledge of the plots. With the king taking the lead in the interview of suspects, more information came out about the plots, some real and some made up to gain reward or to secure personal safety by the transfer of guilt onto others. With the additional information came more arrests, John Rouse, for example, the man who had been planning to capture the Tower offered evidence against Thomas Pilkington, Sir Patience Ward and Sir Thomas Player, all Whig leaders in the city, in exchange for his life.

One of the Whig lords who had managed to go into hiding was Lord Howard of Escrick, but he was later arrested after being found hiding in a cupboard behind a chimney. He rapidly decided to seek a pardon by betraying his erstwhile colleagues. Using his own knowledge of the plots and embroidering them to prove his worth, Howard came up with sufficient damning evidence to convict Essex, Russell and Sidney; this, together with that of Rumsey, West and others, meant that prosecutions could take place.

On 13 July Lord William Russell was brought to trial at the Old Bailey, charged with conspiring to kill the king and wage war against him. The trial was before Chief Justice Pemberton who was believed to be a staunch Tory and the jury had been specially selected as true Tories. To clinch matters, the dedicated Royalist Sir George Jeffreys, led for the prosecution. No sooner had Howard given evidence against his cousin than everyone's attention was drawn to another alleged conspirator. The Earl of Essex was found with his throat cut in his cell at the Tower. By chance, the cell was the same that had held his father, and also his grandfather, before they met their deaths, hardly propitious. Essex had asked for a razor and so his death was probably suicide, but that may not have been the case. Bishop Burnet had spoken to Essex's physician and believed that it was murder because the cut was so deep it had nearly resulted in decapitation. In his own words, 'it was impossible the wound could be as it was, if given by any hand but his own; for except he had cast his head back, and stretched up his neck all he could the *aspera arteria* must have been cut.'[11]

Some said the Duke of York had arranged the murder, but others that Sunderland was the most likely suspect to ensure his final removal as a potential rival. Both theories are rather unlikely. Nevertheless, a Whig lawyer and former member of the Green Ribbon Club, Laurence Braddon, was convinced that Essex had been murdered and began collecting evidence. His investigation did not get far. Braddon was arrested, found guilty of high misdemeanour and fined. The fine was £2,000 (approximately £295,000 today), which it was impossible for him to pay, so he remained in prison for the rest of the reign. Although Essex had been an irritating opponent of the king, Charles had a strong personal bond with him going back to the time when the commonwealth had executed both their fathers within weeks of one another. Assuming Essex had committed suicide rather than face the probability of a traitor's death, he was premature. When the king heard of the suicide he said that he would probably have pardoned him as he 'owed him a life'.[12]

The Russell trial continued, but Essex's apparent suicide enabled Jeffreys to tell the jury that it was proof of his guilt and therefore Russell, his associate, must also be guilty. At the end of the trial Pemberton gave a surprisingly fair summing up, but Russell was found guilty of high treason and condemned to be hanged, drawn and quartered. There was considerable pleading to the king for Russell to be pardoned; he was after all a son of the Duke of Bedford. However, when Lord Dartmouth put the case to the king, Charles replied 'All that is true, but it is as true that if I do not take his life he will soon have mine.'[13] Charles did reduce the sentence to beheading and, at Lincoln's Inn Fields, Russell's head was struck off at the third blow of the axe.

The next person of distinction to be tried was the Republican, Algernon Sidney. The trial was before Jeffreys, who had just been made Chief Justice to replace Pemberton who, it was felt, had not given a sufficiently damning summing up in the Russell trial. It must be admitted that Jeffreys had a debauched lifestyle, even by the standards of the age, and his habitual drunkenness would not normally have marked him out as a suitable candidate for high judicial office. That said, Jeffreys was a protégé of the Duke of York who could be relied upon to use his bullying ways to obstruct the defence and ensure a conviction. Rumsey, Keeling and West were wheeled out to give evidence against Sidney, but did not come over well. Howard owed Sidney a considerable amount of money and spurred on by this, and his hope of a pardon, gave more convincing evidence. However, the evidence of two witnesses was required for a treason conviction. Sidney's house had been searched and the manuscript of an old lampoon of his was found saying that it would be right to rebel against a tyrant such as Nero or Caligula. A few years previously, L'Estrange had extended the definition of libel to include manuscripts and so, with a judge and jury of Tories, Sidney was found guilty of seditious libel. As seditious libel was considered to be the equivalent to the second witness needed for a treason conviction, Jeffreys was home and dry. Sidney was condemned to death and was beheaded on 7 December. Howard received his pardon and Keeling was rewarded for his evidence with £500 and a post in the Victualling Office.[14]

But what of Monmouth? He had been hiding at the home of his mistress Henrietta Wentworth but decided to give himself up before he was pronounced an outlaw. The king wanted to be reconciled with his much loved son, and all he required in return was an assurance of his future loyalty and a frank account of his knowledge of the Whig's plots. Halifax acted as a go between and even drafted Monmouth's letters to the king asking for forgiveness. At last on 25 October, father and son met and it looked as though reconciliation would follow. There then followed a period when Monmouth first agreed, then stepped back, feeling that he was letting his friends down;

then agreeing to sign a statement, but insisting that it should not be made public – and then retracting it. Matters came to a head at the trial of John Hampden, when Monmouth refused to give evidence against him and then fled to the continent. The main evidence came from Howard, but the lack of evidence from a second person, be it Monmouth or anyone else, meant that it was impossible to obtain a conviction for anything other than a misdemeanor. Hampden received a huge fine of £40,000, but kept his life – although being unable to pay the fine, he remained in prison.

Another prominent Whig conspirator had also got off a few months earlier. This was Wildman, who seems to have withdrawn from the Rye House Plot at an early stage after deciding not to put up money to purchase weapons. The evidence against him was from Howard, who accused him of concealing weapons for an uprising but when his house was searched just two old cannon were found in the cellar. Wildman correctly maintained that these were ornamental cannon, which had been given to him by the Duke of Buckingham. Buckingham had retired from the Whig leadership some time ago so was not tainted by the plot and confirmed Wildman's story. Wildman was released under a writ of *habeas corpus* and bail of £1,000; being a rich man, he could afford the bail and returned home. Knowing he was a marked man, he kept a low profile but, being the inveterate conspirator he was, returned to plotting rebellion before a year had passed. Hampden and Wildman had been the lucky ones, but trials of the less fortunate continued. In total twelve people were eventually executed for the Rye House Plot. A few were innocent, such as Henry Cornish, who had been the Whig candidate for Lord Mayor. Although he had taken no part in the plot, Rumsey and Goodenough fabricated evidence against him out of personal animosity, which resulted in his conviction and execution. The majority of those who were executed or imprisoned may not have received the highest standards of justice but had, at the very least, been talking about rebellion. Having been plotting sedition, they must have realised the risk they were running so they were not the innocent martyrs painted by later generations of Whigs.

The Rye House Plot had been exceptionally dangerous. Had it succeeded in murdering the two royal brothers, the country would have been plunged into chaos that could have escalated into a bloody civil war. The discovery of the Rye House Plot had been devastating to the Whig movement, which had been thrown into complete disorder with most of their leaders either dead or fled the country. Charles's next priority was to follow up on this advantage and to enjoy some sweet revenge.

Chapter 18

Peace in His Time
1684–5

'But I must leave dark things to God, and to the great day in which every secret thing will be discovered.'

Bishop Burnet

The Rye House Plot had given the king the perfect opportunity to seize the nation's public opinion from the Whigs. Charles immediately recognised this and determined to ruthlessly exploit the plot just as Shaftesbury had exploited the Popish Plot. A royal proclamation was issued to be read in all churches and chapels, detailing the conspiracy by Whigs and Nonconformists against the king and the Duke of York. There was general horror that radical Whigs and Nonconformists should have come so close to killing the king, just as there had been horror that Papists had been thought to be scheming to kill the king in the Popish Plot. What was more, there was a tide of sympathy for the Duke of York, who many might oppose as a Catholic heir to the throne, but few would want to see murdered. Naturally, there were those whose fear of Popery transcended any sympathy for the king and still less for his brother. Lord William Russell's written speech was handed to the sheriff at his execution. It had probably been drafted by his Chaplain, Reverend Samuel Johnson, who had previously written hard-hitting pamphlets such as *Julian the Apostate*, which compared the Duke of York with the fourth century pagan emperor. The speech was published within hours by John Darby and had numerous reprints. It said that he was innocent of plotting murder for Exclusion, but warned of Popery to come and ended with the stirring words 'Blest be God I fall by the axe not by the fiery trial.'[1]

Robert Ferguson, now safely in Holland, was not slow to publish a pamphlet entitled: *Enquiry into and Detection of the Barbarous Murder of the late Earl of Essex*, saying that the Rye House Plot was all part of a Popish conspiracy organised by the Duke of York. More and more Whig pamphlets were to follow, professing innocence in what they claimed was a Catholic inspired plot and continuing to attack the Duke of York and Louise, Duchess of Portsmouth. It must be remembered that this new Whig propaganda was on top of their huge effort on pamphlets during the previous few years. These included Ferguson's very popular *A letter to a person of honour concerning the King's disavowing the having been married to the Duke of Monmouth's mother*, bringing twenty-one accusations against the Duke of York, including authorising the Fire of London and saying his crimes: 'made him more liable for the axe, while he is aspiring to the sceptre'.[2] The propaganda had taken many forms and included additional wording, which had been added to the plaque on the monument to the Great Fire by a Whig Lord Mayor. The words inscribed were that Papists 'began and carried on that most dreadful burning of this Protestant city'.[3] Another form of successful propaganda were the popular pieces of doggerel which were circulated by hand against Tory ministers and Catholic mistresses, such as this one about Louise:

This French hag's poxy bum
So powerful is of late,
Although it's blind and dumb,
It rules both Church and State.[4]

Despite past and present Whig propaganda, the king was to win the positive public opinion of the great majority of the nation. He had a number of advantages. First, the widespread and genuine feeling of outrage that there had been a plot to assassinate him. This had almost immediately resulted in bonfires celebrating the king's deliverance all over the country. Second, the high quality of Tory propaganda to be found in the only three legal newspapers: Sir Roger L'Estrange's *Observer*, Edward Rawlins's *Heraclitus Ridens* and Nathaniel Thompson's *True Domestic Intelligence*. They took up a theme that had begun almost two years previously by the friend of Nell Gwynn and former spy, Aphra Behn, in her play *The Roundheads or, the Good Old Cause*. This equated Whigs and Nonconformists to the Roundheads, who had been responsible for causing the bloody Civil War. Tory propagandists now took this further. They argued that Anglicanism was the true bulwark of Protestantism. Nonconformists would bring down the state and make it vulnerable to being taken over by Papists, and then fall victim to arbitrary government of the type in France. The logic of this assertion may not have been foolproof, but it was accepted by many and resulted in 283 loyal addresses to the king in England and Wales.[5]

A third reason for the king winning the all-important propaganda war was that, over time, he managed to stifle most Whig printing. Related to this was the progress he was making in forcing through new city charters using the *Quo warranto* procedure. It was made clear that if a corporation surrendered it's charter and received a new one more favourable to the king, it could keep its privileges – such as existing markets – and might be granted additional ones, such as a horse market. Three corporations had agreed to this by the beginning of 1684, but major cities such as London and Bristol had resisted. Once Jeffreys had become Lord Chief Justice, the Kings Bench was under royal control. In order to have a charter removed, it was necessary to prove that a corporation had misused or exceeded its charter. Jeffreys came up with the rather spurious accusation that the city had raised an illegal tax to help pay for the damage of the Great Fire. Naturally the city was found guilty and so rapidly decided to surrender its charter and receive a new one which gave the king power over the election of key figures such as the Aldermen and Common Councilmen and sheriffs, and so control the appointment of London juries. With compliant courts it became simple to carry out successful prosecutions for the many controls of the press that had been instigated by royal proclamation since the lapse of the Licensing Act.

What had been successful in London was used in other parts of the country. Eleven judges were removed during the year and replaced by sound Tories.[6] Having seen that the powerful London corporation had been obliged to give up its charter, borough corporations around the country began surrendering the charters even before *Quo warranto* procedure could be started. They received new ones enabling the king to reserve the right to nominate the aldermen, recorder, town clerk and common council. So many charters were surrendered that the issue of new charters had to be put into priority order. The towns of strategic importance were issued first, then towns such as Taunton, with large numbers of Whig sympathisers in office. The removal of Whigs or Whig sympathisers was extended to justices of the peace and deputy lieutenants.[7] This all took a fair amount of time but by the end of the year, the king could rely on loyal support from the civic and county leaders in most parts of the country.

With an increasingly compliant judiciary, the recent legislation against the press could be enforced. Ordinances had been published by the Stationers' Company requiring all printed pieces to show the name of the printer. Of course, only authorised printers were permitted and they could only print authorised material. This was normally rigorously enforced by L'Estrange's men although they were not unknown to accept bribes to turn a blind eye.[8] Reverand Samuel Johnson, the author of *Julian the Apostate* and Russell's scaffold speech, was arrested for seditious libel. He was found guilty and fined 500 marks (equating to £240 or approximately £36,000 today) which he could not pay and so spent the next four years in gaol for the non-payment of a fine. Others would follow.

The Crown had succeeded in the propaganda war and convinced the majority of the population of the link between political opposition and nonconformity. In the public mind, both Whigs and Nonconformists were linked as enemies of Anglicanism, Protestantism and the state itself. In order to please Anglicans and fully exploit the Rye House Plot, the government returned to the persecution of dissenters. Of course the dissenters had been harassed for some time. John Hilton had been able to report to the king in January that he had dissolved more than forty meeting houses, and the ministers had either agreed to conform to the Anglican Church, or been driven from their homes and imprisoned.[9] Soon after, magistrates were directed to apply the Clarendon Code in full, and those caught attending conventicles were arrested. Now magistrates, the judiciary and juries were largely under royal influence, if not direct control, there was no hope of mercy for dissenters brought to court. Under these circumstances many decided to attend their Anglican church, take any oath of Supremacy that was put to them, but secretly follow their own religion. This course of action was not open to Quakers and some Baptists because they considered it ungodly to swear any oath. Those caught attending a meetinghouse were fined five shillings, but if they were caught again they were likely to be charged with riot and brought before the courts. Conveniently for the authorities, riot was defined as three or more people gathered to commit an illegal act. Large fines were levied. In one year in Bristol alone, fines totalling £16,420 (approximately £2.5 million today) were levied on 191 Quakers for failing to attend church. Many could only pay by selling their homes and possessions, some simply fled, but the majority ended in prison for non-payment. About 500 Quakers were to die in the overcrowded, filthy and infectious prisons.[10]

As far as the court was concerned, life continued with the usual rivalries, scheming and jostling for patronage. There were a few important changes. Following the Rye House Plot the king stepped up his security. He went out only with an escort of guards and charged Christopher Wren with arranging for the many doors and gates to Whitehall and St James's Park to be locked.

It is not known whether Charles really feared assassination, or whether it was all part of the propaganda to gain public sympathy by drawing attention to the threats against him. Earlier in the reign, Charles is said to have joked with his brother that no-one would kill him to put James on the throne. Charles had not considered the Rye House Plot scenario of assassinating both, so he may indeed have begun to be genuinely careful about his personal security. The greatest change that took place in early 1684 was that the Duke of York returned to being a prominent figure at court. He was constantly at the king's side and in May, returned to the Privy Council after an eleven-year absence. Furthermore, James was given the powers, but not the title, of Lord High Admiral, with him running the navy and the king formally signing official documents. The king's propaganda success in winning the moral high ground emboldened him to make other reverses to return to the situation before he had been faced by antagonistic parliaments. Danby was released on bail, but not yet returned to office. Also released were the remaining innocent Catholic peers who had been held in the Tower.

One of those who had been a casualty of the Popish Plot, but was restored thanks to the fallout from the Rye House Plot, was Samuel Pepys. His restoration had begun soon after the discovery of the Rye House Plot, when he received a letter saying no more than to report directly to Lord Dartsmouth at Portsmouth. Up to that time, Pepys had been desperately trying to prove he was innocent of the charges against him. John James, the butler who he had sacked for being caught sleeping with one of the servants, had accused Pepys of being a Papist. Fortunately, James had made a deathbed confession in front of a witness that his allegation had been false. Pepys also gathered enough evidence to prove that the accusation of involvement in piracy was untrue. The accusations of treachery by the swaggering fraudster John Scott had proved more difficult. As Scott had gone to France, Pepys sent his French speaking brother-in-law there to find out as much as he could about him.

What was eventually discovered gives a glimpse of the life of a rogue at that time. 'Colonel' Scott, as he called himself, was the son of a Royalist Colonel who had been transported to Massachusetts under Cromwell, where John grew up. After a number of brushes with the law, Scott got a commission and served in the West Indies in the Dutch War but was court marshalled for cowardice. By then married, he abandoned his wife and family and travelled to Europe, carrying out frauds such as preying on widows, selling non-existent property, and obtaining fees for his pretended powers of alchemy. Whenever he was unmasked he managed to elude the authorities and escape, using one of his many false names and disguises, which even included being dressed as a milliner. He had returned briefly to England but having killed a coachman, fled to Scandinavia and so was no longer likely to cause Pepys any trouble.[11]

This is all Pepys knew about Scott, but there was an even more colourful side to this adventurer: he was also a spy. Scott had met Williamson when he first came to London in 1662 and was later introduced to Arlington as a potential agent. Williamson's attitude to Scott cooled when he found that he had stolen money from his house. Scott was imprisoned for debt, but on release he had killed a page of the Duke of York and fled to the Netherlands, where he joined the Dutch Army. With Scott so well placed, Williamson forgave the theft incident and took him on as an agent. Scott met Arlington and Buckingham when they visited on a peace mission and was instructed to operate in Bruges, but was driven out soon after he arrived. Scott had been providing intelligence reports for Williamson but was also working as a double agent for de Witt, to whom he betrayed English agents. Moving on to Paris, still in the pay of Williamson and de Witt, he was also taken on as an agent by the French Treasury Department. This unauthorised tripartite intelligence exchange came to an end when Scott's value as an agent declined as England was no longer at war. Scott then decided to renew his acquaintance with Buckingham, who took him on to carry out any nefarious work for the Whig cause.[12] It had been in this capacity that he had agreed to make the false allegation against Pepys.

When Pepys reported to Admiral Lord Dartmouth in Portsmouth in August 1683, he was told only that he would be accompanying him and his fleet on a secret mission, the orders for which were not to be opened until after they had set sail. The good news was that Pepys would receive pay of a very welcome £4 a day. Once the fleet had left for open waters, the orders were opened and it was revealed that its task was to abandon Tangier, destroying the fortifications, and return the garrison to England. Tangier had brought no commercial gains to speak of and its maintenance had been a massive cost to the Treasury. The garrison had an uneasy truce with the Moors, which would expire in a year's time, and a commission had reported that it would cost the impossible sum of £4,798,561 to make it defensible.[13] It would only be a matter of time before it would be captured by the great warrior, Sultan Moulay Ismail, who was in the process of conquering the whole of Morocco. He was noted for adorning his city walls with the heads of 10,000 of his slain enemies. Any survivors of an English garrison, which either surrendered or was defeated, could anticipate agonising deaths, for Moulay was not a man to do things by halves. For example, even in his domestic life he is known to have fathered 876 children (525 sons and 342 daughters), which makes Charles II positively monastic in comparison. Charles had reluctantly accepted that it was no longer viable to hold the town. When Dartmouth arrived at Tangier he got to work mining the fortifications and destroying the harbour. Pepys, who had been Treasurer of Tangier before he had to resign his appointments, provided the administrative support for the operation. In early 1684, Dartmouth, Pepys and the fleet returned to England leaving Tangier largely destroyed, and arriving back with about three regiments totalling around 9,000 soldiers as well as their families and others from the garrison. On their return to England, the Tangier troops were sent to barracks in the South of England and made a significant increase to the king's army. Although there was absolutely no sign of any active preparations for rebellion, it must have been reassuring for Charles to have these battle-hardened troops at his disposal.

Pepys was fortunate to arrive back at about the time that his patron the Duke of York had gone back to running the Navy. He was not only invited to return to the Naval Office, but given promotion to the post of Secretary for the Affairs of the Admiralty of England on £2,000 per annum.[14] As Pepys was returning to public life, Sir Leoline Jenkins was bowing out through ill-health. He resigned in April 1684 but did not have long to enjoy his retirement in his home village of Hammersmith, for he died the next year. Jenkins had made a professional job of his secondary role of head of intelligence and had redirected intelligence-gathering to concentrate on Whig radicals, particularly those who had fled overseas. Sunderland took over the senior secretary appointment of the Southern Department but, as was his wont, took no part in intelligence management. Sidney, Lord Godolphin, briefly replaced Sunderland in the Northern Department from April to August and then it was passed to the Earl of Middleton. The Duke of York had been impressed by Middleton during his time in Scotland and in 1682 had made him joint secretary of state for Scotland with the Earl of Moray. Middleton later followed James to England and was made a member of the Privy Council. That Middleton was now appointed secretary of state for the Northern Department was an indication of James's increased influence at court.

Middleton had left a Scotland where Presbyterians were still undergoing persecution, much of which was Middleton's making. In September 1683 a minister called James Renwick came from the United Provinces to Scotland and restarted field conventicles in the South West. As might be expected, soldiers were called out and arrests made. This did not stop Renwick, whose little group of Cameronians and other Covenanters formally declared war on the king in a document called *Apologetical Declaration*. The council responded by saying that anyone who refused to denounce the document would be hanged. Also, for good measure, anyone who refused to take the Test Act would also face hanging, or the apparently equal fate of transportation to Carolina. Such transportation was also widely used for ordinary prisoners to help relieve the overflowing gaols.

Those engaged in the Rye House Plot in England had been working with both Argyll and some of the Scottish Covenanters about coordinating a rebellion in both countries. The investigations following the revelation of the plot led to many arrests in England, including suspect Scots, the most notable of which were Sir Hugh Campbell, William Spence, William Carstares, and Alexander Monro. As no evidence could be found against them, it was decided to send these man and others to Scotland, which had the convenience of allowing torture and did not have habeas corpus. The king decided to clarify the legal position over torture in Scotland and on 14 June wrote about it to the Scottish Council. His limitations were that there should be at least one witness against the accused and that a prisoner could not be tortured again if they failed to confess, and should not be killed under torture.

The Scots felt, under the circumstances, these new-fangled rules did not necessarily apply to William Spence or William Carstares. Spence was the Earl of Argyll's secretary and was thought to know the key to decipher some of the duke's captured correspondence. Spence was subjected to three different types of torture. On 25 July he had the boot and received eighteen blows of the mallet, this was followed by sleep deprivation by putting him in a hair shirt and prodding him with hot pokers whenever he fell asleep or passed out. Although this procedure was often used with success against 'witches', it did not succeed with Spence. The council decided to import a new invention from Russia, the thumbscrew. It is interesting that the Scots seem to have traditionally favoured using mechanical means of torture such as the maiden and the boot. Despite strong commercial ties with Holland, the Scots did not consider simply using a wet rag like the thrifty Dutch who had invented water boarding. Nevertheless, the thumbscrews worked, Spence broke and provided the key to Argyll's code which, when decrypted, showed that he and others were planning to raise a rebel army in Scotland.

The council's interrogators now moved on to Carstares who, having been given the thumbscrews and threatened with the boot, confessed, and named others to be arrested and tortured. Some of those named, like Robert Bailley of Jerviswood, had been in prison without charge for more than a year. As he was ill, it was decided to establish guilt before he died. The evidence of

Carstares was inadmissible but was read to the Jury as background information; Bailley was found guilty and executed the same day. So the process continued with some prominent men such as Walter Scott, Earl of Tarras, having their lands subject to attainder. Eventually the council had succeeded in punishing virtually all suspects who had not fled abroad. Meanwhile, sheriffs such as Claverhouse were continuing to arrest and drag before the courts those who would not take the oath of allegiance, or were found attending Presbyterian meetings. There were occasions when the bureaucracy of the court was omitted and suspects were summarily executed on the spot. Claverhouse himself is believed to have had eight or nine men shot.[16] There was occasional retaliation from the Covenanters, such as when there was a mass attack on a prison in Kirkcudbright, which resulted in a sentry being killed and some prisoners released, but that was very much the exception. Most Presbyterians decided it was prudent to begin attending church and keep their real beliefs strictly limited to friends they could trust. During this period of the 'killing times', over 100 people were executed, several killed during arrest, and many hundreds more gaoled or transported. But the government got its way and Scotland had become outwardly subservient to the Anglican faith.

Back in London it was past the third anniversary since parliament had been dissolved. Halifax thought he should remind the king of the Triennial Act of 1641, which had brought in the law that parliaments had to be called at intervals of no more than three years. The king was not interested, he had had enough of parliaments and in any case there was his undertaking to Louis not to call one. Halifax believed in parliament and was always trying to find middle ground between extreme Whig and Tory positions, but accepted the king's wishes. A public outcry that parliament had not been summoned might have been expected, but times had changed. Gone were the days of civic petitions to call a parliament; the Whigs were in too much disarray to organise them and the corporations had no intention of offending the king while their charters were being scrutinised.

To the Duke of York, Sunderland and Louise, Halifax's suggestion to have a parliament made him no better than a crypto-Whig and they made common cause against him. They also joined forces against Rochester, who was a strong Anglican and supported the United Provinces while they favoured France. Although Halifax and Rochester both wanted good relations with the United Provinces, it did not prevent their intense dislike of each other. As always, power ultimately rested with the king, but Charles had allowed Louise to become a power in her own right. For years she had been more queenly that the queen, regularly taking the queen's place at official events and receiving the French ambassador almost daily. While Queen Catherine had been content with modest accommodation in Somerset House, Louise occupied forty rooms in the Palace of Whitehall and filled them with lacquered cabinets and Gobelin tapestries. She had her own royal yacht called the 'Fubbs' after Charles's nick name for her, and when she had visited France two years previously, she had gone everywhere with four coaches bearing Charles's coat of arms, with coachmen in royal livery and 600 horses.[17] Louise had developed from a pretty, baby-faced mistress with studied innocence and femininity, into someone who was equal with the king's principal ministers in affairs of state and often stood in for the king at official receptions.

Louise, Sunderland and Halifax may not have thought much of Rochester, but he had been done a pretty good job as Lord Treasurer. The farming of customs had been replaced by direct taxation and there was far greater supervision of remaining tax farmers. New concepts were introduced including the edict that all promotions in Customs should be based on merit, and that Excise staff should be given training and receive salaries rather than back-handers from the public. Apart from his efficiency, Rochester had the ability to persuade the king to be less extravagant – except over the obvious ring-fenced expenses of royal mistresses and their children. Rochester was also fortunate. The country was no longer at war, and with Tangier abandoned there would be no further requirement for its costly resupply and maintenance. With peace came increasing trade, which coincided with an increased demand for English cloth, and both imports and exports of colonial products, particularly, sugar, tobacco and calicoes. The king's annual revenue, which was largely from customs, rose from £1.1 to £1.4 million, while his expenditure was about £4.2 million.[18,19] The situation was not quite as rosy as it seemed though because Charles had considerable debts to pay off, but what it did mean was that he was a man of independent means; he did not need parliament.

In August 1684 Halifax saw an opportunity to attack Rochester over supposed mismanagement of the Treasury, alleging that £40,000 of chimney tax could not be accounted for. As a result the king moved Rochester to the post of Lord President of the Council, nominally a more senior role but in reality, it was a move to the side lines. A gleeful Halifax remarked that Rochester had been 'kicked upstairs'. To balance this victory for Halifax, the king made Sunderland's protégé, Godolphin, Lord Treasurer. For some reason the relationship between the king and the Duke of York began to cool during that summer, but there was no doubt that Charles was gradually pursuing his own preference for France and Catholicism. This will have been encouraged by Louise, but was exactly the same direction that James wanted. Another thing the brothers wanted was revenge on those who had made their lives so difficult over the previous couple of years. An obvious choice was Titus Oates. With public opinion now behind support for the king and his brother, it was at last safe to act.

Oates's star was definitely in decline. His pension had been £12 a week but had declined to £2 and was finally removed. Except with a few die hard anti-Papists, his popularity had evaporated. It was a sign of the times that, unbeknown to him, his brother Samuel had become a government informant and was providing information about the remaining Whig clubs. In June, the Duke of York had brought an action for defamation against Oates alleging that he had called him a traitor. The case went before the Kings Bench presided over by Judge Jeffreys and a suitable jury. Jeffreys ruled that Oates should pay damages of £100,000 and costs of 20 shillings to the Duke of York. Obviously Oates could not pay this sum so was placed in irons in the King's Bench Prison. There he was to remain, not realising that far greater punishment awaited him in the next reign when he would be placed annually in the pillory and whipped all the way from Aldgate to Newgate then Newgate to Tyburn, a total of ninety-two miles.

Another area for revenge was on those Whigs, Phanaticks and radicals who had escaped abroad. Most had settled in the United Provinces and Charles had hoped that his nephew William would arrest them. That was not going to happen because Calvinist Holland had a long tradition of welcoming Nonconformist Protestants seeking asylum. Indeed, it was as a result of this disagreement that Sunderland persuaded the king to arrange for James's younger daughter Anne to be married to the brother of the King of Denmark, an ally of Louis and therefore opposed to William. The marriage went ahead and was popular in the country because an English princess was marrying into a Protestant family. William of Orange was less pleased and this made him even less likely to cooperate over harbouring English exiles. Charles had to fall back on the customary way of getting things done in the United Provinces: covert operations.

Sir Leoline Jenkins had been running agents and informants against the Whigs and their allies both at home and abroad. A considerable amount of effort had been expended, directly or through sheriffs and magistrates, to obtain informant information about the potentially dangerous opposition. Following the Whig route after the revelations of the Rye House Plot the intelligence gathering effort concentrated on the United Provinces. That does not mean that intelligence gathering in England was totally neglected. Nonconformists had been largely under government control but it was still important to keep tabs on the Whig clubs with their dwindling membership, and those aristocrats and gentry who had welcomed Monmouth on his tours around the country. Mary Speke and her husband George were gentry who had entertained Monmouth when he visited Ilminster.[20] Mary and her children were some of those who remained strong Whig activists and in the words of the Bishop of Bath and Wells: 'there is not a more dangerous woman in the west than she.' There were also some radicals and Phanaticks like John Wildman to keep an eye on, but virtually all opposition of note had fled abroad. Following Jenkins's resignation there had been something of a vacuum in the government's intelligence management until August, when the Earl of Middleton decided to take on the task. His track record as secretary of state in Scotland showed that he would not be squeamish in undertaking covert activity, and this proved to be the case. The other person who was important to intelligence gathering was the English envoy to The Hague, Thomas Chudleigh, who had been in post for two-and-a-half years. It was Chudleigh who had put Shaftesbury and his small group under surveillance when they fled to Amsterdam, and did what he could to monitor the activities of the Earl of Argyll.

Monmouth's friend and adviser, Sir Thomas Armstrong, had been indicted for treason and subsequently declared an outlaw but had fled first to Cleves with Grey and Ferguson, and then moved to Rotterdam using the alias 'Henry Lawrence'. Armstrong then decided to journey to Amsterdam, Chudleigh heard of this and set a trap. Chudleigh's agents captured Armstrong as he travelled through Leiden, kidnapped him and bundled him into a ship they had standing by to take him to England. He appeared before the King's Bench on 14 June but Judge Jeffreys rejected a request for a trial and immediately sentenced him to execution, which was carried out six days later. Armstrong's head was spiked onto Westminster Hall, three of his four quarters distributed about the City, and one quarter sent to Stafford.[21] The sentence of being hanged, drawn and quartered continued until the Forfeiture Act of 1870 and many more people would receive it before then. What makes Armstrong's execution of note is that it is believed to be the last one in which the prisoner remained alive after hanging and therefore conscious for the remaining parts of the sentence. As a reminder of what those were, this is an extract from the record of one of Judge Jeffreys's sentences:

That you be conveyed from hence to a place from whence you came, and that you be coveyed from there on hurdles to a place of execution, where you are to be hanged by the neck; that you be cut down alive, that your privy members be cut off, your bowels taken out and burned in your view; that your head be severed from your body; that your body be divided into four quarters, to be disposed of at the king's pleasure; and the god of infinite mercy have mercy on your soul.[22]

When Armstrong was captured he was found in possession of correspondence with Monmouth. As Monmouth was perhaps the greatest remaining threat to the royal brothers, his position was rather strange. His indulgent father had not forgiven him, but was sending him money to support himself in exile. Monmouth was still carrying out a bit of intrigue with people like Armstrong and Argyll, but was mainly occupied with having a pleasant time in Holland. He had been welcomed by William and Mary, who liked their charming cousin. Monmouth therefore passed the year hunting, skating, dancing and dining at William and Mary's court in The Hague.

With Monmouth distracted by the pleasures of life in The Hague with his mistress Henrietta Wentworth, the nearest the opposition had to a leader was the Earl of Argyll. He, together with his son Lord Melville, the Earl of Loudoun, and Sir John Cochrane, had fled Scotland to Friesland. Non-Scottish Whigs such as Richard Goodenough, the former London under-sheriff, began associating with them. Argyll began travelling around the United Provinces meeting the Scottish Presbyterian communities in exile and trying to raise money for eventual rebellion. He also managed to get hold of some of the weapons that had been gathered by the Cameronians. While doing this, he was trying to press Monmouth into action but received little but vague words of encouragement in reply.

The main base for English exiled Whigs and radicals was Amsterdam. Colonel Rumsey and Captain Walcot had gone there with Shaftesbury, as had Ferguson, but he had returned to England soon after Shaftesbury's death. Shaftesbury's secretary, John Locke, had also gone to Amsterdam but although he had contact with other Whigs, he does not seem to have been taking part in any seditious activity. Rather surprisingly, women played a significant part in the nefarious operations going on. These ladies were known as 'nursing mothers' in reference to a mother giving succour to a cause in Isaiah 49:23. Many of the nursing mothers mentioned in intelligence reports acted as couriers such as, for example, Constance Ward, an Anabaptist, and

Susannah Nelthorp, the wife of a Rye House conspirator who carried messages to and from England. Suzanne Burger and Jane Hall were also suspect couriers, but some nursing mothers had other roles. Widow Broning was a bookseller in Amsterdam and sold seditious publications including Francis Smith's *Protestant Intelligence*. Her shop was regularly visited by Phanaticks and so was well worth keeping under surveillance. The nursing mothers were not confined to Amsterdam. After Argyll had been rescued from Edinburgh Castle by his daughter-in-law, Lady Sophia Lindsay, he had been hidden in London by Ann Smith until Captain Nicholas Lockyer could arrange a safe passage abroad. Ann's husband William had helped Thomas Walcot with his plans to capture the Tower as part of the Rye House Plot. Ann and her husband decided to flee to Utrecht soon after which William died, leaving her a rich widow. She continued to support the Whig cause and put up other exiles such as Elizabeth Gaunt, a Baptist from Wapping who would later be burnt at the stake at Tyburn for treason. Ann would eventually provide the considerable sum of £ 9,000 to help fund Monmouth's rebellion.[23]

Courageous though the activities of these women were, they did not make any real difference at the time, nor did that of the menfolk. Dissidents were mainly well known personalities who found it hard to be inconspicuous. The agents and informants of Thomas Chudleigh at The Hague Embassy, and Middleton's secretarial intelligence office had the exiled community pretty well covered. The people engaged in this work were mainly scoundrels such as Edmund Everard, who had entrapped Fitzharris and decided to make a career of intrigue. In late 1680 he had been sent to the United Provinces specifically to spy on the Whigs. Having worked in a secretarial position for Monmouth at one time, he had the right credentials to insinuate himself among Whig and Nonconformist groups. In time he established himself as a merchant, and by 1684 he was very much integrated into the exiled community.[24]

A few Whigs, Covenanters and Phanaticks at home and overseas plotted and communicated with each other but nothing came of it. Had they got anywhere near organising a rebellion, the numbers of people needed for the plot meant that it would very likely have been picked up by government informants. In the even more unlikely event that they had actually launched a rebellion, it would have been quickly snuffed out. The king's army was small in comparison with that of Louis, which was 100,000 strong, but Louis had been at war and recently taken possession of Strasburg and Luxemburg. The army in England was 9,000 strong and there were another 2,000 in Scotland and 7,500 in Ireland.[25] Not very large, but there was also the militia whose officers, like those of the Regular regiments, had been purged. The reasonably well trained, disciplined and equipped troops at the king's disposal would have been more than enough to rout any thrown-together band of rebels with makeshift weapons. In short, the king was in a very strong position to crush any armed opposition and, even more importantly, had created the situation in which there was little prospect of serious opposition.

Ireland had remained quiet for years and in Scotland the relatively trivial opposition of the Cameronians had been stamped on without mercy. In England the corporations, sheriffs, magistrates and judiciary were favourable to the Crown and were likely to report, and deal with, any sign of sedition. The remaining Whigs and Phanaticks had mostly fled abroad and their seditious activities, such as they were, were being closely monitored by government agents and informants. Most important of all, thanks to the public reaction to the Rye House Plot and the work of the secretaries of state in winning the propaganda war, the king was popular. The country was becoming more prosperous and the failure to call parliament aroused little concern. There remained considerable public prejudice against Catholics, but the furious hatred of the time of the Popish Plot had burned itself out. There remained concern that the Catholic Duke of York was the heir to the throne but for all anyone knew, he might not outlive his brother and then his Protestant daughter Mary would become heir.

The new year of 1685 saw the government dominated by a triumvirate. It was a bitterly cold winter and the Thames had frozen over, but there had been a thaw in the coolness between the royal brothers. The Duke of York was now firmly by the king's side and supervising much of the administration. Louise was also prominent with Ambassador Barillon in the background and Sunderland had become principal minister. Sunderland had been able to look on smugly as his rival, Halifax, manoeuvred his other rival, Rochester, out of the main stream to become Lord President. Halifax remained Lord Privy Seal but was increasingly side-lined. In order to further remove Rochester, Sunderland encouraged the king to make Rochester Lord Lieutenant of Ireland on the pretext that Ormonde was being too favourable to Catholic officers. This would put Rochester nicely out of the way, with the added bonus that the army of Ireland was to come under the secretary of state rather than the Lord Lieutenant. Charles agreed to this knowing that Sunderland could not become too powerful with the Duke of York taking an active part in government and Louise also at the centre of things and keeping him in the picture.

With the throne secure, no wars or other national misfortunes, and the government under control, Charles could relax and enjoy life. Not that even in the crisis years he had failed to take the opportunity of enjoying himself, but the increase in the royal revenue meant that he could do as he wished without seeking funding from parliament. Charles could get on with his sports and interests, particularly his new palace at Winchester. His private life was also good. He was naturally saddened about the estrangement with Monmouth, but he revelled in the company of his many other children and their offspring. Buckingham had given up politics and was spending most of his time in Yorkshire but returned to court from time to time as an amiable companion. Barbara, Duchess of Cleveland, had recently returned to London and was living at Arlington Street with her latest lover, an actor and former highwayman called Cardonell Goodman, whose nickname 'Scum' gives an indication of his character. Nevertheless, Barbara was welcomed back to court now merely as an old friend. Also welcomed at court as an old friend was Hortense, Duchess of Mazarin, and then there was always the amusing Nell Gwynn. Louise, Duchess of Portsmouth, had long been the real love of the king's life, but Charles enjoyed being in the company of a number of glamorous ladies. John Evelyn's rather censorious description in his diary gives a snapshot of the king's life as he saw it when visiting the Palace of Whitehall on 1 February:

> *I can never forget the inexpressible luxury and profaneness, gaming and all dissoluteness, as it were total forgetful of God (it being Sunday evening) ..... the King sitting and toying with his concubines, Portsmouth, Cleveland and Mazarin, &c, a French boy singing love-songs in that glorious gallery, whilst about twenty of the great courtiers and other dissolute persons were at Basset round a large table, a bank of at least two thousand in gold before them.*[26]

The morning after this relaxed Sunday evening playing cards with old friends, the king looked pale. While having his daily shave he suddenly collapsed in a fit. Physicians were called and he was bled, with sixteen ounces of blood removed. As this did not result in an improvement more physicians were called with additional remedies. For the next five days the best-known medical practices were tried, on top of renewed copious bleeding. Pigeons were put at his feet, which seemed to have helped cure the queen when she had been ill a few years previously, but appeared to have no effect on a male patient. Charles's hair was cut and a blistering agent applied to his skull, some fifty-eight different drugs were administered, often with hideous results, and

234

red-hot irons applied to his head and bare feet. During this ordeal Charles sometimes rallied, but by Wednesday it was clear he was dying. The queen, the Duke of York and Louise all agreed that Charles should die a Catholic. Arrangements were made for Father Huddleston to come to Charles, in disguise, in the queen's apartments through a secret door. Charles welcomed Huddleston and very willingly converted into the Catholic faith, then Huddleston left as secretly as he came. The king was not a religious man but was a Catholic at heart and, by his conversion, joined the faith of his mother, wife, brother and mistress and kept his promise to his cousin Louis.

Thursday was a day of deathbed farewells to Queen Catherine, James, and Charles's many children, who knelt beside him to receive his blessing. The next day, after having been bled of another twelve ounces of blood, the king fell into a coma and died at noon. He was aged 54. The sudden death of a king usually aroused rumours of murder and this was no exception. The Whigs, in particular, began saying that he had been murdered by the Papists so that James could become king. They also came up with a story that Charles had been murdered by his brother because he had decided to make Monmouth his heir. At the time, the royal physicians all agreed that the death was from 'apoplexy', but modern medical examination of the records of his illness suggest that Charles had died of a chronic glandular kidney disease with uraemic convulsions. He was not poisoned, or even killed by the bizarre medical practices of the day; his kidney disease would have killed him anyway.[27]

Precautions had already been taken as the king lay dying. Louise, for example, had sent much of her jewellery and valuables to Barrillion at the French embassy in case she might have to make a hurried exit. The council had ordered extra guards to be deployed around Whitehall, warships to be stationed at sea, and all ports closed to ensure word of the king's illness did not get to Monmouth. These were sensible precautions but turned out to be unnecessary. The transition of government was to run very smoothly. Quarter of an hour after Charles had died his brother, now King James II, held a council meeting and confirmed all the current appointments. He later issued a proclamation that he would protect the Church of England and call parliament. There was a general outpouring of goodwill towards the new king. Church bells rang and celebratory bonfires were lit all over the country; conduits of wine even flowed in Oxford, Southampton and Ludlow. When parliament sat in May it had a Commons largely composed of Tory MPs thanks to the work of the secretaries of state during the last few years in purging Whigs from positions of influence. A compliant parliament voted supplies to the king without delay.

This smooth takeover of the new administration was briefly interrupted by the Monmouth Rebellion, but even that ended satisfactorily. Monmouth, urged on by Argyll and Wildman from London, had decided that it was now or never to return and start Protestant rebellions in England and Scotland. Naturally the government agents in the United Provinces became aware of this and Secretary Middleton was informed of Monmouth's intentions by the envoy in The Hague. Soon after, Middleton received intelligence of Argyll's plans for landing in the Highlands. Argyll did set off with 300 men in three ships in early April but stopped in Orkney, where his secretary disembarked but was arrested, tortured and gave the code to decipher Argyll's intercepted letters. By the time Argyll sailed round to the West Coast, the Edinburgh government had received information of his plan. They called out the militia and dispatched a force of 3,000 Regulars to meet him. When Argyll landed he rallied some of his clansmen, but his ships were captured and very soon his army melted away as government forces approached. Argyll fled but was captured and executed on 30 June. Charles's reign in Scotland may have seen repression, but the government had learnt how to deal with rebels.

Monmouth landed in Lyme with eighty men on 11 June and did not fare much better. Mayors, deputy lord lieutenants and their informants kept Middleton abreast of developments. Monmouth moved to Taunton where he was proclaimed king. His force rose to nearly 4,000 but was composed of artisans and farmers whose enthusiasm for the Protestant religion did not make up for their lack of arms and military training. The promises of support from Whig gentry and magnates did not materialise; in fact, many were falling over themselves to profess loyalty to the king. The county militia had been called out and Monmouth did not have the capability to capture any towns, so moved to Bridgewater to await the arrival of a government force of 3,000 regulars. This force had seventeen cannon and its soldiers consisted of hardened infantry newly returned from Tangier, and cavalry commanded by John Churchill (future Duke of Marlborough). Monmouth decided his best hope was to take his army on a night attack on the army of the government encamped at Sedgemoor. The night advance was chaotic as they floundered into the deep water-filled ditches in the area, and the battle at daybreak proved a complete disaster. Monmouth's disorderly army was put to rout and cut down in their flight. Monmouth fled the field, was captured and executed on 15 July. His unfortunate supporters were rounded up and brought before the Bloody Assizes of Judge Jeffreys.

The swift end to the Monmouth rebellion was thanks to the legacy of Charles II's standing army, intelligence organisation and, most of all, the goodwill towards the king. The majority of the nation had been shocked by the rebellion and rallied to the Crown. James could have exploited this just as Charles had exploited public opinion after the Rye House Plot but he was of a different mould. Instead, James overplayed his hand, insisting on having a 14,000 strong army and commissioning Catholics as officers. The next three years would see James receiving the papal nuncio, putting more and more Catholics into positions of power, and generally moving the country towards Catholicism. He issued a Declaration of Indulgence, removing the penalties against Catholics and Nonconformists. When the Archbishop of Canterbury and six other Anglican bishops asked him to reconsider, he had them arrested for seditious libel. James was exhibiting the worst symptoms of the type of arbitrary government that Louis was conducting with his persecution of Protestants. In blatantly supporting Catholicism, James alienated the ninety-five per cent of his English subjects who were Protestant and so revived the worst fears of Popery that had existed during the Popish Plot. When his queen produced a male heir it was feared that instead of Protestant Mary succeeding to the throne, there would soon be a Catholic dynasty. Some leading Protestant peers agreed that in order to stop England becoming a Catholic country, they would invite William and Mary to accept the throne. William landed with an army at Torbay in November 1688; many Protestant officers, such as John Churchill, defected to him and he advanced without opposition to London. James fled for France and in February the next year, parliament invited William and Mary to be co-sovereigns.

James had lost his throne in just four years. The fact that it could be lost so quickly shows the powerful forces that could have endangered his brother Charles's seat on the throne had he not been an astute politician with some effective ministers, particularly as secretaries of state. As it was, Charles reigned for quarter of a century and succeeded in withstanding the threats against him, which gradually developed from Republicans, Phanaticks and Covenanters into Whigs. Charles was indolent and pleasure-seeking, but he had a good understanding of what would be acceptable to his subjects. Control of the press helped him to win the support of his people and his intelligence service enabled him to identify those who opposed him and take action against them. This combination brought peace and prosperity to the last years of his reign. The fact that his legacy was soon squandered by his brother does not mean that we should lose sight of that legacy.

Appendix 1

Stuart Family Tree

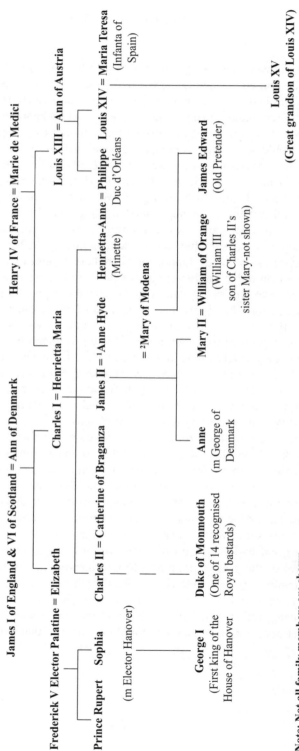

Note: Not all family members are shown

Appendix 2

Dramatis Personae

Ladies

Aphra Behn, agent in Dutch War became famous as playwright, poet and novelist, died 1689.

Barbara Palmer neé Villiers, Countess of Castlemaine, Duchess of Cleveland, mistress of Charles II 1660–73, hated Clarendon. After many other lovers died of dropsy 1709.

Frances Stuart, Charles wanted her as a mistress from 1663–67 but she eloped with Duke of Richmond, died childless 1702.

Hortense Mancini, Duchess Mazarin, mistress of Charles II 1675–6, died in debt, London 1699.

Louise de Kéroüalle, Duchess of Portsmouth, Catholic mistress of Charles II 1671–85, died in debt in France 1737.

Mary of Modena, second wife of James Duke of York, later queen 1685–8, died in exile in France in 1718.

Minette, nickname for Henrietta-Anne the sister of Charles II and wife of Duke of Orleans the brother of Louis XIV of France.

Nell Gwynn, actress, Protestant mistress of Charles II 1668–85, died 1687.

Queen Catherine of Braganza, neglected wife of Charles II, returned to Portugal and became Regent, died 1705.

Queen Henrietta Maria, mother of Charles II, widow of Charles I and aunt of Louis XIV died 1669 in France.

Courtiers and Royalists

Arlington, Henry Bennet Earl of Arlington, hated Buckingham, secretary of state 1667–74 then Lord Chamberlain until death in 1685.

Barrillion, Paul, Marquis de Branges, French ambassador to London 1677–1688, died 1691.

Buckingham, George Villiers, second duke, childhood friend of king became a Whig, involved in various plots, hated Clarendon, Arlington, Ormonde and Danby. Died, having exhausted most of his fortune, in 1687.

Burnet, Gilbert, made Bishop of Salisbury by William III, knew most of main characters of the period and wrote about them in *History of my own Time*, died 1715.

Clarendon, Edward Hyde, Earl of Clarendon, chief minister to Charles II, he lost the confidence of the king, fled and died in France 1674.

Claverhouse, John Graham of Claverhouse, soldier who put down Covenanter uprisings with savagery. Later Jacobite, made Viscount Dundee, killed at Battle of Killiecrankie 1689.

Coleman, Edward, former secretary of Duchess of York and ardent Catholic falsely accused in Popish Plot by Oates and Bedloe, and executed in 1678.

Coventry, Henry, Secretary for North 1672–4 and South 1674–8. Retired through ill-health, died 1686.

Danby, Thomas Osborne Earl of Danby, Lord Treasurer 1673–1679, hated Buckingham. Lord President of Council under William and Mary and made Duke of Leeds, died 1712.

De Croissy, Charles Colbert, Marquis, French ambassador to London 1668–76, then Louis's secretary of state for foreign affairs, died 1696.

Downing, Sir George, Cromwell's Resident in The Hague then supported Charles II and became the king's ambassador in The Hague. 1660–65. Ruthless and effective intelligencer, died 1684.

Evelyn, John, diarist and author close to the court, died 1706

Halifax, George Savile, Earl of Halifax, Privy Councillor 1679–81, orator against Exclusion and for reconciliation between Whigs and Tories. Hated Rochester. Became Marquis and Lord Privy Seal under William and Mary, died 1695.

Hollis, Lord Denzil, Presbyterian and former Parliamentarian, ambassador in Paris 1663–65, supported Whigs, died 1680.

Holmes, Sir Robert, pugnacious English admiral in Dutch wars, Governor of Isle of Wight, died 1692.

James, Duke of York, Catholic brother of Charles II, became James II, died in exile in France 1701.

Jeffreys, Sir George, partisan Royalist Lord Chief Justice, became a baron and Lord Chancellor under James II, conducted the 'Bloody Assizes', died 1689.

Jenkins, Sir Leoline, Judge, secretary of state 1680–84 and government lead on intelligence, died 1685.

L'Estrange, Roger, Royalist propagandist and newspaper publisher who, as Licenser of the Press, suppressed opposition publishing. Knighted by James II, died 1709.

Lauderdale, John Maitland, Duke of Lauderdale, devious and deeply unpopular but supported by Charles II and dominated management of Scotland1660–81, died 1682.

Middleton, Charles, 2nd Earl of Middleton, Secretary of State for Scotland

1682–4, then Secretary of State for English Northern Department 1684–8, followed James II into exile, died 1719.

Middleton, John, 1st Earl of Middleton, Scottish general, supported bishops opposed by Lauderdale, High Commissioner to Scottish Parliament 1661–63, died 1674.

Monck, George, Duke of Albemarle, successful general who persuaded army and parliament to invite Charles back as king. Captain General and Admiral in Dutch Wars, died 1670.

Monmouth, James Scott, Duke of Monmouth, illegitimate son of Charles II and Lucy Walter, allied with Whigs, hoped to succeed father, led rebellion against James II and executed in 1685.

Morris, Sir William, secretary of state for North 1660–68, relation of Monck died 1676.

Nicholas, Sir Edward, loyal royal servant to Charles I and Charles II, secretary of state 1660–63.

Rochester, John Wilmot, Earl of Rochester, wit, poet and rake, died of syphilis 1680.

Rochester, Laurence Hyde, Earl of Rochester, First Lord Treasury 1679–83, Lord Treasurer 1683–4, Lord President 1684–5. Hated Halifax. Made Lord Lieutenant of Ireland under William and Mary, died 1711.

Scroggs, Sir William, Lord Chief Justice, hated Catholics, died 1683.

Sharp, James, Archbishop of St Andrews, former Covenanter, became Anglican at Restoration and made Primate of Scotland, mercilessly put down Covenanters, assassinated by them in 1679.

Sunderland, Robert Spencer, Earl Spencer, ambitious secretary of state 1682–88, died 1702.

Williamson, Sir Joseph, government lead on intelligence management 1663–79, secretary of state 1674–79, died 1701.

Prominent Whigs

Argyll, Archibald Campbell Earl of Argyll, Chief of Clan Campbell, Whig who fled to Holland joined Monmouth Rebellion, executed 1685.

Armstrong, Sir Thomas, army officer, Whig and adviser to Monmouth, executed for Rye House Plot 1684.

Essex, Arthur Capell, Earl of Essex, Lord Lieutenant of Ireland 1672–77, Whig, accused of Rye House Plot, died in Tower 1683.

Ferguson, Robert, Whig pamphlet writer.

Howard, William, Baron of Escrick, Whig involved in Rye House Plot but gave evidence against his friends to save his life, died 1678.

Locke, John, philosopher, writer and Whig activist who became Shaftesbury's physician, fled with him but returned under William and Mary when he produced his major works, died 1704.

Russell, Lord William, Whig leader executed for Rye House Plot 1683.

Shaftesbury, Anthony Ashley Cooper, Earl of Shaftesbury, Chancellor of Exchequer 1661– 1672, Lord Chancellor 1672–73. Lord President 1672. Whig leader, fled and died in France 1683.

Sidney, Colonel Algernon, Republican Parliamentarian politician and writer, on diplomatic mission at time of Restoration, later returned, joined Whigs, involved in Rye House Plot, executed 1683.

Wildman, John, former Leveller, serial conspirator and Whig extremists. Became MP, Post Master General and knighted under William and Mary, died 1693.

Rogues, Spies and Rebels

Atkinson, Captain Robert, Presbyterian, took part in Northern Plot, became government informant, imprisoned and executed 1664.

Atkinson, John, Phanatick, ex-soldier, stockinger, took part in Northern and Tower plots arrested 1665.

Barkstead, Major General John, Cromwell's Lieutenant of the Tower and chief interrogator, Regicide, fled at Restoration, kidnapped in Holland and executed 1662.

Bampfylde, Colonel Joseph, soldier, adventurer and spy who was an agent for Charles I, Cromwell, Charles II as well the French and Dutch.

Barebone, Praise-God, Anabaptist preacher, Fifth Monarchist, prominent member of Cromwell's National Assembly (known as Barebone's Parliament) Republican writer and activist, died 1679.

Bedloe, 'Captain' William, confidence trickster who, like Oates, gave false evidence in Popish plot, died 1680.

Blood, 'Colonel' Thomas, Phanatick, Irish officer involved in Dublin, Northern and other plots, then caught stealing the Crown Jewels, pardoned and became government agent, died 1680.

Cameron, Richard, religious leader of a group of extreme Covenanters called 'Cameronians' who carried out minor uprising but were defeated, Cameron killed at Airds Moss in 1680.

Carr, Colonel Gilby, Presbyterian Phanatick, took part in Tonge, Dublin and Tower Plot, went to Netherland in 1674.

Dangerfield, Thomas, forger and criminal who gave false evidence in Popish Plot, imprisoned, died in brawl, 1685.

Dugdale, Stephen, opportunist who gave false evidence in Popish Plot, died 1683.

Ferguson, Robert, Scottish Presbyterian minister and Whig pamphleteer, landed with William of Orange but became disenchanted and conspired with Jacobites, died in poverty, 1714.

Fitzharris, Edward, Irish soldier and adventurer who intrigued against Whigs with Duchess of Portsmouth, recanted, tried and executed, 1681.

Greathead, Major Joshua, involved in Northern Plot but gave it away as an informer.

Jones, Captain Roger, Phanatick, took part in Northern Plot and London plot, author of *Mene Tekel*.

Leving William, Phanatick, took part in Northern Plot and then became a government informer. Possibly because of what he knew about Buckinghams's Radical contacts was murdered 1668.

Lockyer, Captain John, Phanatick took part in Northern, Tonge and Whitehall Gates Plots, pardoned through Blood.

Ludlow, Major General Edmund, Republican, Parliamentary general and Regicide who fled to Switzerland and plotted against Charles II.

Mason, Captain John, Phanatick, took part in Northern and Whitehall Gates plots, imprisoned but rescued by Blood.

Marsden, Jeremiah, Phanatick, took part in Tower Plot.

Oates, Titus, Anglican cleric and perjurer who invented the Popish Plot and caused many innocent deaths, imprisoned but pardoned by William and Mary and given £300 year pension, died 1705.

Okey, Colonel John, Congregationalist, Parliamentary soldier and Regicide, fled to continent but kidnapped and executed, 1662.

Scot, Thomas, Republican Secretary of State, intelligencer and Regicide, executed 1660.

Scot, William, son of Thomas, Republican exile in United Provinces.

Scott, 'Colonel' John, fraudster, government agent and false accuser of Pepys.

Strange, Captain Nathaniel, Phanatick, Fifth Monarchist took part in Tonge and Northern Plot.

Prance, Miles, Catholic craftsman who gave false evidence in Popish plot then recanted. Imprisoned under James II, died in France in 1690.

Riggs, Edward, former minister took part in Tonge Plot, became Williamson's agent in Rotterdam.

Tonge, Dr Israel, paranoid anti-Catholic clergyman who conspired with Oates to invent the Popish Plot, died 1680.

Tonge, Thomas, ex-soldier tobacco seller, 1662 plot named after him, executed 1662.

Venner, Thomas, Fifth Monarchist, led Venner Rising and executed 1661.

Appendix 3

Notes on Cryptography

Cryptology, the art of covert writing was well established, if little used, in England at the start of the Civil War in 1642. The need for secret correspondence in the Civil War led to a greater use of covert writing so that by 1660 it was widely used by government and, indeed, those plotting against the government. Then, as now, covert writing took two forms. The first is called steganography coming from the Greek *steganos* meaning 'hidden' and *graphein* meaning 'to write'. The usual way to produce this hidden writing was with secret ink, which was often called 'white ink' in the mid-seventeenth century. The most common secret inks were concoctions based either on lemon juice or urine, which left no mark on the paper but appeared when heated by a fire or candle. Many years later steganography would become more sophisticated, particularly when the microdot was invented by the Germans in 1941. Microdots are photographs of text or images that have been compressed to the size of a full stop that can later be expanded to reveal the full information. They were used with great success by the KGB and GRU throughout the Cold War for covert communication with agents. In the mid-seventeenth century however, steganography almost always meant dipping a quill into urine or lemon juice.

The other form of covert writing is cryptography, coming from the Greek for 'secret' and 'writing'. This is a matter of making the writing unintelligible to the reader and has two forms: codes and ciphers. Codes replace whole words or phrases with another word or symbol. As the Civil War developed so did the use of codes. They have always been particularly useful for referring to military operations and activities such as 'Overlord' for the Allied invasion of Europe in 1944, or Operation 'Nimrod', the SAS attack on the Iranian embassy in London in 1980. During the Civil War they were used by both sides, with Royalist letters using 'Mr Cross' or 'my mistress' as substitutions for the king. The New Model Army went so far as to have a standardised code book. After the Civil War codes remained much in use to protect correspondence between either the government and its agents, or the Royalists and their adherents. For example, Thurloe and Williamson's agent,

APPENDIX 3

Joseph Bampfylde, often used codes, such as 'Mr Phoenix' for King of France, and 'Mr Spencer' for King of Spain. With the realisation of the government's growing ability to intercept mail, so grew the greater use of code words as a basic method of retaining secrecy.

A more sophisticated method of keeping meanings secret in cryptography is to use a cipher. This is a system of concealing the meaning of a message by replacing each letter in the original wording with another letter or symbol. When a document is enciphered, the original wording (called 'plaintext') is replaced by a scrambled version that is unintelligible to the reader and is termed 'ciphertext'. The types of cipher used are termed 'encryption algorithms' and each algorithm is defined by a key that provides the specific method of enciphering by the sender and deciphering by the recipient.

Cryptography in the seventeenth century, as indeed today, was divided into two methods, transposition and substitution. Transposition is the oldest method, which was first recorded in Sparta in the fifth century BC. In transposition the letters of the message are re-arranged, thus generating an algorithm. For example the word 'king' could be represented in transposition as 'ingk', 'gnik', 'nikg', 'ikgn'. However, to be a workable system for sender and recipient, it needs to have a reasonably simple key. One way of doing this is for the key to be that every other letter is put on a second line, then all the letters are put together, for example:

Plaintext:	the king has arrived
Cipher:	t e i g a a r v d
	h k n h s r i e
Ciphertext:	TEIGAARVDHKNHSRIE [Conventionally always in capitals.]

Another example of transposition would be to switch letters, for example the first with the second, the third with the fourth, the fourth with the fifth etc. For example:

Plain text:	the king has arrived
Ciphertext:	HTKENIHGSARAIREVD

Needless to say there are numerous ways of doing transposition but it will be seen that in all cases the letters keep the identity they had in the plaintext but their order is changed. In substitution, the other main method of cryptography, each letter changes its identity but retains its position in the plaintext. Transposition was invented in India in the fourth century BC. It was most famously used by Julius Caesar for military correspondence during the conquest of Gaul. On some occasions he merely substituted Roman letters for Greek letters which would mean nothing to the Gallic tribes. More often he used what has become known as the Caesar shift cipher. This was a matter of replacing each letter in a message with a letter a certain number along in the alphabet. If the key was 'two' in a Caesar shift cipher algorithm for example, it would mean that the letter was replaced by a letter two along from it in the alphabet as shown below:

Plain alphabet: a b c d e f g h i j k l m n o p q r s t u v w x y z
Cipher alphabet: CD E FGHI J KLM NO PQ R STUVWXY ZA B
[Conventionally always in capitals.]

Plaintext: the king has arrived
Ciphertext: VJCMKPIJCUCTTKXGF

Although the transposition method was well known, it was the substitution cipher that was almost always used. In many cases, the cipher was simply a matter of replacing each letter of the alphabet with another letter or symbol without any logical sequence, as is the case in the Caesar shift. An example would be:

Plain alphabet: a b c d e f g h i j k l m n o p q r s t u v w x y z
Cipher alphabet: D P E H Q Z T M B A W S N J F V Y K C X R L
                           O G I U

In this case the cipher alphabet becomes the key.

A more convenient variation of transposition was also quite common and that was using a word or phrase as a key that could easily be remembered by both sender and receiver, and placing that at the front of the alphabet to create the ciphertext. For example if the key phrase was 'God bless the king' then the cipher alphabet would be as follows:

Plain alphabet: a b c d e f g h i j k l m n o p q r s t u v w x y z
Cipher alphabet: G O D B L E S T H E K I N P Q R U V W X Y Z
                           A C F J

Naturally, as no letter can be used twice, it means that the second recurring letter in a key word or phrase must be left out and the letters used in the key word must be omitted from the remainder of the alphabet following on from the last letter of the key word or phrase.

At this stage, it is worth turning to cryptanalysis, the art of working out plaintext from ciphertext without knowledge of the key. Although the art of cryptography is old, it did not start being used in Medieval Europe until about the thirteenth century when the English Franciscan monk and scientist Roger Bacon wrote a book on the subject. From then on it became gradually more and more widely used, first by the Church, and then by states for diplomatic correspondence. Naturally, when an enemy intercepted a communication and found that it was unintelligible, they realised that it was enciphered, tried to determine what type of cipher algorithm was used and then tried to work out the key. However, it was not until the early sixteenth century that there was the first breakthrough in cryptanalysis. This achievement is credited to the Venetian Giovanni Soro and his technique, which is referred to today as 'frequency analysis', soon spread to most of the courts of Europe.

The concept of frequency analysis is to examine the number of times each letter or symbol occurs in the ciphertext and the relationship between the letters. This came about when it was discovered that certain letters are, on average, used more frequently in each language. For example, in English 'e' is the most frequent letter, followed by 'a' and then 'o'. By looking at a ciphertext and seeing which is the most commonly occurring letter or symbol, it is likely that that letter or symbol is 'e', and then the same process is followed to determine the likely symbol for 'a' and 'o'. Other factors relating to the structure of the English language can then be used to try to determine certain letters. In English for example, 'e' never occurs before 'h' but often after it. As the word 'the' will be common in most messages, it may be possible to identify the cipher letter or symbol frequently coming before what has been decided is 'e', to establish 'h', and then work out the cipher letter or symbol for 't'. As the word 'and' is also probably going to be used in a message, and the cipher letter or symbol for 'a' has become known, it may be possible to identify 'n' and 'd'. By progressing in this way with much trial and error, the cryptanalyst, using frequency analysis, would hope to build up sufficient of the cipher alphabet to put enough plain alphabet letters into the encrypted message to make sense of parts of it and, in doing so, identify new letters and hopefully end up decrypting the whole message. Thus, frequency analysis provided the potential to counter all the forms of transposition described above.

As the frequency analysis cryptanalyst technique was well known to those responsible for creating ciphers, various improvements to transposition encryption were invented. The earliest and most significant at the time was the use of what are termed 'nulls'. These are letters or symbols which are not substitutions for letters in the plain alphabet, but blanks meaning nothing. These nulls can be scattered among the ciphertext in a way that could totally confuse a cryptanalyst carrying out frequency analysis. They are particularly useful if symbols are being used for a cipher alphabet because additional symbols can be added at the end, which can be included in the ciphertext key by the message sender and will be disregarded by the recipient. Even using an ordinary cipher alphabet, the cipher letters for the infrequently occurring plain alphabet letters 'z' and 'x' could be used as nulls and distributed in such quantity among the ciphertext to make them appear an 'e' and an 'o'.

Another way to confuse frequency analysis was simply by having several different numbers or symbols to represent a particular letter, so for example 'e' could be 7, 13, or 45 in the cipher alphabet. When there are alternatives in a cipher alphabet, these are called homophones. This could be further complicated by combining a cipher alphabet with a small number of code words, a system that is called 'nomenclatures'. In this case symbols (or numbers) would have to be used for the cipher alphabet and so the key would show the plain alphabet above the cipher alphabet (in symbols) and then a list of symbols with their meaning (such as '*' for 'king', '↑' for attack and '⊥' for 'London'), and then possibly the list of any symbols for nulls.

In the mid-fourteenth century, the great Renaissance man Leon Alberti came up with the idea of having more than one cipher alphabet. This is called 'polyalphabetic' [as opposed to 'monoalphabetic' for a single cipher alphabet]. He invented the cipher disk, which were two copper disks, the outer one larger than the inner, and both with the letters of the alphabet marked on them. The inner disk, which was the plaintext alphabet in jumbled sequence, could rotate and each letter opposite on the static outer disk would be the cipher letter. Both the originator and recipient of the cryptograms would have the same disk and would have a key such as starting with 'a' plaintext opposite 'k' ciphertext and after four words, moving the inner disk so that 'a' moved, say three spaces, to be opposite 's' and after a further four words, moved again three spaces and so on. Alberti also added more complex nomenclatures versions of the cipher disk system.

Another form of polyalphabetic cipher was published by the Frenchman Blaise de Vigenère in his *Traicté des Chiffres* in 1586. The 'Vigenère cipher' as it became known, made frequency analysis very difficult because it used twenty-six cipher alphabets, each based upon an additional Caesar shift. In other words:

Plain alphabet: a b c d e f g h i j k l m n o p q r s t u v w x w z
Shift 1:   B C D E F G H I J K L M N O P Q R S T U V W X Y Z A
Shift 2:   C D E F G H I J K L M NO P Q R S T U V W X Y Z A B
and so on for twenty-six shifts.

In this system the key would state which number of shifts would be used. If, for example, it was 2, 16 and 24, the first letter of the ciphertext would use the cipher alphabet letter corresponding to shift 2, the second letter of the ciphertext would use the cipher alphabet letter corresponding to shift 16, the third would use the cipher alphabet letter corresponding to shift 24, and then the next would go back to the cipher alphabet letter corresponding to shift 2. This was further refined by expressing the key not as the numbers of the shift lines, but as an easily remembered key word. The key word is then placed above the message plaintext and repeated again and again. Each letter of the key word shows which shift number cipher alphabet should be used. For example, if the key letter was B, it would mean that Shift 1 should be used and if it was C, it would mean shift 2 would be used.

Although both the cipher disk and the Vigenère cipher were known to be highly effective, they were also regarded as being too complicated for practical purposes and so were just not used in the mid-seventeenth century. In 1641, a young English chaplain called John Wilkins published a book called *Mercury, or the Secret and Swift Messinger.* This described most of the types of cryptology by then invented, but neither he nor anyone else seems to have put this knowledge into practice in the Civil War. During the period covered by this book, encryption was carried out simply using monoalphabetic substitution, often with homophones, nomenclature and nulls. Cryptanalysis relied upon frequency analysis and letter characteristics. If it was intended to use homophones, nomenclature or nulls, numbers were used as substitutes for letters. Because the use of cipher was time consuming, it was normally reserved only for sensitive sections of the text. A typical example of encryption found in letters intercepted by Thurloe is the following extract from an intercepted letter from the Dutch ambassador in July 1653:

We think ourselves bound to tell you plainly, that we think the constitution of the government and the interest of the governors

25.64.15. 48. to have learnt to know them so well. That we make certain 13. 16. 50. 44. 17. 48. 5. 18. 52. and not only to 24. 8.37 ...

The same principle was used in Thurloe's ciphers for communication to agents, for example, this short extract from agent S's letter of intelligence to Thurloe dated 20 March 1655:

159.6.36.9.36.9.36.3.28.5.12.3.31.30.39.3.19.17.25.30.36.19.41.31.11. 40.37.1.35.40.3.19.41.16.30.35. I am sure it is 35.40.18.28.12.28.41. 31.40.37.5.25.36.7.6.37.12.
Pray sir be pleased to decipher this letter yourself.

This cipher is monoalphabetic substitution, with homophones as follows:

Plain alphabet: a b c d e f g h i/j k l m n o p q r s t u/v w y

Cipher alphabet: 9 18 17 16 12 11 10 7 6 5 3 2 1 27
                 19 29 25 26 22 23 25 21 43 42 40 39 38 37 36 35
                 34 33 31
                 30 28 41

It also contains nomenclature in so far as a symbol is used for 'Lord Protector', also the code word 'Overton' means 'Cromwell' and there are other numerical code words such as 158 [designs], 159 [Hull], 82 [from], 81[which], 67[England].62 [army]. 1[Charles Stuart as well as n].

Now knowing the basic cipher, the reader might like to 'decipher' the letter from S, bearing in mind seventeenth century spelling. If this proves too much of a challenge, it will be understood why Charles II's intelligence staff preferred to use simple substitution of key words. This was a quick and effective in hiding the text from the average person, but would not withstand good cryptanalysis. Charles II's principal intelligencers such as Sir Joseph Williamson were good, but they did not achieve the rigorous professional standards of Thurloe.

Even today there is little fundamental change in the cryptology techniques that had been invented by the mid-seventeenth century in that it is still based on ciphers that are substitution, transposition or, more usually, a polyalphabetic combination of the two. The great difference is the advances in technology. First, a combination of mechanisation and simple circuits enabled the Enigma encryption machine to be invented in 1919 to exploit the strength of the Vigenère algorithm. This had revolving disks with the letters of the alphabet that could be set to a particular order based on a code book used by the originator and recipient, and was used by the Germans in the Second World War. Each time a letter was typed on the keyboard and encrypted, the discs would turn to change the algorithm. The Enigma cipher was broken by the Government Code and Cipher School at Bletchley Park in 1940, largely due to the work of mathematician Alan Turing, who invented a machine called 'bombs'. Based upon his work, in 1943 Bletchley were able to decode the similar, but more complex, German Lorenz SZ40 cipher machine used for communication between Hitler and his generals. This was done using 'Colossus', the first ever computer, running on 1,500 valves.

After the War GCHQ was formed, and in 1952 the US established the National Security Agency (NSA), which soon became the largest employer of mathematicians in the world. Computers began to be used for encryption because they were able to mimic vast numbers of mechanical scramblers. In 1960 IBM began using computers for encryption, and in 1977 the US government introduced the Data Encryption Standard (DES). About the same time, the problem of key distribution and control was resolved by the creation of Public Key Infrastructure (PKI) and the RSA standard for PKI encryption was created. Since then, cryptology has remained centred on computers and has developed with the same amazingly rapid advances of Information Technology. Data today can be encrypted to several standards, with the difficulty of cryptanalysis depending upon the key length. An 8 bit key allows 2 power 8 (256) permutations, which modern computers could crack very quickly. Most encryption today uses 128 bit Advanced Encryption Standard (AES) which has 2 power 128 i.e. 340 followed by 36 zeros of possible permutations. Higher level encryption uses 256 bit AES and other, more complex standards, which make cryptanalysis extremely challenging even with the aid of exceptionally powerful computers. For all that, cryptanalysis still depends upon men and women with the mathematical and analytical skills exemplified by Dr John Wallis, who served both Cromwell and Charles II with equal distinction.

Bibliography and Sources

Ashley, Maurice, *John Wildman Plotter and Postmaster* (London: Jonathan Cape, 1947)

Barber, Sarah, *A Revolutionary Rogue, Henry Marten and the English Republic* (Stroud: Sutton Publishing, 2000)

Baxter, Stephen, ed, *England's Rise to Greatness 1660-1763*, (University of California Press, 1983)

Bryant, Sir Arthur, ed, *The Letters of King Charles II* (London: Cassell, 1968)

Black, Jeremy Black and Jeremy Gregory, eds, *Culture Politics and Society in Britain 1660-1800* (Manchester University Press 1991)

Burnet, edited by Osmund Airy, *History of My Own Time,* Vol 1 (Oxford: Clarendon Press, 1997)

Childs, John, *The Army of Charles II* (London: Routledge & Kegan Paul, 1976)

Clark, Sir George, *The Later Stuarts 1660-1714* (Oxford: Clarendon Press, 1967)

Cowan, Ian B, *The Scottish Covenanters 1660-88* (Southampton: Camelot Press Ltd, 1976)

De Krey, Gary S, *Restoration and Revolution in Britain – a Political History of the Era of Charles II and the Glorious Revolution* (Palgrave: Macmillan, 2007)

Evelyn, John, *Diary,* ed Guy de la Bèdoyére (Woodridge: Boydell Press, 1995)

Foss, Michael, *The Age of Patronage – the Arts in Society 1660-1750* (London: Hamish Hamilton, 1972)

Fraser, Antonia, *Charles II* (London: Weidenfeld and Nicolson, 1979)

Greaves, Richard L, *Deliver us from Evil, The Radical Underground in Britain 1660-1663* (Oxford University Press, 1986)

Greaves, Richard L, *Enemies Under His Feet Radicals and Nonconformists in Britain, 1664-1677* (Stanford University Press, 1990)

Glassey, Lionel, *Reigns of Charles II and James VII and II* (New York: St Martin's Press, INC 1997)

Haley, K.H.D, *Politics in the Reign of Charles II* (Oxford: Basil Blackwell, 1985)

BIBLIOGRAPHY AND SOURCES

Haley, K H D, *The First Earl of Salisbury* (Oxford University Press, 1968)

Hanrahan, David C, *Colonel Blood, The Man who stole the Crown Jewels* (Stroud: Sutton Publishing, 2004)

Hanrahan, David C, *Charles II and the Duke of Buckingham, The Merry Monarch & the Aristocratic Rogue* (Stroud: Sutton Publishing, 2006)

Harris, Tim, *Politics Under the Later Stuarts, Party Conflicts in a Divided Society 1660 -1715* (London and New York: Longman 1993)

Harris, Tim, *Restoration, Charles II and his Kingdoms 1660 -1685* (London: Penguin Group 2005)

Harris, Tim, *London Crowds in the Reign of Charles II – Propaganda and Politics from the Restoration to the Exclusion Crisis* (Cambridge University Press, 1987)

Harris, Tim, Paul E Seaward and Mark Goldie Editors *The Politics of Religion in Restoration England* (Oxford: Basil Blackwell, 1990)

Holmes, Geoffrey, *The Making of a Great Power, late Stuart and Early Georgian Britain 1660-1722* (London and New York: Longman, 1993)

Hutchinson, Robert, *The Audacious Crimes of Colonel Blood, The Spy who Stole the Crown Jewels and became the King's secret Agent* (London: Weidenfeld and Nicolson, 2015)

Hutton, Ronald, *Restoration, A Political and Religious History of England and Wales 1658-1667* (Oxford: Clarendon Press, 1985)

Hutton, Ronald, *Charles the Second King of England, Scotland and Ireland* (Oxford: Clarendon Press, 1999)

Jenkinson, Matthew, *Culture and Politics at the Court of Charles II 1660-1685* (Woodbridge: Boydell Press, 2010)

Jones, J R, *The First Whigs The Politics of the Exclusion Crisis 1678 – 1683* (Oxford University Press, 1966)

Jones, J R, *Charles II Royal Politician* (London: Allen Unwin, 1987)

Keeble, NH, *The Restoration, England in the 1660s* (Oxford: Blackwell, 2002)

Kenyon, John, *The Popish Plot* (Portsmouth: William Heinemann Ltd, 1972)

Lee, Maurice, Jr, *The CABAL* (University of Illinois, 1965)

Ludlow, Edmund, *The memoirs of Edmund Ludlow* 1625-1672 Edited by C H Firth Vol II (Oxford: Clarendon Press, 1894)

Marshall, Alan, *Intelligence and Espionage in the Reign of Charles II, 1660-1685* (Cambridge University Press, 2002)

Marshall, Alan, *The Age of Faction – Court Politics, 1660-1702* (Manchester University Press, 1999)

Masters, Brian, *The Mistresses of Charles II* (London: Constable, 1997)

McElligot, ed. Jason, *Fear, Exclusion and Revolution, Roger Morrive and Britain in the 1680s* (Aldershot: Ashgate Publishing Ltd, 2006)

Miller, John, *Popery & Politics in England 1660-1688* (Cambridge University Press, 1973)

Miller, John, *Charles II* (London: Weidenfeld and Nicolson, 1991)

Miller, John, *After the Civil Wars, English Politics and Government in the Reign of Charles II* (London and New York: Longman, 2000)

Morrice, Roger, Jason McElligot eds, *Fear Exclusion and Revolution, and Britain in the 1680s* (Aldershot: Ashgate Publishing Ltd, 2006)

Nenner, Howard, ed, *Politics and the Political Agitation in Later Stuart Britain* (University of Rochester Press, 1997)

Norrington, Ruth, *My Dearest Minette – The Letters between Charles II and his sister Henrietta, Duchess d'Orleans* (London: Peter Owen, 1996)

Ogg, David, *England in the Reign of Charles I* (Oxford University Press, 1984)

Ollard, Richard, *Clarendon and his Friends* (London: Hamish Hamilton, 1987)

Ollard, Richard, *The Image of the King, Charles I and II* (London: Phoenix Press 1997)

Oxford Dictionary of National Biography (Oxford University Press, 2004)

Patrick, John, *Courting the Moderates Ideology, Propaganda and the Emergence of Party 1660-1678* (Montano: University of Delaware Press, 2010)

Pepys, Samuel, *The Diary of Samuel Pepys – A new and complete transcribed edition,* eds Robert Latham and William Matthews (London: Bell and Sons, 1976)

Petherick, M, *Restoration Rogues* (London: Hollis and Carter, 1951)

Pincus, Stephen C A, *Protestantism and Patriotism: ideologies and the making of English foreign policy, 1650-1688* (Cambridge University Press, 1996)

Singh, Simon, *Code Book, The Secret History off Codes and Code-breaking* (London: Fourth Estate Ltd, London, 1999)

Southcombe, George Southcombe and Grant Tapsell eds, *Restoration Politics, Religion and Culture Britain And Ireland, 1660-1714* (London: Macmillan, 2010)

Spencer, Charles, *Prince Rupert, The Last Cavalier* (London: Weidenfeld & Nicolson, 2008)

Smyth, Jim, *The Making of the United Kingdom 1660-1800* (London: Pearson Education, 2001)

BIBLIOGRAPHY AND SOURCES

Spurr, John, *England in the 1670s, This Masquerading Age* (Oxford: Blackwell, 2000)

Tapsell, Grant, *The Personal Rule of Charles II 1681-85* (Martlesham: Boydell Press, 2007)

Tomalin, Clair, *Samuel Pepys, The Unequalled Self* (London: Viking, 2002)

Uglo, Jenny, *A Gambling Man Charles II and the Restoration* (London: Faber and Faber, 2009)

Webber, Harold, *Paper Bullets, Print and Kingship under Charles II* (University of Kentucky, 1996)

Western, J.R, *Monarchy and Revolution, the English State in the 1680s* (London: Blandford Press London 1972)

Whitehead, Julian, *Cavalier and Roundhead Spies, Intelligence in the Civil War and Commonwealth* (Barnsley: Pen & Sword, 2009)

Williamson, Derek, *All the King's Women* (London: Hutchinson, 2003)

Zook, Melinda S, *Radical Whigs and Conspiratorial Politics in Late Stuart England* (Pennsylvania University Press, 1999)

Notes

Abbreviations used
Burnet – *History of my Own Time*
DNB – *Dictionary of National Biography*
Evelyn – *The Diary of John Evelyn*
Pepys – *Diary of Samuel Pepys*

Introduction
1. Gary S. De Krey, *Restoration and Revolution in Britain – a Political History of the Era of Charles II and the Glorious Revolution* (Palgrave Macmillan, 2007), p. 100.

1. Homecoming – 1660
1. Evelyn entry for 29 May 1660, p. 265.
2. It is not known for certain that Barbara Palmer slept with Charles on his first night in London. It was assumed so as she gave birth to her first Royal bastard on 25 February the next year, but then the child could have been the daughter of Lord Chesterfield or even her husband Roger Palmer.
3. Manchester was well regarded by Burnet and Clarendon as 'universally beloved…and a virtuous and generous man' (Burnet, vol. 1, p. 175) and did support the Restoration but the fact remains that he joined the Parliamentary army in the Civil War and was the Major General commanding the Roundhead troops at Marston Moor whose victory lost Charles the north of England.
4. Julian Whitehead, *Cavalier and Roundhead Spies – Intelligence in the Civil War and Commonwealth* (Pen and Sword, Barnsley 2009), ch. 7 to 11 provide details of Cromwell's intelligence organisation.
5. Pepys entry for 14 February 1668.
6. Burnet vol. 1, p. 184.
7. Alan Marshall, *Intelligence and Espionage in the Reign of Charles II, 1660-1685* (Cambridge University Press 2002), p. 21. Alan Marshall, DNB, vol. 59, p. 352.
8. Following seemingly endless wrangles with the French over protocol, it was not until July 1663 that Holles took up his appointment.

NOTES

2. Seeds of Dissent – 1661

1. W. C. Braithwaite, *Second Period of Quakerism* (London, 1919), p. 22.
2. Sir George Clark, *The Later Stuarts 1660-1714* 2nd ed. (Clarendon Press 1965), p. 27. (It was not until 1871 that Oxford and Cambridge were open to Protestant Nonconformists.)
3. Richard L. Greaves, *Deliver us from Evil, The Radical Underground in Britain 1660-1663* (Oxford University Press 1986), p. 12.
4. Jason McElligot, *Fear Exclusion and Revolution, Roger Morrice and Britain in the 1680s* (Ashgate 2006), p. 202.
5. Richard Ollard, *Clarendon and his Friends* (Macmillan 1987), p. 128.
6. John Miller, *After the Civil Wars, English Politics and government in the Reign of Charles II* (Longman 2000), p. 73.
7. Richard L. Greaves, *Deliver us from Evil, The Radical Underground in Britain 1660-1663* (Oxford University Press 1986), p. 67. Moyer had been a member of Cromwell's Nominated Assembly which was nicknamed 'Barebone's Parliament' after Barebone, a leather seller and Congregationalist leader who was a prominent member. Harrington had been a Cromwellian Lord Mayor of London and Ireton was brother of Cromwell's son-in-law General Henry Ireton.

3. Plots and Risings – 1662–63

1. N. H. Keeble, *The Restoration, England in the 1660s* (Blackwell, 2002), p. 151 see also. Sir George Clark, *The Later Stuarts 1660-1714,* Second Ed (Oxford Clarendon Press 1965), p. 28.
2. Sir Arthur Bryant, *The Letters of Charles I* (Cassell, London 1968), p. 126, letter to Clarendon dated 21 May 1662.
3. Richard L. Greaves, *Deliver us from Evil, The Radical Underground in Britain* (Oxford University Press 1986), p. 91.
4. Alan Marshall, *Intelligence and Espionage in the Reign of Charles II, 1660-1685* (Cambridge Studies in Modern History 1994), p. 268 for a full description of the operation.
5. Ibid., p. 292. Also see C. H. Firth ed., *The Memoirs of Edmund Ludlow 1625-1672,* vol. 2 (Clarendon Press 1894), p. 331.
6. Richard L. Greaves, *Deliver us from Evil, The Radical Underground in Britain* (Oxford University Press 1986), p. 103.
7. Ibid., p. 113.
8. Burnet, p. 99.
9. John Miller, *Charles II* (Weidenfeld and Nicolson, London 1991), p. 99.
10. Richard L. Greaves, *Deliver us from Evil, The Radical Underground in Britain* (Oxford University Press 1986), p. 113.

11. John Miller, *Charles II* (Weidenfeld and Nicolson, London 1991), p. 99.

4. Plots Spread – 1664
1. Sir Arthur Bryant ed., *The Letters of King Charles II* (Cassell, London 1968), p. 136.
2. For details of Blood's early life seen David C. Hanrahan, *Colonel Blood – The Man who Stole the Crown Jewels* (Sutton Publishing 2004), pp. 14-16.
3. Ibid., for details of the plot see pp. 33-37.
4. Ibid., p. 94.
5. Richard L. Greaves, *Deliver us from Evil, The Radical Underground in Britain* (Oxford University Press 1986), p. 174.
6. Ibid., p. 167.
7. Ibid., p. 181.
8. Sir Arthur Bryant ed, *The Letters of Charles I* (Cassell, London 1968), p. 154, letter 16 March 1663/4.

5. The Apocalypse Years Begin – 1665
1. Ruth Norrington, *My Dearest Minette The Letters between Charles II and his sister Henrietta, Duchess d'Orleans* (Peter Owen, London 1996), p. 52 letter 4 January 1662.
2. According to Brian Masters, *The Mistresses of Charles II* (Constable, London 1997), p.70, James Hamilton, Lord Sandwich and Henry Jermyn had all tasted her delights.
3. Maurice Ashley, *John Wildman, John Wildman Plotter and Postmaster* (Jonathan Cape, London 1947), p. 156.
4. Sir Arthur Briant ed, *The Letters of King Charles II* (Cassell, London 1968), p. 168, letter 24 October 1664.
5. John Miller, *After the Civil Wars, English Politics and Government in the Reign of Charles II* (Longman 2000), p. 84.
6. Jim Smyth, *The Making of the United Kingdom 1660–1800* (Pearson Education 2001), p. 37.
7. Gary S. De Krey, *Restoration and Revolution in Britain – a Political History of the Era of Charles II and the Glorious Revolution* (Palgrave Macmillan 2007), p. 64.
8. Ronald Hutton, *Charles the Second King of England, Scotland and Ireland* (Clarendon Press 1999), p. 232.
9. Marie Bous Hall, DNB, vol. 41, p. 675.

NOTES

6. Fire and Sword – 1666

1. David C. Hanrahan, *Colonel Blood, The Man who Stole the Crown Jewels* (Sutton Publishing 2004), p. 46.
2. Jenny Uglow, *A Gambling Man Charles II and the Restoration* (Faber and Faber, London 2009), p. 324.
3. Richard L. Greaves, *Enemies Under His Feet Radicals and Nonconformists in Britain, 1664-1677* (Stanford University Press 1990), p. 52.
4. Ibid., p. 80 for details of the retributions.

7. Toppling the Chancellor – 1667–8

1. Under the Treaty of Troyes in 1420 the King of England was made heir to the Kingdom of France. Although this was all very reasonable considering the victory at Agincourt, the claim to the French throne became increasingly tenuous after England's defeat in the Hundred Years War and when Calais, the last foothold in France, was lost in 1558. Despite this the fleur-de-lis remained on the royal coat of arms until 1801.
2. David C. Hanrahan, *Charles II and the Duke of Buckingham, The Merry Monarch & the Aristocratic Rogue* (Sutton Publishing 2006), p. 90.
3. Stephen, C. A. Pincus, *Protestantism and Patriotism: ideologies and the making of English foreign policy, 1650–1688* (Cambridge University Press 1996), p. 510.
4. Jenny Uglow, *A Gambling Man, Charles II and the Restoration* (Faber and Faber, London 2009), pp. 405–410 for a description of the Medway attack.
5. Marie Bous Hall, DNB, vol. 41, p. 675.
6. Pepys entry for 17 July 1667.
7. Burnet, vol. 2, p. 99.
8. Jenny Uglow, *A Gambling Man, Charles II and the Restoration* (Faber and Faber, London 2009), p. 429.
9. David C. Hanrahan, Colonel Blood, *The Man who Stole the Crown Jewels* (Sutton Publishing 2004), p. 52.
10. Alan Marshall, *Intelligence and Espionage in the Reign of Charles II, 1660–1685* (Cambridge University Press 2002), p. 80 for a detailed description of intelligence and the Post Office.
11. Julian Whitehead, *Cavalier and Roundhead Spies, Intelligence in the Civil War and Commonwealth* (Pen and Sword Books Ltd, Barnsley, 2009), pp. 15 and 110 for Wallis in the Civil War.
12. Pepys, entry for 14 January 1668.
13. Jenny Uglow, *A Gambling Man Charles II and the Restoration* (Faber and Faber, London 2009), p. 453.

8. The Secret Treaty – 1669–70
1. Ruth Norrington, *My Dearest Minette. The Letters between Charles II and his sister Henrietta, Duchess d'Orleans* (Peter Owen London 1996), Letter 8 April 1665.
2. Ibid., letter 20 January 1669, page 170.
3. Ibid., letter 22 March 1669, page 173.
4. John Miller, *Charles II* (Weidenfeld and Nicolson London 1991), p. 160. says that on 25 Jan 1669 on Feast of Conversion of St Paul, Charles spoke to York, Arlington, Clifford and Lord Arundel of Wardour of his conversion and asked their advice on when to declare himself a Catholic. This information was taken from J. J. Clark ed., *The life of James II. Collected Out of memoirs writ of His Own Hand* (London 1816), pp. 441-43 but as *The life of James II* was put together by others from James II's notes many years after his death, it may not be correct.
5. According to p. 507 of Jenny Uglow's *A Gambling Man, Charles II and the Restoration*, the text was first published in 1826 in *The History of England* by the historian John Lingard.
6. A good account of suspicions of Minette murder is given in Ruth Norrington *My Dearest Minette. The Letters between Charles II and his sister Henrietta, Duchess d'Orleans* (Peter Owen London 1996), pp. 214-231.
7. Buckingham, *The Works of His Grace George Villiers, late Duke of Buckingham London 1715,* vol. 1, p. 80.
8. Details of Charles' pay off to Castlemaine are given in Derek Williamson's *All the King's Women* (Hutchinson London 2003), p. 283.
9. Details of the attack are given in David C. Hanrahan's, *Colonel Blood, The Man who stole the Crown Jewels* (Sutton Publishing 2004), pp. 70-83.
10. M. Petherick, *Restoration Rogues* (Hollis and Carter, London, 1951), p. 33.
11. David C. Hanrahan, *Colonel Blood, The Man who stole the Crown Jewels* (Sutton Publishing 2004), p. 82.

9. Implementing a Secret Treaty – 1671
1. Geoffrey Holmes, *The Making of a Great Power, late Stuart and Early Georgian Britain 1660-1722* (Longman London and New York, 1993), p. 91.
2. David C. Hanrahan, *Colonel Blood, The Man who stole the Crown Jewels* (Sutton Publishing 2004), p. 111.
3. Robert Hutchinson, *The Audacious Crimes of Colonel Blood, The Spy who Stole the Crown Jewels and Became the King's Secret Agent*

(Weidenfeld and Nicolson London, 2015), p. 138 – Extract from *Notes by Williamson on information received by Thomas Blood and others*.
4. Ibid., p. 140.
5. Evelyn, entry for 10 May 1671.
6. Richard L. Greaves, *Enemies Under His Feet Radicals and Nonconformists in Britain, 1664-1677* (Stanford University Press 1990), p. 222.
7. Pepys, entry for 27 December 1668.
8. Sir Arthur Bryant editor, *The Letters of King Charles II* (Cassell, London 1968), p. 246 – letter from Charles to Downing January 1672.
9. John Spurr, *England in the 1670s, This Masquerading Age* (Blackwell 2000), p. 283.

10. Indulgence for Tender Consciences – 1672-3

1. Lionel Glassey, *Reigns of Charles II and James VII and II* (St Martin's Press, 1997), p. 93.
2. Sir Arthur Bryant ed, *The Letters of King Charles II* (Cassell, London 1968), p. 25, letter of 4 July 1672.
3. Ibid., p. 252, letter of 26 July.
4. Robert Hutchinson, *The Audacious Crimes of Colonel Blood, The Spy who Stole the Crown Jewels and became the King's secret Agent* (Weidenfeld and Nicolson, London, 2015), p. 167.
5. Richard L. Greaves, *Enemies Under His Feet Radicals and Nonconformists in Britain, 1664-1677* (Stanford University Press 1990), p. 229.
6. Brian Masters, *The Mistresses of Charles II* (Constable, London 1979), p. 144.

11. Muddling Through – 1674–78

1. John Spurr, *England in the 1670s, This Masquerading Age* (Blackwell 2000), p. 63.
2. Ibid., p. 73.
3. Ibid., p. 222.
4. Robert Hutchinson, *The Audacious Crimes of Colonel Blood, The Spy who Stole the Crown Jewels and Became the King's Secret Agent* (Weidenfeld and Nicolson London, 2015), p. 175.
5. John Patrick, *Courting the Moderates Ideology, Propaganda and the Emergence of Party 1660-1678* (Montano, University of Delaware Press, 2010), p. 259 Memorandum to the King, 17 March 1674.

6. Robert Hutchinson, *The Audacious Crimes of Colonel Blood, The Spy who Stole the Crown Jewels and Became the King's Secret Agent* (Weidenfeld and Nicolson London, 2015), p. 173 for details of plot.
7. Brian Masters, *The Mistresses of Charles II* (Constable, London 1979), p. 90.
8. Calendar of Clarendon State Papers, vol. 5, p. 154.

12. The Popish Plot – 1678
1. John Kenyon, *The Popish Plot* (William Heinemann Ltd 1972), p. 24.
2. Burnet, p. 159.
3. Sir George Treby, *A collection of letters and other writings relating to the horrid Popish Plot* (London 1681), p. 166.
4. Further detail about the interview of Oates is given in John Kenyon, *The Popish Plot* (William Heinemann Ltd 1972), pp. 94-5.
5. Ibid., p. 82.
6. Ibid., p. 84-85.
7. Alan Marshall, DNB vol. 4, p.787.

13. Anti-Papist Hysteria – 1679
1. A. C. Bickley, DNB vol. 17, p. 151.
2. Alan Marshall, DNB vol. 45, p. 209.
3. John Kenyon, *The Popish Plot* (William Heinemann Ltd 1972), p. 136.
4. Alan Marshall, DNB vol. 59, p. 355.
5. Antonia Fraser, *Charles II* (Weidenfeld and Nicolson London 1979), p. 369.
6. Lords Journals 31 Car II 1679 p. 348.
7. Melinda S. Zook, *Radical Whigs and Conspiratorial Politics in Late Stuart England* (Pennsylvania State University Press, 1999), p. xi.
8. Stephen Baxter, Clayton Roberts eds, *England's Rise to Greatness 1660-1763* (University of California Press 1983), p. 190 for power of patronage in parliament.
9. Clair Tomalin, *Samuel Pepys, The Unequalled Self* (Viking, London, 2002), p. 318.
10. *Isabell Sharp and the Servants account of the assassination* in Sharp's Mausoleum.
11. John Childs, *The Army of Charles II* (Routledge & Kegan Paul London 1976), p. 202. (There are varying figures for the number of rebels killed in the battle.)

NOTES

14. The Crisis Deepens – 1679

1. Harrold M. Weber, *Bullets Print and Kingship under Charles II* (University Press of Kentucky 1996), pp. 156 and 162.
2. John Kenyon, *The Popish Plot* (William Heinemnn Ltd 1972), p. 137.
3. Burnet, p. 286.
4. Antonia Fraser, *Charles II* (Weidenfeld and Nicolson London 1979), p. 385.
5. David C. Hanrahan, *Colonel Blood, The Man who stole the Crown Jewels* (Sutton Publishing 2004), p. 156.
6. Harris, *Politics Under the Later Stuarts, Party Conflicts in a Divide Society 1660-1715* (Longman 1993), p. 84.
7. Ibid., p. 105.
8. K. H. D. Harley, *Politics in the Reign of Charles II* (Basil Blackwell 1985), p. 46. (As the Royal army only numbered 6,000 the numbers must have been exaggerated but whatever they were they would not have been far off enough to form an army.)

15. The Whigs Begin to Mobilise – 1680

1. Robert Hutchinson, *The Audacious Crimes of Colonel Blood, The Spy who Stole the Crown Jewels and became the King's secret Agent* (Weidenfeld and Nicholson London, 2015), p. 181.
2. David C. Hanrahan, *Charles II and the Duke of Buckingham, The Merry Monarch & the Aristocratic Rogue* (Sutton Publishing 2006), p. 206.
3. David C. Hanrahan, *Colonel Blood, The Man who Stole the Crown Jewels* (Sutton Publishing, 2004), pp. 164-78 for details of buggery case.
4. Gary S. De Krey, *Restoration and Revolution in Britain – a Political History of the Era of Charles II and the Glorious Revolution* (Palgrave Macmillan 2007), p. 172.
5. Melinda S. Zook, *Radical Whigs and Conspiratorial Politics in Late Stuart England* (Pennsylvania State University Press, 1999), p. 49.
6. Tim Harris, *Restoration, Charles II and his Kingdoms 1660 -1685* (Allen Lane, Penguin Group, 2005), pp. 249-50 for full description of the *Committee.*
7. Antonia Fraser, *Charles II* (Weidenfeld and Nicolson, London 1979), p. 392.
8. Ibid., p. 394.
9. Sean Kelsey, DNB, vol. 13, p. 46.
10. Ian B. Cowan, *The Scottish Covenanters 1660-88* (Camelot Press Ltd, Southampton, 1976), p. 105.

11. Alan Marshall, DNB, vol. 18, p. 780.
12. Alan Marshall, DNB, vol. 19, p. 869.

16. Rebellion in the Air – 1681
1. Geofrey Holmes, *The Making of a Great Power, late Stuart and Early Georgian Britain 1660-1722* (Longman, London and New York 1993), p. 131.
2. Antonia Fraser, *Charles II* (Weidenfeld and Nicolson London, 1979), p. 401.
3. Grant Tapsell, *The Personal Rule of Charles II 1681-85* (Boydell Press, 2007), p. 36.
4. Ibid, p. 36.
5. K. H. D Haley, *Politics in the Reign of Charles II* (Basil Blackwell, 1985), p. 658.
6. Grant Tapsell, *The Personal Rule of Charles II 1681-85* (Boydell Press, 2000), p. 120.
7. Ibid., p. 28.
8. Gary S. De Krey, *Restoration and Revolution in Britain – a Political History of the Era of Charles II and the Glorious Revolution* (Palgrave Macmillan, 200), p. 148.
9. Ian B. Cowan, *The Scottish Covenanters 1660-88* (Camelot Press Ltd, Southampton, 1976), p. 109.
10. Ibid., p. 111.
11. Charles Middleton, 2nd Earl, son of General John Middleton, 1st Earl, who died while Governor of Tangier in 1674.

17. The Road to Rye House – 1682-83
1. Antonia Fraser, *Charles II* (Weidenfeld and Nicolson London 1979), p. 418.
2. Tim Harris, *Politics Under the Later Stuarts, Party Conflicts in a Divided Society 1660-1715* (Longman 1993), p. 106.
3. Howard Nenner ed., essay by Mark Goldie, *Politics and the Political Agitation in Later Stuart Britain* (University of Rochester Press, 1997), p. 43.
4. J. R. Jones, *The First Whigs The Politics of the Exclusion Crisis 1678 – 1683* (Oxford University Press, 1966), p. 205.
5. Tim Harris, *Politics under the Later Stuarts, Party Conflicts in a Divided Society 1660-1715* (Longman, 1993), p. 148.
6. Burnet, p. 340.
7. Tim Harris, Paul E. Seaward and Mark Goldie eds, *The Politics of Religion in Restoration England* (Basil Blackwell, 1990), p. 149.

8. Ibid, p. 152.
9. John Miller, *Popery & Politics in England 1660-1688* (Cambridge University Press, 1973), p. 366.
10. Tim Harris, Paul E. Seaward and Mark Goldie eds., *The Politics of Religion in Restoration England* (Basil Blackwell, 1990), p. 152.
11. Burnet, p. 372.
12. Antonia Fraser, *Charles II* (Weidenfeld and Nicolson, London 1979), p. 423.
13. Ibid., p. 429.
14. Garry S. De Krey, DNB, vol. 31, p. 23.

18. Peace in his Time – 1684–5

1. Melinda S. Zook, *Radical Whigs and Conspiratorial Politics in Late Stuart England* (Pennsylvania State University Press, 1999), p. 121.
2. Ibid., p. 97.
3. Ibid., p. 16.
4. Williamson, *All the King's Women* (Hutchinson, London 2003), p. 290.
5. Howard Nenner ed., *Politics and the Political Agitation in Later Stuart Britain* (University of Rochester Press, 1997), p. 317.
6. Antonia Fraser, *Charles II* (Weidenfeld and Nicolson, London 1979), p. 421.
7. J. R. Western, *Monarchy and Revolution, the English State in the 1680s* (Blandford Press, London 1972), p. 74.
8. J. R. Jones, *The First Whigs, The Politics of the Exclusion Crisis 1678-1683* (Oxford University Press 1966), p. 210.
9. Howard Nenner ed., essay by Mark Goldie, *Politics and the Political Agitation in Later Stuart Britain* (University of Rochester Press, 1997), p. 43.
10. Tim Harris, *Restoration, Charles II and his Kingdoms 1660-1685* (Allen Lane, Penguin Group 2005), p. 103.
11. Clair Tomalin, *Samuel Pepys, The Unequalled Self* (Viking, London 2002), p. 325.
12. Alan Marshall, DNB vol. 49, p. 411.
13. John Childs, *The Army of Charles II* (Routledge & Kegan Paul, London 1976), p. 230.
14. Clair Tomalin, *Samuel Pepys, The Unequalled Self* (Viking, London, 2002), p. 339.
15. Tim Harris, *Restoration, Charles II and his Kingdoms 1660-1685* (Allen Lane, Penguin Group 2005), p. 366.
16. Ian B. Cowan *The Scottish Covenanters 1660-88* (Camelot Press Ltd, Southampton, 1976), p. 133.

17. Brian Masters, *The Mistresses of Charles II* (Constable, London 1997), p. 167.
18. Garry S. De Krey, *Restoration and Revolution in Britain, A Political History of England of Charles II and the Glorious Revolution* (Palgrave Macmillan 2007), p. 206.
19. K. H. D. Haley, *Politics in the Reign of Charles II* (Basil Blackwell 1985), p. 74.
20. Melinda S. Zook, *Fear, Exclusion and Revolution, Roger Morrice and Britain in the 1680s* (Ashgate Publishing Ltd, Aldershot, 2006), p. 191.
21. Richard Greaves, DNB, vol. 2, p. 44–5.
22. John Kenyon, *The Popish Plot* (William Heinemann Ltd 1972), p. 195.
23. Melinda S. Zook, *Radical Whigs and Conspiratorial Politics in Late Stuart England* (Pennsylvania University Press, 1999), p. 191 for more details on nursing mothers.
24. Alan Marshall, DNB, vol. 18, p. 780.
25. Lionel Glassey, *Reigns of Charles II and James VII and II* (St Martin's Press 1997), p. 219.
26. Evelyn, entry for 4 Feb 1685.
27. Antonia Fraser, *Charles II* (Weidenfeld and Nicolson London 1979), pp. 443-457.

Index

INDEX

INDEX